Just
Play Ball

Joe Garagiola

foreword by Yogi Berra

NORTHLAND
PUBLISHING

To Audrie, my wife,
without whom
the book would not have been written.

To Gina, our daughter,
without whom
the book would not have been finished.

To Joe and Steve, our sons,
who are a part of everything we do.

FRONTISPIECE: Joe Garagiola. *Reprinted from The Saturday Evening Post magazine,* © *1963.*
Saturday Evening Post Society

www.northlandbooks.com

Composed and Printed in the United States of America

Edited by Claudine J. Randazzo
Designed by David Jenney

FIRST IMPRESSION 2007

ISBN 10: 0-87358-923-8
ISBN 13: 978-0-87358-923-9

07   08   09   10   11   5   4   3

Library of Congress Cataloging-in-Publication Data
Garagiola, Joe.
    Just play ball / by Joe Garagiola.
        p. cm.
        ISBN-13: 978-0-87358-923-9 (hc)
        ISBN-10: 0-87358-923-8 (hc)
    1. Baseball—United States.   I. Title.
GV863.A1.G375   2007
796.357—dc22

CONTENTS

Yogi Berra. They called him a bad ball hitter, but he said, "It ain't bad if I hit it."
Courtesy National Baseball Hall of Fame Library, Cooperstown, N.Y.

FOREWORD

BEFORE I SAY ANYTHING I wanna tell you something. You're gonna like this book a lot, and I'll bet Joe makes you laugh out loud. He made me laugh with his other book, Baseball is a Funny Game, and this is a new one.

See, I've known Joe all my life—and that's a long time. I'm not gonna tell you how old we are because you can look it up. I'll tell you this, that there are guys who come up to me that look like they're one hundred and twenty years old, and they tell me they saw me play when they were a kid. I tell 'em okay, but it's déjà vu all over again for them, and they laugh. That's what I'm trying to tell you about this book. Joe lived right across the street. I lived at 5447, and he lived at 5446 Elizabeth. Growing up they called me Lawdy because my mother had trouble calling me Lawrence, and he was Joey. When we went to play pro ball I was Yogi, and he stayed Joe. We were catchers.

When we were kids we did a lotta things together. We played on the same team, and we never played against each other until I went to the Yankees, and he was with the Cardinals. That was in spring training. We went to the same movies together and belonged to the same club. It was named the Stags Athletic Club (Stags AC for short). I'm trying to tell you we saw all the same things, but he heard 'em different.

We were always playing some sport.

I remember one time playing hockey on roller skates. Joe was the goalie, and he didn't have a mask. We were lucky to have roller skates. The only protection he had was shin guards, which were those thick *National Geographic* magazines we got from the library. It's true we didn't read 'em, but we used 'em. The puck was made out of wood, and it was easy to raise it. I took a shot that sailed and hit Joe right over the eye. He was bleeding real bad, and we all got scared. I felt bad, but when he came back from the doctor he told us that he put in some stitches, and in a couple of days he was okay. See, we never had a fight. We never even had an argument. I mean a real one, not one about baseball because we were always arguing about that. I still remember what he told me when I told him I felt bad I hit him with the puck. He said it was a good shot and then laughed and said, "but I stopped it."

When we were kids we played any place that none of the other guys wanted to play. I was a pitcher or outfielder, and Joe was a first baseman most of the time. When we went to play pro ball we were both catchers. That was a good position for us because you hear a lot of stuff. I liked being a catcher because I like to talk to the batter, and you find out a lot of things and a lot of it ain't about baseball. Joe liked being a catcher because he remembers everything he ever hears if it makes him laugh.

A lotta people tell me I say funny things, but they just come out that way. I read some of the things they write, and I know I didn't say all the things I said. Joe says sometimes I just leave out a couple words. I don't try, but that's why it comes out funny. I know my wife and kids and Joe know what I mean, I think.

Like the time when Joe was sick and getting better. I called him up in Arizona, and while we were talking I asked him if he was playing golf yet. He said no, so I told him not to worry because you always play better when you don't play. He knew what I meant, and I bet if you play golf you do, too.

I remember in 1973 when I was the manager of the Mets. We were in fifth place in early September, but the teams were all bunched together, and we had to play 'em all. They said we were dead. When the writers asked me about it I told 'em, "It ain't over till it's over."

Okay, so I say things funny and Joe says funny things. When I used to go back to St. Louis in the off-season I would get invited to banquets to make a speech. I always told the people the same thing; I'll go and make a speech if Joe talks. I like to answer questions.

You'll see what kind of guy my pal Joe is when you read this book. He's done a lot of things—especially in TV—but I know baseball is number one with him. He knows the game, and with this book you'll see baseball through the eyes of a catcher and a broadcaster. In his rookie year he played in a World Series for the Cardinals against the Red Sox. He's done enough broadcasting that he's in the Hall of Fame with all the great broadcasters.

There is one World Series game that I'll never forget. It has nothing to do with the game, but what a memory it gave me.

It was the 1964 World Series, and I was managing the Yankees against the Cardinals. The game was in St. Louis, and it hit me. I was managing the Yankees, and my pal Joe was upstairs broadcasting. It was hard to believe. It was almost spooky. Could this be the same two kids from the Hill who used to sit by the lamppost in front of Pucci's house holding a handful of dirt one of them had scooped up from the Sportsman's Park infield after watching their favorite team, the Cardinals, play?

You will laugh with Joe in this book, and I'll bet you'll say, "Geez, I never thought of that." I promise you will learn from it, too. If I ever manage again, I'm gonna ask him to be my bench coach, so he can keep me loose and laughing like he did when we were kids.

— YOGI BERRA

A 1946 Cardinal rookie catcher—and there was hair under that cap. I could cry.
Courtesy Joe Garagiola.

How It All Began

BASEBALL IS A COLLECTION OF memories and people, not steroids and human growth supplements. Those two things top the list of what I'm tired of hearing about—and you can add statistics to that list. To me, baseball is a great game played by real people. The players don't run on batteries or computer game chips. When it comes to statistics, I don't mind if they make sense like a batting average, earned run average, home runs, or RBI's. But when you start telling me about the "steals after the number of pick-off throws to first," that's a little more than I need. How old a player is and how much he weighs is enough for me. And I even wonder about those things when I hear "but that's his baseball age" or "he got weighed with his clothes on."

I did learn, last baseball season, that the record for the longest pair of last names on the right side of the infield in major league history belongs to Mark Grudzielanek and Doug Mientkiewicz. That information probably won't win you any games, but you could spend half the game just reading the back of their shirts.

At the ballpark, sitting in the dugout as a player (which I've done), or sitting in the bullpen (which I did a lot), or sitting in the stands (like I do now) there's a common thread, besides watching the game. It's talking to the guy next to you. That's how this book got started—through a conversation with a fan who came to the game to watch the teams just play ball. One of his thoughts really hit me.

"You should be a contest."

"Whadda you talking about?" I asked.

Our outfielders made throws that came with a flight plan and frequent flyer miles. Courtesy United Press International.

"Well, I sit here and a lot of times I don't think anything is going on, then you tell me something and it's like you're showing me the game you don't see. You tell me about the players you know or who they remind you of when you played. My favorite is when you tell me what the catcher is talking about when he goes to the mound. If you were a contest, the winner would get to sit next to you. Or maybe you should write a book."

"I don't have time to write a book," I said.

Then my wife joined in. "Why don't you make some notes, put them in a drawer, and one day when you have time, get them out and see what happens."

I listened to my wife, made those notes, and put them in a drawer, and found time to take them out and turn them into this book. Along the way they became more than notes; they made the bubble gum cards come alive, and they let me visit teammates and old friends. Baseball has a way of turning back the clock, recalling a certain game, maybe a special World Series or a favorite player. Your memory becomes your remote control to review the past.

Just Play Ball is a book of funny stories, some pitching and hitting theories that might have you scratching your head, and funny one-liners, said by guys who played the game hard but realized it wasn't life or death. Simply said, people just like you.

The Past Always Looks Better
Than It Was Because It Isn't Here

CHAPTER 1

"Did anybody throw ninety miles an hour when you played?" Curt Schilling asked me. How could I give him a straight answer after a question like that?

"Catching a ball on one bounce was an out when I played, so we didn't have to throw ninety miles an hour," I said.

When the Arizona Diamondbacks, an expansion team, made it to the World Series in 2001 to play the Yankees, the New York writers were ready.

How do you think the Diamondbacks will do in Yankee Stadium? Will the team be intimidated by the history and tradition? One of the most asked questions was: *Will the aura and mystique of playing the Yankees in Yankee Stadium be a factor?*

Curt Schilling defused the situation with his own question and answer to it, "Aura and mystique? Sounds like the names of two strippers in Phoenix." One quick comeback and the writers' verbal rallies were over. I know Schilling would have made a good bench jockey in my day.

The job of the bench jockey was to sit on the bench and needle players—ride them during a game. Your personal life was fair game, and it could get nasty.

Bench jockeying is not a lost art, and like most things in baseball today it has a new, MTV-style name: trash talk. Today's players think they play the game the way it should be played, not the way the "old guys" played it. I said the same thing in 1946 when I broke in, and it's repeated today, camouflaged with different words.

The history will always be there, but most players focus on today. It's a real bonus when players want to talk about the greats of yesterday, but it's the rare player, like Curt Schilling, who can. Hall of Famers have a chance of being remembered, but for the rest of us it's *Jeopardy* time. When did you play? Were you a regular? Were you on a baseball card?

In 1972 Gene Tenace was a utility player with the Oakland A's. He hit only five home runs during the regular season. Oakland played the Cincinnati Reds in the World Series, and the A's won the opening game by a score of three to two. In that game Gene Tenace hit home runs in his first two at bats, a World Series record. His two home runs drove in all the A's runs. Even though it's easy enough to find out if your coaches or manager played in the big leagues (an old catcher with knuckleball fingers found at least ten Web sites with this information), Gene still had this conversation, or non-conversation, while a coach.

"Did you ever play in the big leagues?" The question came from one of his players who wasn't hitting the New York City area code of 212 at the time. Tenace gave him the only answer that fit the scene. He looked, smiled, and walked away.

I promised myself that when my baseball career was over I wouldn't be an "old ballplayer" and tell everybody how tough it was when I played. No stories about walking ten miles barefoot to a tryout camp with a borrowed glove to show what I could do. We played on decent fields. We didn't have to clear away broken beer bottles and rocks, although I remember seeing a picture of Yogi batting right-handed while barefoot with a hunk of concrete for home plate. I wouldn't tell any horror stories about the different reasons a pitcher would knock you down, either. You wouldn't hear me say, "In my day the pitcher would deck you if you had bad breath." I knew I'd never tell stories about batting in the big leagues without a batting helmet and then say that we just let our hair grow thick. Old timers told me that if a foul tip nicked a finger you spit on it and stuck it in the dirt. No pitcher threw hard enough to make you rub the spot where he hit you. I heard them all, but I wasn't going to use any of them.

It goes with any profession. A retired plumber told the story about when he broke into the business. "I'll tell you how tough it was. My boss had his own way of teaching us how to fit pipes. While we were trying to connect them he would turn the water on and you had to stay ahead of the flowing water." You have to admit that's a tough way to learn your trade, but I'd be willing to bet his boss also told him how he walked barefoot to school through a blizzard with a foot of snow on the ground.

Finley Peter Dunne once said that the past always looks better than it was because it isn't here. Yogi couldn't have said it any better. People refer to me as a legend or one of the greats of the game. That means two things: one, the only thing that kept me out of the Hall of Fame is that I had to play; and two, I'm old.

But, there's one big advantage to that—I know that whatever happens in a baseball game more than likely is something I've seen. The adage goes: the more things change, the more they stay the same. That's definitely true in baseball. I'm not talking about the players and the equipment or their salaries, but the game itself.

The language has changed, but it's still mostly centered on the pitcher. The "old" pitcher threw a fastball, a curveball, and a change-up. Then came the slider. The trick pitch was the knuckleball or the forkball. As kids we had pitchers who could throw an upshoot, a drop, and some had a fade-away. Today I hear pitchers who can "bring it," and they clock the speed of what they bring on the scoreboard. They don't bring a fastball, but they do bring hard cheese, heat, gas, high octane, and dead red. They throw seeds, aspirin, and peas at the knees and throw them through brick walls. Pitchers have two-seamers, four-seamers, runners, cutters, sinkers, tailers, sliders, back door sliders, splitters, and I'm sure a few I've missed. But you get the idea. They don't bring curveballs, but they do have yakkers, 12 to 6s, and Uncle Charley—or an exceptional Sir Charles. Some even call it a snapdragon. Talking to these guys you think you should have brought along a translator.

Every era seems to develop a language of its own. After a while they become clichés, but in my day it was not unusual to hear a pitcher talk about being beaten and yet hardly hear a baseball expression.

"I sawed the bat off in his hands, and I know all he got was a fist full of bees, but he got enough of it to hit a dying quail that beat me." Translation: The batter got a broken bat single that drove in the winning run.

"Dumb-dumb threw him a cantaloupe and that ping hitter hit a big can of corn but Clang-clang tried to hotdog the ball and it was good enough for a ribby." Translation: Dumb-dumb is the pitcher. Cantaloupe is the bad pitch. Ping hitter is the weak hitter. Big can of corn is a lazy fly ball. Clang-clang is the slow moving outfielder. Hotdog is the show- boating attempt. Ribby is the run batted in credited to the batter.

"He's got a good hose but bad wheels." Translation: Has a good arm but is a poor runner.

One of the great things about being part of the NBC *Game of the Week* broadcasts was seeing a different game every week. Watching the game from the best seat in the house, and getting paid for it, was like winning the lottery before the million dollar jackpots. Talking to the players was always a treat, and it was the major reason for getting to the park early.

Dennis Eckersley, a recent inductee into the Hall of Fame, was one of my favorite guys. Eck, as he liked to be called, never ducked anyone and always had time to talk. He's my choice as the father of this new baseball language. I'd hear cheese or gas or yakker when he talked about pitching, but there was more. A Dennis Eckersley sentence could sound like this: "It was a Bogart. I had good gas and I get good iron to do what I do, so I don't need to have anybody take me to the bridge. I gotta get the cheese into the kitchen or at least let him know about the yakker. I can't let it end up where he ding dongs me in front of thirty-five grand."

This translation from the Eckersley dictionary should help:

Bogart: a big game

Good gas: good fastball

Good iron: gets paid well

To the bridge: hit a home run off him

Cheese: Eckersley's fastball

Into the kitchen: throwing his fastball inside

Yakker: any breaking ball, curve, slider

Ding dongs: batter hits a home run

Thirty-five grand: the crowd

Dennis Eckersley. One of my all-time favorites, but I felt like I always needed an interpreter when I talked to him. Courtesy Oakland A's.

Some pitching coaches almost become evangelists and preach about the "point of release." You hear phrases like, "tight rotation on your breaking ball." The three words you hear the most from a pitching coach are movement, location, and velocity. But for me, nothing tops Eck's description of pitching: "Pitching is simple: give 'em cheese in the kitchen and a yakker for the kudo." Is there a better way to say "throw your fastball inside and then strike him out with your curveball?" You can see why Eck was a favorite.

I wonder sometimes who started some of the other things you see in today's game. Who was the first player to wear his pants down to his ankles?

The first time I saw this down-to-the-shoe-tops style was when I was broadcasting a Detroit Tigers game and George Hendrick was modeling. Some pants give the impression that the player is wearing spats like dancer Fred Astaire, and watching some of them play the outfield, maybe that's appropriate. They must have a reason for wearing their pants so low, but the answer I get is that "they feel good low." I don't like that style because there's no consistency. Some players wear them so low they cover their shoes while others just cover their ankles. Most look like they just fell off the truck on their way to a fashion photo shoot for *Popular Mechanics*.

Tight pants and shirts are another problem for me. Loose, billowing shirts were the style when I played, and they were encouraged because of the chance that an inside pitch might nick your shirt and therefore you had been hit by a pitch. You felt no pain and found yourself on first base. And on some of the teams I played for, a man on first was a rally. Some players' pants are so tight they look sprayed on. I often wonder how the "tight pants" player handles the low throw without splitting his pants. One player gave me his reason for wearing tight pants. Phil Linz of the Yankees said, "I don't know why, but I always felt I ran faster if my pants were tight." To that I can only say, "OK."

Now players wear sunglasses and earrings while playing. I remember seeing Raul Mondesi, then with the Dodgers, wearing an earring so big that I figured if he went 0 for 4 he'd be in a slump, but if he lost that earring the country would be in a depression.

Picking up a handful of dirt was the old system for making your hands feel dry. Now dirt is obsolete. Moises Alou revealed a unique way of toughening his hands; he urinates on them. That makes it easier to understand why players offer their closed fist instead of a handshake to congratulate him when he hits a home run. The straight congratulatory handshake has retired anyway. Now it's the closed fist against a teammate's closed fist or it's a high five or a low five or bumping chests to a dance ritual made up by the players. With some teams it's a tap on the helmet when they reach the dugout. The only prediction I'll make here is not that there will be a new congratulatory gesture, but that the team will have to hire a handshake coach.

Players have batting gloves, sliding gloves, weighted bats, and doughnut rings to make bats feel lighter, and the list goes on. The next time you're at the ballpark, take a look at the on-deck circle of the team batting. It looks like the inventory of a sporting goods store getting ready for a sidewalk sale.

The ballparks have changed, too. Scoreboards make you feel like you're at a movie. Games broadcast on the scoreboard have you either rooting for a hot dog to win a foot race or trying to figure out which cap is hiding the baseball. You're told when to get on your feet and when to cheer, and a noise meter tells you how loud you're cheering. Yet, with all the new technology, teams still win by using the Willie Mays Theory of Winning Baseball: "When they throw the ball I hit it, and when they hit it I catch it."

Scouts now use laptops and radar guns to check the speed of a pitch. Advance scouts give their team an up-to-date report on the strengths and weaknesses of the opposition. Curt Schilling is constantly referring to his notes and his computer, and he has the best reasons. He has invested in building his own personal library on every hitter he has faced. I've seen him sit on a plane with his laptop and watch himself pitch against every hitter who will face him in his next start. You can put your own label on all of this. Is it overkill? Too much preparation? Schilling doesn't care what the label is because it's his road to Cooperstown. Nothing in his game is an accident; everything is planned. His preparation is so detailed that you get the feeling he had ancestors at the invasion of Normandy in World War II.

As a kid, when I heard a scout was watching our game, I could never figure out which guy sitting in the stands was a scout. The biggest bonus we heard about was given to a player for the Detroit Tigers named Dick Wakefield. Wakefield went to the University of Michigan and the Tigers gave him a then record fifty-two thousand dollars. With this background, we thought a scout would be a guy dressed in a tuxedo with money coming out of every pocket, smoking a cigar, and arriving at the game in a big limousine like the ones we saw at funerals. That was not the case.

For the most part, scouts were former players who went out and looked at young players. There were tryout camps with hundreds of youngsters running, hitting, and throwing—hoping to fulfill their dream. You signed up; you were given a canvas patch with a number painted on it; and you were on your way. Scouts with clipboards and pencils were watching. No stop watches. No charts. The notes said things like: number 106, can't run. No speed. Number 214, good arm but can't cover any ground.

The message was to the point. No scouting report said more with fewer words than the famous Mike Gonzalez report. Looking at an infielder, the St. Louis Cardinals' coach wrote, "Good field—no hit." Birdie Tebbetts came close to that report when he wrote about a player, "He has a 400 batting stroke but 200 legs."

Paul Krichell, the famous Yankees' scout, summed up a manager who should have been winning more games with the caliber of players he had. Krichell wrote, "He knows a lot of baseball but he can't ever think of it."

Scouts on the payroll of a major league team also had "bird dogs" that watched high school games or pickup games and reported back to the scout that he just saw "the next Bob Feller" or "the next Babe Ruth."

The over-simplification is that there were scouts who beat the bushes and high school fields to find future big leaguers and scouts who followed the other big league teams and reported to the parent club. This helped in trying to win games and in making trades.

If there has been one big improvement in baseball, it's the scouting reports. I still have several official scouting reports from my days in the mid-40s to 2004. You be the judge.

In 1946, Harry Brecheen, my teammate on the Cardinals, won three games in the World Series against the Boston Red Sox. Another star pitcher on the team was Howard Pollet. In a comprehensive report covering the entire National League that year (figure 1) here's what the Chicago Cubs' scout had to say about Brecheen and Pollet. On Brecheen: "I like him. A champion. He wants to beat you." No numbers were given, but it gave you a good idea of Brecheen's makeup and desire.

```
ST. LOUIS CARDINALS COVERAGE - A.

BRECHEEN, L.H.P. - Hits L. : The outfielder played this fellow for a pull hitter.
    Certainly respected his hitting ability. Hitting against all R.H.P. They pitch
    him low and away. He walked one time and they made him hit the low curve away t
    other two times he was up. He beat the ball into the dirt.

    He pitched a smart game, winning it all the way. Good control. Pitched to spot
    Fast ball just average which goes for his curve and a dandy screw ball. He did
    not hesitate to brush the hitter back when he was ahead and every pitch seemed t
    have some motive behind it. In on the handles, away etc. Helped himself by
    fielding the ball hit back and bunted to him. I like him. A champion. He wants
    to beat you.

BRAZLE, L.H.P. - Hits L. : The outfield played him straight away and 3B. back. He only
    hit one time and against pitcher Karl. He didn't look so hot against the knuckle
    ball.

    Brazle relieved and only pitched a short time in the second game. He had a good
    sinker ball. He only threw three curve balls, but that sinker was a dandy and he
    did a swell job relieving.

MUNGER, R.H.P. - Hits R. : Outfield played him straight away. 3B. even with the bag.
    R.H.P. Johnson side armed him curve and fast low away. He got one hit off a curv
    ball shoulder high to C.F. Did not look so good on the side arm low away.

    This fellow had good stuff, fast, curve and change. He was behind the hitter all
    night and had to come in with the good pitch too much. He lost his stuff in the
    seventh inning and was relieved by Brazle.

POLLET, L.H.P. - Hits L. : Outfield played for left field hitter. 3B. over and even
    with the bag. Hitting against L.H.P. Spahn who pitched him high tight. He only
    hit one time and went out 2B-1B.

    Pitched good ball for 5 innings. Masi hit home run and triple off him good for
    two runs and he was taken out for pinch hitter. This pinch hitter led the inning
    off. It is possible that Pollet was having arm trouble. His stuff although did
    look okay.
```

Figure 1.

As the manager, Whitey Herzog could have used the starter's flag from the Indianapolis 500 for his steal sign. Left to right: Willie McGee, Vince Coleman, Whitey Herzog, Ozzie Smith, Jack Clark, and Tom Herr. Courtesy St. Louis Cardinals Hall of Fame Museum.

The last line of the report on Howard Pollet (who won twenty-one games in 1946) gives an idea of what to expect when facing him as a batter. "His stuff although did look OK."

When the St. Louis Cardinals had Ozzie Smith, Willie McGee, and Vince Coleman in their lineup it was the understatement of the year to say they had good speed. One of that team's best weapons was the groundskeeper. He'd make sure that the area in front of home plate was kept hard so all any of these speedsters had to do was hit down on the ball, get a big hop, and off they'd go. Instead of "Play ball," the umpire should have hollered, "Gentlemen, start your engines."

If you were scouting that Cardinals' team today, the computer would tell you how fast they were, which base was their favorite to steal from, what pitches they favored, and on and on. The information with this system is much better. Today's scout is better trained and more equipped to do his job, but the scout of my day made it much easier to understand. You wouldn't be confused if you read the Cardinals' scouting report (figure 2). The first sentence told you pretty much all you needed to know. Again, there are no numbers or a computer printout, just information

---

ST. LOUIS CARDINALS

This is a running ball club and they will steal your ass off. They will steal when they are ahead and also when they are two and three runs behind.

Most of the bases were stolen on the first and second pitches. Namely Coleman and Lonnie Smith. These two will also steal third base against left handed pitching, also, if given the chance, will go against right handed pitching.

This club will also hit & run. Their favorite count was 2 balls, 1 strike and 1 ball, no strikes. They used the squeeze play one time in six games.

Herr was the hitter with count 1 ball and no strikes. Coleman was the runner at third base.

Cards did not show much power at all. They scored most of their runs by good base running, singles & doubles. PLEASE run on Lonnie Smith in leftfield.

Their bullpen is not that impressive. Allen has to carry a big load in the bullpen. Outside of Andujar there were pitching was just fair.

I feel that they have the best double play combination I've seen this year.

VINCE COLEMEN - OUTFIELD

High ball Hitter from both sides. Likes the ball out over plate. Must keep ball in on him and down. Play him shaded to left field. When hitting from left side, give him rightfield line. He will bunt from both sides. Coleman will run, be careful, he will also try to steal third base. He has great speed and will gamble on bases. Play your third and first basemen in on grass. He will bunt, push and drag.

OZZIE SMITH - SHORT STOP

High ball hitter from both sides. Keep ball down. Will chase bad pitches with two strikes. Play him straightaway from rightside and shade to left field from left side. He will run and take a big lead off of first base. He will bunt.

Figure 2.

gathered by watching the Cardinals play. No computer could be as definite as the first sentence in the report or the pleading of "PLEASE run on the left fielder."

The reports got a little better as charts were added to the verbal reports. Where the batter hit a particular pitch became important as the defense was set up accordingly. Once the scouting report was given to the manager the intrigue began. It was a double-edged sword as you tried to figure out the strengths and weaknesses of the opponent but also

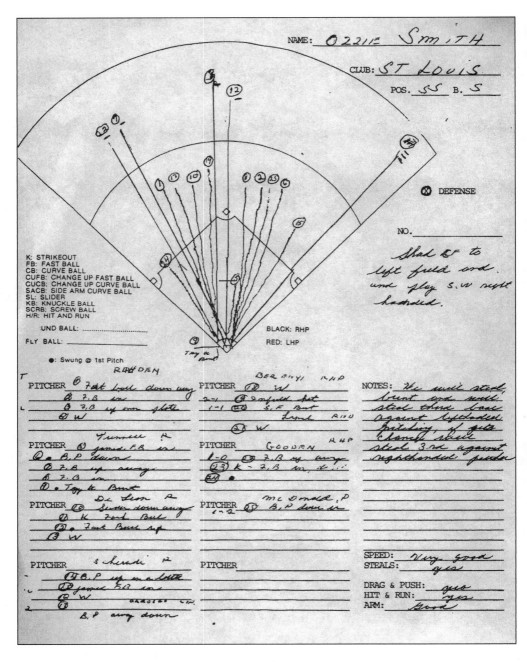

Figure 3.

tried to "decode" your scout's report. Good penmanship was not a requirement, and some scouts were never participants in the class spelling bee. So most teams brought in the scout who wrote the report in hopes that he knew and remembered what he wrote.

The report shown on (figure 3) would mainly tell you that your defense should be bunched from left-center field to right-center field. There appears to be only one ball hit down the line and that was in right field. Many pitchers, though, don't like to hear about where the pitches were thrown. I agree. For example, no two pitchers' fastballs are alike. In the 2006 World Series, Detroit pitchers Verlander and Zumaya were regularly clocked in the high nineties. Both pitchers flirted with the one hundred mile per hour mark on the radar gun and got that high a couple times. Cardinals' pitchers didn't come close to that speed. While Cardinals' pitchers tried to hit particular spots in the strike zone, it seemed like the Tigers' fireballers just released the ball toward the general vicinity of home plate.

As a catcher, it was important to know the opposing players who played hit and run or would try to steal a base. It was also important to know the players who could beat out a bunt for a hit.

This scouting report was an improvement over "they will steal your ass off" but doesn't come near the reports of today. Rather than explain pitches and draw lines the new reports describe tendencies. Take a look at Pedro Martinez's tendencies (figure 4, page 17) and you have a good idea what he will do when he has two strikes on you or what he will do when he's behind in the count with runners on base. That is solid information.

The question comes up today whether all that information is too much. I've heard more than one hitting coach warn a hitter to be careful of too much information as you may end up with the prescription for a slump. Your bat will suffer from "paralysis by analysis."

Batters get their information, but so do pitchers. The day is over when a pitching coach walked out there and, as the myth goes, he and the pitcher talked about the blond in the first row. The pitching coach will remind the pitcher about the strategy meeting before the game and end up getting him to say what pitch he will make. It will be a positive statement, and the pitcher will think he thought of it. One team's report on Moises Alou had this information: Over 40% of the time he will hit the first pitch. Against right-handers he hit .356. Against left-handers he hit .368.

You can be sure the coach will visit the mound and say something like, "Don't make that first pitch a fastball right down the middle."

The latest technology used (and it probably will continue to change) is the video iPod. The technology's gone from film to tape to DVDs that players can take home so they can watch themselves on a laptop. Now it's all in the palm of their hands. The hitters can watch their every at bat and see how the upcoming pitcher worked on them.

How specific does it get? According to one newspaper story, Todd Helton has every one of his hits since 1998 stored by the month in his iPod. When things go badly and Mr. Slump comes around, Helton can go to his iPod and look at his swing when he was getting base hits. An excellent month to check would be August of 2000. He can pick any date. He had fifty hits and batted .476 for the month.

For me, one thing hasn't changed at all. Baseball is an unpredictable game. It always has been and always will be. Over the years I've seen so many things happen that tell me you can never be sure of a "sure thing."

Look at the 2001 World Series between the Yankees and the Diamondbacks. In game five, manager Joe Torre played the infield back, and when Diamondbacks outfielder Reggie Sanders hit a line drive up the middle, Alfonso Soriano made a diving catch for the out. He saved at least two runs and probably saved the game for the Yankees. In the seventh game, Torre played the infield in, and Luis Gonzalez drove in the deciding run of the game *and* the Series with a little blooper over shortstop Derek Jeter's head. If Torre had played the infield back, like in game five, Jeter could have caught Gonzalez's pop fly bare-handed or with a pair of tweezers.

What could Torre have done? Gonzalez's hit itself was unpredictable. Here's a player with fifty-seven home runs for the year who wins the game with a ball that slips just over the shortstop's head and barely lands on the outfield grass—hit so softly it hardly moved a blade. To use

Inside Edge
SCOUTING SERVICES

Pitcher Profile

Martinez, Pedro

Mets   *vs. LHBs*

Throws: Right	**# Pitches Charted:** 439
Ahead in the count %: 42%	**Pitches per Pl. App.** 4.06

E D G E   N O T E S

Covering Scouted Games from 2006 Season

Pitches
- Fastballs (49%): 4-seam (87-94); 2-seam sinks (85-88); Cutter (83-86)
- Curves (9%): 12/6 break (68-79)
- Sliders (23%): Sharp (83-86)
- Changeups (19%): Sinks/runs (75-83)

Moves
- Quick feet: Mixes in slide step: Will hold the ball

Notes
- Times to plate: 1.32 to 1.46
- With slide step: 1.03 to 1.13

Strengths
- Good Fastballs (.128) & Changeups (.182)
- Hitters chase his Sliders (36% chased)

Weaknesses
-

Tendencies
- Likes to backdoor the CB to LHBs w/2 strikes
- Low strike zone % with Curves (34%) & Changeups (29%)
- High strike zone % with Sliders (61%)
- More Fastballs to RHBs (60%) than LHBs (49%)
- More Changeups to LHBs (19%) than RHBs (5%)
- Throws more Fastballs with 2 strikes (56%)
- Throws more Sliders when he's behind (33%) & with runners on base (36%)

P I T C H   T I P S

Pitch	% of pitches	All Counts	First Pitch	Early Counts	Two Strikes	Pitcher Ahead	Pitcher Behind	With RISP	Strike Zone %	Chase %	Opponents' Scouted BA	
	Fastballs	49%	50%	44%	56%	50%	52%	43%	58%	23%	.128 (6/47)	Very High
	Curves	9%	4%	7%	12%	15%	2%	5%	34%	20%	.111 (1/9)	High
	Sliders	23%	26%	28%	13%	14%	33%	36%	61%	36%	.263 (5/19)	Avg. or unsure
	Changeups	19%	20%	21%	19%	21%	12%	16%	29%	37%	.182 (4/22)	
	5th Pitch											Low
	Total Scouted Pitches	439	108	246	153	185	84	61	51%	29%	.165 (16/97)	

P I T C H   Z O N E

vs. Fastballs

LEGEND:

Number of pitches

Very Favorite Zones

Favorite Zones

	9	6		30
5	7	8		
5	14	11	36	10
	11	13	21	
4		7		19

vs. Other Pitches

	7	1		12
	4	5	6	
3	10	4	22	8
	10	16	22	
26		21		46

Very High
High
Avg. or unsure
Low
Very Low

Figure 4.

golfer Lee Trevino's description, "The ball landed like a butterfly with sore feet."

For me, the beauty of the game is its unpredictability. Baseball still starts with the pitcher. No clock can run out, and kneeling with the ball cannot end the game. The pitcher still has to throw the ball, and after he does it becomes somebody else's responsibility. In games four and five of the 2001 World Series between the Yankees and the Diamondbacks, somebody else's responsibility was a euphemism for the term "walk off home run." Ken Harrelson, the player turned general manager turned broadcaster, pointed out that in baseball, when a team is on offense the defense has the ball. That alone makes baseball a unique game.

A great pitcher will seem to be playing a simple game of catch with his catcher with the batter standing between them. Yet there's no assurance that when the pitcher throws the third strike the catcher will catch it. Sometimes the catcher drops the ball, and he has to throw to first for the out. We can't be sure he'll make an accurate throw or throw in time to get the runner. The pitcher got his man, but the catcher didn't get *his* man. Unpredictability!

A famous person, not Yogi, once said, "Beauty is in the eyes of the beholder." That may be, but I like to switch the word "beauty" for "funny" and say that funny is in the eyes of the beholder.

Many of the players I played with said funny things, and many of today's players say funny things. The big difference is that today's players are paid better, and that should make it easier to laugh.

People often tell me how much they enjoyed watching baseball back when I played because "you guys played for fun and love of the game." Sorry, not true. We played for as much money as we could get, but with no union we had no leverage. We were owned by the teams since we had signed a contract. You were with the team until they decided to move you. There was no free agency. You signed; you played; and you got paid what the team said. You can't win an argument with the general manager who finishes his contract conversation with, "We finished last with you and we can finish last without you."

Until the Major League Baseball Association was born and people like Marvin Miller, Donald Fehr, and Gene Orza came on the scene, all a player got was advice from everyone and ultimatums from club owners. You can go back to a 1908 article in *Collier* magazine by Billy Sunday and read the great advice he gave to ballplayers: "Fellows, listen to me! You will not always be in the spotlight. Your eye will grow dim. You will get a glass arm or a charley horse. Down will come the 'is' and up will go the 'was' and you are all in. You work hard for your money. GET ALL YOU CAN AND CAN ALL YOU GET!"

From Billy Sunday in 1908 we go to third baseman Ken Boyer, who played most of his career with the St. Louis Cardinals and was in the major leagues from 1955 until 1969. When it came to the myth about playing for fun and love of the game, he said it best for all players: "True, I'm in this game for love, not money. But the more money I make the more I love it."

Today's managers may also have a better sense of humor but don't get much of a chance to show it. Now television runs the show to the point that the manager is interviewed during a game. He not only has to think of what he can do to help his team win but think of an answer for the TV audience that makes sense while saying nothing.

When it comes to telling baseball stories, though, all that have really changed are the names. Every year during the banquet season I hear the following two stories, and the only change is that a current player's name is substituted for a former player. I first heard these stories back in 1946.

Story number one. _____ (any pitcher) is on the mound. He's really getting rocked. It's the first inning and nothing but line drive base hits. The first _____ (put in any number) batters really hit him hard. _____ (any manager) comes out, calls to _____ (catcher) and says, "What about it? What kind of stuff does he have?" _____ (catcher) says, "I don't know, I haven't caught one yet."

The other faithful story that shows up every year has the catcher arguing with the umpire. Once again you substitute the names you want.

CATCHER: That wasn't a strike.

UMPIRE: It was because I called it a strike.

CATCHER: Well, it wasn't because I say so.

UMPIRE: Just be quiet and catch or I'll bite your head off.

CATCHER: Do that and you'll have more brains in your belly than in your head.

I don't think I've watched a ballgame since my "Golden Years" began that I don't think of a similar play or a conversation that had the same cast of characters. I was lucky to have been a catcher because that's where the action is. I don't mean the game action. I'm talking about the meetings on the mound, the discussions with the umpire, visits with the opposing players, and listening to the bench jockeys. In my baseball life the real insult comics were on the other team's bench:

—"You're so ugly you ought to shave your neck and walk backwards."

—"Next time you go into a sauna why don't you reshape your face when the steam makes it soft?"

—"Every other Italian goes to umpiring; where's your indicator?"

—"Great throw. Umpire should've called it an infield fly."

—"Need to put hinges on that swing."

—"Throw in a salad once in awhile. We need a bus ticket to get around you."

Bench jockeys spared no one. It was open season even on the guys who were skinny:

—"Why don't they use you as a foul pole?"

—"You could be a dipstick at the Texaco station."

—"You're built like a TV antenna. Put a dish on your head. We can get the game."

Sitting in the stands is a new experience for me, and I like it. One fan told me, "Now you're sitting in the stands like real people." That's true, and now I hear things, not from press releases but from real people. Sometimes I hear one that gets my attention right away.

I was at a home game between the Diamondbacks and the Yankees. Now, I'm used to hearing things like, "he's taller than I thought," or "he's cuter than his pictures," or "I didn't think he was so big." But how about this conversation:

FIRST FAN: Bernie Williams is a big surprise. I didn't picture him like that.

SECOND FAN: Whadda you mean? How did you picture him?

FIRST FAN: Well, look at him. Don't you see it?

SECOND FAN: See what? I don't know what you're talking about.

(By now I'm all ears as I want to hear this big secret.)

FIRST FAN: Look. Bernie Williams has high knees.

SECOND FAN: High knees? What the hell are you talking about?

FIRST FAN: Look—he's got high knees. Can't you see?

SECOND FAN: He's like everybody else—his legs start at his feet and go all the way up to his ass. That's what I see.

FIRST FAN: You're blind.

I don't know what he meant, and I agreed with fan number two, but I have to admit that every time Bernie Williams went up to hit I was checking his knees.

Here's a question I tried to answer but was unsuccessful. The conversation was simple.

FAN: Mr. Joe, this is my first professional game. I have a question that my husband can't answer, and he told me you played and are now on TV and you would be able to answer.

ME: I'll try.

FAN: Why is that one man standing on a hill and all the others have to stand on the flat ground?

I stick by my statement of "I'll try." I did, and I failed. Test your baseball knowledge and try to explain the pitcher's mound to a non-fan.

Since I sit in the same seat for every game, I've gotten to know my seat neighbors. One night my friend's daughter came to the game with some of her friends, all college-age (but then it seems like everybody looks college-age to me these days). During the game, my friend's daughter asked if I would show her friend my St. Louis Cardinals World Series ring.

"Sure, I'll be glad to show her," I said, as I took it off and handed it to her. She was admiring it, and I was puffing up when her innocent question took all the air out of the balloon.

"Wow, 1946. That's a long time ago. Did you play with Babe Ruth?"

"No," I said, laughing. "I had one chance to play with him, but I had to go to the theater with a guy named Lincoln."

Many people want to show me that they know their baseball and will swear that they saw me with my old team. The problem with this is that my "old team" always turns out to be the Gas House Gang, the Cardinals' team of the 1930s.

"Hey, Joe. I'll bet that Dizzy Dean was something to catch."

"I guess he was, but I never caught Dizzy Dean. He was before me."

"C'mon, I used to watch you guys. Pepper Martin, Joe Medwick, Diz, and his brother Daffy. You were there."

"No, I wasn't, but I did root for them because they were my favorite team when I was eight years old."

"Really? I'd swear I saw you with them."

"No, honest. I was a little boy once and they were my team." Sometimes I have to pull out my driver's license to show I was born in 1926 and the Gas House Gang was my team in 1934. You'd be surprised how many people walk away muttering that they're sure I was with them. Too bad I've never been given credit for being the only eight-year-old to play in the big leagues and in a World Series.

Getting old doesn't have many pluses but memories take some of the potholes out of this road called life. Memory lets me watch and enjoy a baseball game like I never did before and many times lets me leave the park saying, "How about that game!" Baseball is the only sport that doesn't jump at you. When you watch a football game on television you get the "sounds of the game." That means a collision, usually between two guys big enough to have license plates on their uniforms instead of numbers.

Basketball used to be considered a non-contact sport, but if you watch it today you know that's a myth. Former Notre Dame coach Digger Phelps put it into perspective when he said, "I wouldn't go under the basket now even if I had a tetanus shot."

I like hockey, but comics say it best when they talk about going to a fight and a hockey game breaks out. It's knocking people against the boards, and when that gets boring it's a fight. When the fight is over usually the next thing you hear is, "Did you see how he beat him up when he got his gloves off?"

The only time I even hear the word "beat" at a baseball game is when fans say they're leaving to beat the traffic. Of course, I live by the baseball cliché that I heard in a Class C league, the Western Association. My manager, Runt Marr, wanting to get the players out of the clubhouse would say, "You can't see the whole game if you don't see the first pitch." Add to that, "You can't see the whole game if you don't see the last out." I never care about beating the traffic. That's the whole idea of baseball— spending a leisurely night at the ballpark watching a great game unfold and watching the teams *just play ball*.

Even Charlie Brown's Catcher Would Rather Play the Piano

CHAPTER 2

Being a catcher is like being a fire hydrant at a dog show. If a catcher was asked to march in a parade, they'd make him march behind the elephants. He'd have the same lousy view the whole parade and get dumped on at the same time. Thinking of it that way makes it easy to understand that even Charlie Brown's catcher would rather play the piano. When you stop to think about it, the name for the position is an unfinished sentence. Catcher of what? Stares from pitchers? Second guessing from the manager? Catchers can't complain about the name, though, because it is an upgrade. Look in The New Dickson Baseball Dictionary and you'll learn that the catcher, per 1845 Knickerbocker rules, was called the "behind." Mention that to a pitcher today and he might say something like, "You got that right, he is a behind, a real dumb ass."

Courtesy Charles M. Schulz Creative Associates.

Maybe this is why, in the early days, they called the catcher "the behind." He was almost behind the umpire. Ty Cobb at bat. Courtesy National Baseball Hall of Fame Library, Cooperstown, N.Y.

Curt Schilling agreed. "Great name. Should have kept it." It's hard to argue with a guy who has a computer record of every hitter he ever faced, but that was not the argument he used that left me speechless.

"How would you like to have the catcher you're working with come out to the mound and tell you he's not sure if you're using the second sign or adding the first two signs? He's supposed to be calling pitches from the game plan we talked about in the meeting, and he's not sure what fingers to flash. Now, is he a behind or not?"

I have to agree with Schilling. But being behind the plate is not exactly like being the Grand Marshal at the Rose Parade, either. The catcher is a grunt, a real groundhog. The uniform of a catcher should be a construction hardhat or a coal miner's hat with a lamp on it. Some pitchers make you a neighbor to the grub worms in front of home plate. You live in the dirt. After the game, you really appreciate a shower. In fact, a long trip on a raft would be great. Think of it as the worst job you can get, maybe like a septic tank cleaner. You take just as much of the septic tank product except that you don't see or smell it.

All summer you get foul tips off your fingernails, your Adam's apple, your legs, and your feet. Your body feels like a one-wall handball court. Even when the foul balls miss you, there's always the chance that your pitcher might miss the signal and throw a fastball when you're expecting a curve. There's an old joke about a catcher walking into a saloon and ordering four beers by holding up his index finger and little finger. The inference is that the other two fingers are somewhere around home plate because the pitcher missed the catcher's signal.

One of my favorite writers, the late Jim Murray, pegged it right when he wrote, "The catcher is the Sultan of Squat. Not even Cinderella was on her knees as much as a big league catcher. Being the catcher is the submarine job of baseball."

As a catcher, you can study all the hitters and remember how to pitch to all of them. You can set up the hitter perfectly, block the plate, and make the tag for a crucial out. You can keep a couple of fifty-five- foot curveballs from bounding past you and make sure the runner stays at third base. Now your team wins the game and nine out of ten times, all you hear about is how the pitcher had command of all his pitches. In the post-game interview the pitcher might give credit to the catcher with the magnanimous phrase, "I didn't shake him off one time." I remember a couple of my not-so-favorite pitchers saying that. All I could think of was that even from the bench I could tell they didn't shake off the catcher because I didn't hear a rattle.

Catching is the only position that can warrant a full blown strategy meeting after a key hit. The catcher is blamed for giving up a run, and he hasn't even touched the ball.

After a home run or a key hit, here's how it went when I played:

MANAGER: "What did he hit?"

CATCHER: "Fastball."

MANAGER: "How the hell can you give him a fastball when all we talked about was that we were going to show him the fastball and make him hit the breaking ball? How dumb can you get?"

Now, depending on the manager, this can go on for two minutes or two days or every time he sees you from then on. Rarely does the catcher get a chance to tell the manager, "We were trying to show him the fastball but he hit it." You also learned very early in your career that the worst way to begin a sentence after a big hit is, "I thought." That's as far as you get.

I'm not sure that happens much today because when I see a manager's reaction after a key hit, I put the binoculars on him as soon as the third out is made. Seldom do I see contact between the catcher and the manager. I guess the manager knows that in some cases, today's catcher could buy the team and fire him. I also feel a catcher's agent figures into the mix. Neither situation was around when I was playing ball.

Crossing up a catcher is not uncommon, but you better not go out and start screaming at the pitcher, or you will find that he will have a personal, private catcher for his next start, and it won't be you. Even when a rookie pitcher crosses you up the catcher has to go into his tender loving care mode. The great Hall of Fame catcher Bill Dickey had the best method to handle the situation. In his best Southern drawl he told this story:

> I got crossed up when I called for a curve and got a fastball and that is the worst kind of cross up. I got this rookie pitcher out there and I know he can't ask me out of the lineup if I get on him, but I didn't want him to be upset for the rest of the game, so I walked out to the mound real calm. 'Listen, I told him, don't be nervous out here 'cuz it's the same as pitching in college except here in the big leagues the catchers are dumber. See, they have to know what's coming.

When a catcher gets an industrial strength hit from a foul ball a couple of scenarios may unfold. If he's hit hard enough and goes to his knees there's a chance the trainer will come out and check on him. It's always, "How do you feel? Does it hurt?" Most of the time, if you get any sympathy, you get it from some umpires. Notice I said some umpires because often the umpire will check the ball first. I don't know why, but maybe once he had to put an injured ball out of the game.

Umpires try to help catchers, and it's an unwritten reciprocal agreement. The routine goes something like this: catcher gets hit by a foul tip on the arm. Down he goes. Everybody in the park—fans, players in the dugout, players on the field, ushers, and vendors—are all watching the catcher. The overall feeling is that it hit him on the arm and since his arm's not lying on home plate it must still be attached to his body. So, he can't be too badly hurt. But here comes the umpire to the rescue. If you're on good terms he might ask you how you're doing as he passes you to get to the plate. This is his act of mercy and for this he should get the Humanitarian of the Year Award. He dusts off home plate to give you enough time to see if your arm is really still attached.

The degree of the umpire's compassion depends on where you're hit. I once got a foul tip in a very vulnerable area. Down I went and was almost kicked out of the game. The umpire leaned over and asked, "You all right? Where did it hit you?"

"Do I look like I'm all right?" I said. "You saw where it hit me. The least you can do is rub it."

If you're really lucky the opposing catcher will come up to bat, and then you might get some real sympathy. Outside of your immediate family only another catcher knows what you're going through.

Unless you can swing a big bat àla Johnny Bench, Yogi Berra, Roy Campanella, Carlton Fisk, or Mike Piazza, you're a grunt. What other position gets the benefit, if you want to call it that, of having a special description. Many think the ultimate compliment is to be described as a great handler of pitchers. Show me a catcher who's described that way and I can probably show you a batting average under .230. A former catcher had it right when he said, "The best handler of pitchers is the catcher who drives in the winning run."

Infielders are never described as great handlers of ground balls. Have you ever heard an outfielder described as a great handler of fly balls? Baseball people say you can shake a tree and four gloves will fall out but you'll never see a bat coming out of a tree.

When I broke into professional baseball with the Springfield Cardinals in the Western Association, a Class C league, catchers were treated as

No, I wasn't praying. I was hoping I was still in one piece. Courtesy Joe Garagiola.

special people. It wasn't much, but you weren't just another name in the
lineup. I was sixteen years old, and how I loved to play against the Fort
Smith Giants. Why? Close your eyes and think about a deep voiced six-
footer with a megaphone in his hand starting in the right field corner
and going all the way around to the left field foul pole announcing the
starting pitcher and his catcher. I felt special, but never more than when
we had one particular pitcher starting for us. His name was Arthur
Cyralewski. What an audition for the "megaphone man" to announce:
"And tonight's battery for the visiting Springfield Cardinals, Arthur
Cyralewski pitching and Joe Garagiola catching." Even though he was
practically winded by the time he got to third base, it did make a guy
feel special.

Forget the given or baptismal names of catchers. They're usually the first to get saddled with a nickname, and it's never going to be the Yankee Clipper or the Georgia Peach. When catchers get nicknames they're usually brutal and they stick. Names like Smokey, Shanty, Fats, Hoss, Tank, Mule, Porky, Gabby, and Yogi are just a few. One catcher with a name that I thought really elevated the position was the Phillies' Clayton Errol Dalrymple. Carlton Fisk was another great name, but his teammates just called him Pudge. Catchers always have the nicknames you figure were left over from the plumber's union meeting.

The Peanuts Gang, Charlie Brown's team, has lost more games than any team I know. I remember one comic strip where Charlie Brown blamed part of their eternal losing streak on the fact that catchers have too much time to think. Charlie Brown really understands catchers. Maybe he started out as a catcher but somebody, like Lucy, turned him into a pitcher. But for me, Charlie Brown is the hero of the catcher. As a pitcher he never wins a game, but he has a competitor's heart. All catchers love the pitcher with "questionable" stuff who never blames the catcher.

The catcher is my favorite guy to watch for a few reasons. Number one, I was a catcher. Number two, anything that's worth watching usually happens to or near a catcher. Number three, it's my book, and no catcher will look bad in my book.

Good baseball fans know a catcher is many things. He doesn't just strap on the equipment and go out there to be the pitcher's best friend and the umpire's conversation partner.

First, the catcher is like a census taker. He has to make sure that in every inning all his players are on the field. He has to be able to see and count eight guys standing in front of him in fair territory. Sound simple? Let me tell you what I think about when I see the catcher checking his defense.

Catcher Del Wilber was playing for a Texas League team called the Houston Buffaloes. They had a left fielder named Lou Novikoff who had played in the big leagues with the Chicago Cubs. He was nicknamed the Mad Russian. With Houston leading and going into the top of the ninth inning, Wilber noticed there was no left fielder. Everyone assumed Novikoff had run out to his position, but he wasn't there, and nobody could figure out where he went. The batboy was sent to the clubhouse to look for him but came back saying he wasn't there. It was a big mystery, but the game had to go on, so a new left fielder came into the game. After one, two, then three innings the Houston team headed for the clubhouse with a victory. There to greet them was the Mad Russian. The batboy had checked the clubhouse but not everywhere. The next day's paper cleared up the mystery with the headline, WHEN YOU GOTTA GO...YOU GOTTA GO. Of course, the catcher received no credit for being an alert census taker.

A catcher is also like a foreman on a construction job. In the clubhouse meetings before the game the team talks about setting up the defense. The pitcher pitches a certain way to try to make the batter hit to where the defense is set up the strongest; for example, pitch a right-handed pull hitter inside, and set the defense to play him to pull. It's up to the catcher to see that the infielders and outfielders are playing him to pull. Night games make it easier because during day games the outfielders drift to where the shadow of the light standard falls on the field. Like a construction worker, the outfielder likes the shade too. If you check most outfields in parks using natural grass you'll usually see a spot that by August is worn thin. Like sheep, most outfielders will graze in the same spot. So much for printouts and laptops; just let me find the shade of an old oak tree or light standard.

Sometimes the way a park is built dictates how an outfielder plays on defense. A good example is Wrigley Field. Let's look at left field. The wall has an indentation, which is like a lighthouse to a lost ship. The left fielder, regardless of who he is, and regardless of who the hitter is, will line up even with the indentation. Why? The answer's always the same: "'Cuz I know if I have to go to my right and back I have more room."

Finally, the catcher is like a peace negotiator. When the umpire makes a call that riles the pitcher, it's up to the catcher to calm him down. Then he has to try to convince the umpire that his pitcher wasn't referring to him when he screamed but was yelling because the catcher called for the wrong pitch. It's not easy to convince an umpire he's not the target when the pitcher is screaming and at the same time questioning the umpire's intelligence and suggesting that his father and mother should have gotten married.

One of the toughest chores for the catcher is trying to be a diplomat when the manager comes out to visit with the pitcher and motions that he wants the catcher in on the conversation. It's usually late in the game and the pitcher is really tired and sweaty. He's wide-eyed and hardly able to breathe, but he waits for the manager. Here comes the manager, having just left an air-conditioned dugout wearing a uniform that looks like it just came from the dry cleaners. Then he asks the pitcher, "What's the matter, you tired?"

I always hoped I'd hear the pitcher answer truthfully. "Sure I'm tired. Don't I look like I'm tired? My eyeballs are behind my ears." The worst part for the catcher is when the manager looks at him and asks, "Has he still got it, whaddya think?" Try to think of a diplomatic answer while the pitcher, who looks like he was just run over by an eighteen-wheeler, is listening.

The catcher knows he's on his own out on the field. The infielder misses the ball so the outfielder picks it up, and the error sign goes up on the scoreboard. The outfielder misses the ball, and the wall stops it, and after he picks it up he can check the scoreboard to see if they gave him an error. If the catcher misses the ball, there's no outfielder or wall. When the inning ends after a play like that, I watch the dugout. The manager and the catcher usually choose to sit at different ends of the dugout. Those dugouts are so big now that they probably have different zip codes, so communicating will take a couple of days.

Whenever a catcher goes out to the mound the announcers usually say it's due to one of two things. Either they're changing signals or the catcher is trying to settle down his pitcher. To that I say, not necessarily. Pitchers will call you out and ask you to look at the scoreboard to see what so-and-so is doing because "my friend is pitching that game." Get in a pennant race and the trips are frequent because managers don't like pitchers to be scoreboard watchers. The catcher becomes the messenger and scoreboard checker.

Many people are convinced that being a catcher is the most dangerous position on the field. The hazardous part of the job is not the foul tips that nick you or the runners who try to bowl you over. It's an unseen enemy.

On a hot, humid day in a city like St. Louis or Cincinnati, some players and umpires ought to wear warning signs stating that getting near them is hazardous to your health. Imagine yourself stuck between the batter and the overweight umpire who had spaghetti smothered in garlic the night before. Even his mask reeks of garlic. You know you're in trouble early in the game when you start sniffing and the umpire asks, "Did you do that?" The tip-off on who the culprit is turns out to be easy to figure, since the batter hasn't reached home plate yet.

I always have to smile when I'm watching a game on TV and nothing seems to be going on and yet the catcher calls time and goes out to the mound. No base runner is on second base to make you think any sign stealing is going on, and the pitcher hasn't had any trouble, so why the conference on the mound?

Some batters in my day took great delight in delivering this unwanted gift. I won't name the player but he was a teammate of mine at one time. When he came back to the bench it was funny to hear him tell us what he did in the batter's box. Then I got traded and learned up close and personal about chemical warfare in the batter's box. When it came to passing gas he was a Hall of Famer, delivering almost on cue. He was the only person who would brag, "I had great follow through with that one." Playing against him, I learned he'd make it a point to drop his package sometime during the game. He'd announce it at the proper time. As he tapped home plate he'd relieve himself, and his timing was uncanny. I'm sure the people in the first row on the third base side sometimes heard his effort.

If it was a hot, humid day (and it seemed like they all were when he did it), you tried to protect yourself. Like the condemned man, I knew it was coming, but unlike the condemned man I didn't know when. Up he'd come to begin his ritual. He'd tap the plate twice and say, "Joey, this is for you." You were doomed. Sometimes you heard it and other times it was as if a rattlesnake was in the batter's box. All you heard was a hiss. You'd squat lower...you'd rise up...but nothing worked. The smell just hovered and regardless of the game situation you had to get help. All you could do was leave. The umpire would walk to the ball boy next to the dugout and pretend he was getting some more baseballs and you headed for the mound. With watering eyes you'd make it to the mound only to hear the pitcher scream, "What the hell are you doing out here? Whadda you want?" More than once, sometimes gasping, I'd answer back, "Fresh air...fresh air, that's what I want."

It all starts as kids on the playground. When you throw the bat in the air and start the climb up the bat hoping your hand is last so you can choose first, you already know the name of your first choice. In my neighborhood it was Lawdy, who grew up to be Yogi Berra. He wasn't a catcher then, and he could play where he wanted because he could hit. I'm sure the routine was the same in all neighborhoods. The left-handed thrower played first base and was usually nicknamed Lefty. The big kid was the pitcher. The can't-do-anything-but-usually-owned-the-ball kid played right field because that seemed like the place to hide him. Then came our hero, the fat kid. He was always the catcher. I think the catcher had to be built like the term used for the catcher, the backstop. He didn't catch many balls, but he could stop them. You rarely see a catcher endorsing a product, but most people think the perfect product would be a Zamboni.

Two thoughts about catching help justify why you chose the position in the first place. If you have a good pitching staff you're getting plenty of strike-outs and very few foul tips or wild base runners to tag. If you have a bad pitching staff you have the safest spot in the park because, thanks to the batter, the ball will stop about two feet in front of you. Although the bad pitching staff will make you feel like a head-waiter at a busy restaurant. The runners keep crossing the plate, and you greet them as they come across.

Which position gives you the most laughs? The answer in a landslide is the position of catcher. I'm not talking about when he is under a foul ball on a windy day. That can be funny to everybody except the catcher. Humor comes with the position because the catcher is around the batter, the umpire, and the pitcher.

Is it any wonder that Bob Uecker became a broadcaster, made people laugh in the TV series *Mr. Belvedere,* and was often on the *Tonight Show with Johnny Carson?* Would an infielder think of saying, "I made a great contribution to the team this year; I came down with hepatitis." Or "I wound up my career with a lifetime .200 average, which tied me with Don Carter." (Carter was a champion bowler.)

Some of the most fun I have at a game is watching the speed of the catcher. I want to agree when a fan says to me, "You probably had speed when you got to the big leagues, but with all the getting up and down your knees went bad and you slowed down." Sounds good, but it's not true in most cases. Most of us catchers ran like we were either in quicksand or had suction cups on the bottoms of our shoes. But there were some exceptions. Yogi was always quick, so quick that he made an unassisted double play at home plate. On a suicide squeeze play, John Beradino, Cleveland second baseman, bunted. Yogi got out from behind the plate so fast that he tagged Beradino before he could start toward first base. The runner coming in on the other end of the squeeze play was an easy room service out. Yogi had to wait so he could tag him out. If you're wondering, yes, he was the same John Beradino who became an actor and went on to play Dr. Steve Hardy on *General Hospital.*

Tim McCarver, a catcher, stole home in the World Series. Some catchers were even given the steal sign. When it comes to speed, though, you have to be able to accept the description "he has good speed for a catcher."

Like every other player, you tried to catch the ball with the hand wearing the glove, but foul tips could detour the ball right into your knuckle. Today's catcher is much smarter, and with no base runners will catch everything one-handed and keep the bare hand behind his back. The catcher with a guaranteed contract will catch everything with one hand, and if the ball gets by him he'll probably call his agent to get it. When you shake hands with today's catchers it's like gripping a nice soft, fluffy pad that's been using the mildest detergent possible. Shake hands with the old timer and it's like grabbing a handful of old peanuts that have been left out in the rain.

Today's catcher does what's called "framing the pitch." It's a more

With my salary, I could hardly pay the shoemaker who patched this glove, but I did use it in the 1946 World Series.
Courtesy Joe Garagiola.

sophisticated way of stealing a strike call. When you talk about framing pitches, most catchers will look at you with the most innocent eyes since kindergarten and say, "I'm not trying to steal a strike. I just don't want to lose the pitch that is a strike." Sure, and Willie Sutton didn't want the keys to the bank because he wanted the challenge. I've watched catchers use the glove so well that on a low, borderline pitch the umpire sees only the back of the glove and not the ball. The ball is out of the strike zone, but the glove is in the zone. Some catchers are so good they can put the glove on the corner, the webbing outside the strike zone, and catch everything in the webbing. In my day you were taught to catch the low ball coming up to give the umpire a good look, but that's not the case today. Jabbing or pulling the ball in or out doesn't get the job done. Today's good catchers have soft hands and give the impression they're catching an egg, not a baseball. I like the modern style.

I believe the old mitt I used was designed by a government committee at midnight, by candlelight, in a dark basement. It was the worst glove ever designed for many reasons; I'll give you just a few.

First, all the padding was around the pocket. This forced you to catch every pitch with both hands with no protection for your hands. It was impossible to catch a pitch with just one hand.

The webbing wasn't much more than a rumor. Two pieces of leather string ran across the top. The webbing is the most important piece in the design of today's catcher's mitts. It's the Bermuda Triangle for foul tips. The new glove has top-of-the-line leather that breaks in easily and even has an opening to protect your index finger by keeping it outside the glove. Some catchers will tell you that the finger outside gives them better control of the glove. It sounds good, but some of the gloves are so big you can sleep a family of six in them, so what is there to control unless it's the rent? As always, the great philosopher, Yogi Berra, gave the best explanation. "I keep my finger out there because it don't hurt as much when I catch the ball."

The glove is the first thing I look at when a new catcher is playing. If I were a manager I'd insist he use a glove with big webbing. Once the ball hits there it closes like a trap door and you've caught the foul tip. You can't practice catching a foul tip. The catcher doesn't have to do a thing except hope the ball hits into the webbing.

I don't stop at checking the glove. I'm envious of the new, modern equipment. Catchers wear a form-fitting chest protector (some are even silver) with state-of-somebody's-art mask and shin guards.

The chest protector for today's catcher deadens the ball when it hits, keeping it in front if he blocks the ball at all. It is seventeen inches long and weighs one pound, 3.3 ounces. I think the old ones had straps that weighed that much. The old front was made of canvas and was filled with cotton, felt, kapok, or a smelly unknown substance. It seemed to fit only the fat bartender who played on Sunday afternoons with a keg of beer at second base.

The shin guards are now described as "twelve inch injection-molded, fitted for the right and left leg. Wings provide full leg protection. The knee caps are protected by three separate parts and there are two dual caps to protect the top of the foot and toe. All this weighs only four pounds."

I'd like to have used the "regular game stuff," but what I'd really like to have tried is the Knee Saver. This is a wedge-shaped foam pad that fits at the back of the knee right in the bend and is supposed to ease the strain. The least that baseball could do is give old catchers a set of these

This was our first batting helmet. The first time Frankie Frisch saw it he said it was great because we could use it for a soup bowl at night. Joe Garagiola, 1952.
Courtesy Pittsburgh Pirates.

foam wedges to use if they go to High Mass and have to kneel a lot.

The mask is made of ultra-light wire frame. Deer skin leather gives you comfort and absorbs the moisture. The catcher comes out today and I think he's ready to walk on to a movie set and be the lead actor in a Sci-Fi film. I smile and think the equipment we wore got us ready to jump on the truck and collect the leftover scrap iron.

When we came out with batting helmets in Pittsburgh in 1952, Mr. Rickey, the general manager, made catchers wear the helmet while behind the plate. It was torture. The helmet was the same one we wore to hit, but it had an extended bill so when you wore it backwards and tried to find and catch a foul ball the sharp edges of the bill dug into the back of your neck. To avoid being stabbed in the neck you flipped it off and tried to catch the ball bareheaded, which wasn't too bad if you had hair. But if you were bald the bench jockeys had a field day. Your ego was bruised, but at least you didn't bleed to death.

The inside of the batting helmet had a ring of foam rubber that was supposed to give you protection when you were batting. Behind the plate was another story. You dreaded the hot day when you'd break a sweat just shaking hands. When the foul tip hit you head on, the foam rubber compressed and the moisture (sweat) you were collecting streamed down your face like you were in the middle of a rain forest. A towel helped, but windshield wipers would have been better. Do you get the feeling that I'm watching catchers today and wondering if I played so long ago that a guy named Columbus was recruiting sailors for a boat trip?

The most pathetic scene in the ballpark for me is watching catchers try to catch a knuckleball. It's like watching a surgeon perform a delicate operation with an axe. The pitcher doesn't know where the ball is going most of the time, and if the wind is blowing against the pitcher it's a nightmare. It's like the baseball wants to personally visit every fan in the park before it decides to cross home plate. The least a pitcher can do is holler "good luck" when he throws it.

If the catcher happens to catch the ball and thinks it's a strike but the umpire calls it a ball, the umpire's explanation sounds like something between Abbott and Costello. "He threw it and didn't know where it was going. The batter didn't know where it was going so he took it. You didn't know where it was going and were lucky to catch it, and you want me to get the call right? Why don't you shut up and just try to catch the next one."

The knuckleball is thrown so softly that I don't think the speed even registers on some radar guns. It's also embarrassing when the throw to first base to pick a runner off is faster than the pitch to the plate. From the stands it looks so easy that you can't understand why the catcher is having trouble. Doug Rader said that knuckleballer Charlie Hough burned more calories while reading than pitching.

A picture of catcher Rick Ferrell jumps front and center when I see a knuckleball pitcher. Rick Ferrell is one of my heroes. He's in the Hall of Fame, and I know he belongs there without even looking up his batting average or his fielding average. When he was catching for the Washington Senators he had four knuckleball pitchers on his team: Dutch Leonard, Roger Wolff, Johnny Niggeling, and Mickey Haefner. From Opening Day until the last day of the season he had nothing to make his day better. I'm sure his only chance to relax was to see a "No Game...Rain" sign.

Paul Richards, while managing the Baltimore Orioles, developed an oversize jumbo catcher's mitt to help the poor catcher. It's one of the few pieces of equipment used today that came from the "old guys." The glove is so big that every pitch is a two-step process for the catcher. First, he has to try to catch the ball. Second, he has to find it in that big glove.

I see a knuckleball pitcher come into a game and I think of the day I was warming up Hall of Famer Hoyt Wilhelm and he motioned, "Here comes the number one knuckleball." I put my glove where I thought the ball was going to be, and it hit me right on the kneecap. Today the knuckleballer is on the endangered species list. I'm still looking for the catcher who's unhappy over that news.

I sit in the stands sometimes and wonder if I'll ever see a left-handed catcher as the number one man rather than a novelty. I really don't know why a left-handed catcher is such a rarity. The only explanation I ever heard was that on throws to the bases, especially to second, the ball would move too much. It might be an old wives' tale, but there's a saying in baseball that a left-handed thrower can't throw a ball straight. That's great for a pitcher but not for a catcher.

Hall of Famer Bill Dickey is the only person I ever heard make a case for a left-handed catcher. Dickey felt the left-handed catcher would even have some advantages and no disadvantages. "There are more right-handed pitchers," he said, "so the curveball would break to his glove side and be easier to catch. On the bunt down the third baseline he'd be ready to make the throw to first base when he picked up the ball." I agree. I think there's room for left-handed catchers in the big leagues.

I saw only one in my career, Dale Long of the Pittsburgh Pirates. Dale was known mostly for his hitting and playing first base. The only drawback to being a left-handed catcher that Dale Long talked about was the catcher's mitt. He was convinced that for the right-handed throwing catchers, the leather they used came from the front of the cow, but for the left-handed throwers it came from the back. I think there's some truth to that because for some reason every time I see the make-believe horse at the circus I have the same thought. You know the one I mean— it has two people inside of it, and they clown around to the amusement of all. Whenever I see this so-called horse I'm convinced a pitcher is the front end and the catcher is the back end.

The Oakland Raider guard, Gene Upshaw, once said something about offensive linemen that I agree with one hundred percent in regards to catchers. Upshaw said, "I've compared offensive linemen after a game to the story of Paul Revere. After Paul Revere rode through town, everybody said what a great job he did. But no one talked about the horse. I know how Paul Revere's horse felt." Catchers also know how the horse felt.

I see certain plays and certain moves by a catcher and I immediately think of the guys that I played against who made the same play. The year 1946 was my first as a St. Louis Cardinal. As years went by I saw plenty of catchers that, in certain areas, I wished I could be like. I wished I could make catching a pop foul look as easy as Roy Campanella did. I always thought Campy could catch an egg from a hundred feet up and not crack the shell.

I wished I could throw the ball to catch a base runner like Del Crandall. I wished I was built like Jim Hegan, over six feet tall and as graceful as Baryshnikov. At least I'd look good in the team picture. If I had to build a catcher I'd use Jim Hegan as the blueprint. But it was Ernie Lombardi who did two things I wished I could do.

They called Big Ernie "Schnozz" for the obvious reason. Lombardi was with the New York Giants when I met him, but he was the star catcher for the Cincinnati Reds when they played the Yankees in the World Series. I remember the newspaper picture of him sprawled at home plate after being "the victim" of a slide by Charlie Keller that allowed DiMaggio to score. The headline read "DiMaggio Scored While Schnozz Was Snoozing." Once again it shows that when a run scores it's the catcher's fault even if he's almost knocked unconscious.

I remember the first time I was on the same field with Ernie Lombardi. He was walking across the field in the Polo Grounds, and after admiring him as the guy who was one of my favorites on the bubble gum cards, I realized he wasn't carrying a glove. Infielders and outfielders could fit their gloves in their pockets, but show me another catcher who could carry his catcher's mitt in his back pocket. I wished I could do that.

Ernie Lombardi. He was one of my heroes. They called him Schnozz, and you can see why. For me, though, it was his hands and fingers, which were so big they looked like salamis hanging from a rack. Courtesy National Baseball Hall of Fame Library, Cooperstown, N.Y.

Ernie Lombardi would take out most of the padding, and it seemed like all that remained were two pieces of leather, as if he threw the glove away and kept the wrapping. He could then fold it up and put it in his back pocket. For a rookie like me, that was almost scary.

Once I saw the size of his hands I could understand a little better what he did to the glove. The hands were double X jumbo size. His fingers were so big they looked like salamis hanging from a rack. I think he wore a glove only because the other catchers did.

The other move that made him number one on my "I Wish I Could Do That" list was the way he rubbed up a baseball. Many times during a game the umpire would hand you a new ball, and if it felt slick, you'd take off your glove and rub up the ball before you threw it to the pitcher.

Big Ernie never came out of his crouch after a foul ball; he just put his bare hand back, which looked like a serving tray, and the umpire placed a new ball in his hand. He never took off his glove, just took his time as he rubbed up the ball with one hand.

Lombardi had his own way to send a message to his pitcher to make him throw harder. Some catchers do this by throwing back the ball hard after a pitch. Lombardi would call for a fastball, then reach out and catch the ball with his bare hand. He didn't shift his body an inch, just reached out and caught the ball. I don't think that gave his pitcher a lot of confidence in his "stuff," but it did fire him up to throw harder.

The most embarrassing time for a catcher is not when you're asked to go out and get the rosin bag because it's raining, but when you block a ball with base runners on and it bounces off you and you don't know where it is. Everybody in the stands can see where it is, and most times you see only the umpire and he's jumping around trying to get out of the way. If he's not moving it's because he's so big that he's not only blocking your view but you'd get winded trying to get around him. The fans are screaming, the manager is screaming, and here comes the pitcher running toward you, but he has lockjaw. He isn't saying a word, just pointing. You want the ground to open up so you can fall in.

After you read what happened to Hank Foiles you'll think of him whenever you see the ball get away and the catcher can't find it. One of the worst cases of trying to do the job and getting the "no good deed goes unpunished" medal happened to him.

The Angels held a slim lead in the late innings of a game at Minnesota. The Twins loaded the bases against Dean Chance. He threw a curveball where it should have been thrown, low and away, but it was one of those fifty-five footers in the dirt. Foiles reached for it and then spun and raced to the backstop screen where he searched for it but couldn't find it. With everybody screaming and Foiles not able to find the ball, all three runners scored before he thought to look in his glove. The ball had been there all the time, and I'm willing to bet that when he saw that ball it was smiling.

Watch how a catcher shows his confidence. He has to sell that confidence to his pitcher, manager, and the opposition. The pitcher has to believe in the catcher's pitch selection. Although most pitchers have the right to shake off a catcher and choose another pitch, the catcher better be on the same page most of the time or he won't be playing much.

The manager has to believe, too. The opposing club has to learn to respect the catcher's arm and not think it's a track meet when runners get on base. I always watch the throw to second base between innings because a good catcher uses that opportunity to say, "I'm ready and I'll get you if you try to steal." The successful stolen base is a blow to the catcher's ego.

Catchers have different ways of selling this confidence. One of the best stories comes out of the Negro Leagues. The catcher was nicknamed Trap, short for Speed Trap. He had a great arm and great legs. Trap didn't hide the fact that he was good. Not only did he have Speed Trap painted on his chest protector but when a base runner got on he would sing behind the plate. "De di doe that's alright baby. Let 'em go 'cuz the speed cop gonna get him. Let him run cuz the Speed Trap will get him."

No other position is given a formula for an out. The infielder gets the ground ball and sometimes takes a step, maybe two, and pounds his glove before throwing the ball to get the out. The outfielder waits for the ball to come down and land in his glove. On a base hit and runners on, the outfielder will get the ball back to some infielder and, like throwing a hand grenade, wait for the results. No stop watches on those plays.

The catcher is told and/or shown the formula for throwing out base stealers. All parts have to work or it's a stolen base. The first base coach used to be like a greeter when you got on base. He gave you two pieces of advice: number one, get a good lead but don't get picked off; number two, keep making left turns. Check today's first base coach and he's probably checking his stopwatch. The opposing pitcher throws to first base and you hear the "click." Inning over, out comes the book to record the time it took to throw over to first base. The runner breaks for second; again it's "click" to see how long it took the catcher to release the ball and get it down to second. Today's first base coach is a better clock tower than Big Ben.

The pitcher delivers the ball in 1.4 or 1.5 seconds. It's great if the catcher gets rid of it in 1.8. The ideal formula is the pitcher at 1.4, catcher at 1.8. Get it to second in 3.6 or less and you'll get your man. The average catcher release time is 2 seconds. This came right out of a first base coach's book. This formula eliminated a scouting report like "You can run on this pitcher," or "The catcher is slow getting rid of the ball." Today you may need a calculator to figure it out, but the guesswork is eliminated.

I once asked Dave McKay while he was coaching for the Cardinals to do a typical run down if I were a base runner. Here is the report he gave me with a left hander pitching. Obviously, he didn't give me the name, but the left hander was a big league pitcher.

Has a hang move with a speed snap throw to first. It's a decent move. He is good at holding runners at first and second with a consistent slide step. Showed a very average step off move, will sometimes fake a throw to first. (Here's where the stopwatch comes in):

Average Time		Slide Step	
To 1st Base	1.63–1.77	To 1st Base	1.18–1.28
To 2nd Base	1.74–1.80	To 2nd Base	1.22–1.32

One statistic tells you the success rate of a catcher in throwing out base runners on attempted steals. Many pitchers are slow with their delivery to the plate, so the catcher has no chance, but the successful steal still figures in the statistic. Let me tell you about one scoring decision that again proves that being a catcher means you're the human toxic waste dumping grounds. The logic seems to be, "I don't know what to call it, so blame the catcher."

In a game between the Arizona Diamondbacks and the Detroit Tigers, Diamondbacks pitcher Casey Fossum picked off the base runner at first base, Eric Munson. He was in no-man's-land, so Munson kept running. The first baseman, Shea Hillenbrand, was looking to throw to get him, but nobody was covering second base. Munson kept running, arrived safely at second, and was credited with a steal. Obviously, it will figure in the statistic of base runners caught stealing, yet the catcher, Robby Hammock, didn't even touch the ball. His middle infielders decided to go into the Witness Protection Program so Hammock had to take the blame.

The collision at the plate is always sure to wake me up. The catcher is usually a victim with the base runner causing him to leave the scene of the accident. Most times on this play you hope somebody got a license number. Some catchers use the "just missed him" play. Here comes the

This really wasn't a collision since I didn't leave the scene of the accident. It was just his way to say hello. Courtesy Pittsburgh Post-Gazette.

throw and up the line he goes to catch it, then does his best Olympic dive and just misses the runner. Some catchers get up and look around like they're looking for the judges' score.

The opposite of the "just missed him" play was perfected by the Dodgers' Mike Scioscia, who earned the nickname The Human Dead End. When he got the ball he planted his feet in front of home plate and you couldn't get through with a passport in a Hummer. He must have felt some aches at times, but it always seemed like the base runner would get up and check to see if he had all his body parts.

Catchers are important on the field, of course, but they're also important in the bullpen.

Next time your seat is near the bullpen, check out who's doing the most talking and you can bet it's a catcher. You can add to the bet that the talk is not about strategy, either. The bullpen is the closest thing to a late night talk show, and like a talk show you need storytellers. Catchers make the best bullpen talk show hosts. Like Bob Uecker:

"I was with the Phillies and got stopped by the police at four o'clock in the morning."

"What did they do to you?"

"Not much. The judge fined me seventy-five dollars for being drunk and four hundred dollars for being with the Phillies."

He also said, "I had two highlights in my career. I got an intentional walk from Sandy Koufax and in 1962, I got out of a rundown against the Mets. I have a tape of that, too."

Managers may think it's hard to embarrass us, but catchers don't run on batteries. We have feelings too. Like this story from catcher Ed Bailey:

I'm with Cincinnati and we're playing in the Polo Grounds. I'm out in the bullpen and it's a long way to the dugout. In the eighth inning they call up and tell me to come in because I'm going to pinch hit. I start trotting in and then run a little faster to make it in time. I'm swinging two or three bats, then drop a couple, and I'm taking practice swings with my favorite bat. Durocher brings in a left-hander, and now they pinch hit for me. All that work and all I got out of it was winded.

That happened to me, too. The Cardinals were playing the Dodgers in Ebbets Field. I had my usual spot in the bullpen, down the left field line. In the eighth inning I'm told they want me on the bench. As I made my way in I was thinking all kinds of endings. I'll hit a pinch-hit home run with runners on, and, being a local St. Louis boy, I'll get my picture in the paper. All kinds of thoughts were running through my head. I got to the bench and even before I could get to the bat rack, Manager Dyer said, "Give Rice your glove, his webbing broke."

Catchers are like the neighborhood welcome wagon, as far as some hitters are concerned. Hitters will walk up and some will just say hello or they might tap your shin guards with the bat like the Diamondbacks' Luis Gonzalez does. That's just a friendly hello.

I liked visiting with hitters because I felt that if I could break their concentration I'd get an edge. It works with some and not with others. Some players walk up and immediately tell you to just shut up and catch because they're not going to talk to you. Any player who played against Yogi Berra will tell you that Yogi had the best gossip and trade rumors and used the material to distract you.

Some catchers will think out loud. "Let's see, you got a hit on a curveball. Should I call for it again? Should I try the fastball? I don't think you can hit the curveball again so I'm calling it." If it was the curveball and you took it for a strike the next thing you heard was, "Believe me next time." But the catcher has you thinking now.

A couple of times my manager, Fred Haney, would have me tell the hitter what was coming. It usually happened when the hitter was wearing you out and hitting nothing but line drives for base hits. The thinking was simple. The batter won't believe you anyhow, but if you tell the truth on at least the first two pitches, the batter doesn't know what to believe and you got him thinking about what you're saying.

But it's a two way street, and sometimes the batter gets the catcher. My Army buddy, Joe Ginsberg, was catching for the Orioles when Earl Torgeson came up as a pinch hitter for the White Sox.

"Torgy comes up to hit and you know how friendly he is," Joe started. "He looks down at the third base coach and steps out of the box and is knocking the mud out of his spikes, really moaning."

"Ain't that great. I sit on the bench for two weeks. They don't even know I'm here. Now I get a chance to hit and they give me the take sign. Take! Take! Take! After two weeks on the bench, I get the take sign. I gotta get outta here."

Joe said, "I kinda smiled to myself and thought 'I'll get ahead of him with the first pitch.' So I called for a fastball. What a mistake. The next thing I know Torgy hit that fastball and tore out a row of seats in the upper deck for a home run that won the game. Last time I'm gonna believe anybody."

With a man on second base, take a good look at the pitcher. His expression may give you a hint that strange things are about to happen. The mound is the place where weird things are seen, done, and said. Some pitchers get spooky when there's a man on second. They're convinced that the base runner is stealing the signals and relaying them to the hitter. Sometimes the base runner is a former teammate and you're positive he doesn't even know his own team's signals. When you get a pitcher like that on the mound you do everything to make him feel at ease.

"Okay, you called me out here. I'm here. What's going on?"

"I know he's trying to steal our signs. I know it."

"Okay, we'll change them. Let me give a bunch of signals but you concentrate on just the first two finger flashes you see. Add them, and if they total three it's a fastball, if they add up to four it's a curveball, and if they add up to five it's the change of pace. OK? Just add the first two flashes of fingers you see. Got it?"

"Yeah, got it."

Walking back to the plate I could almost hear the wheels turning, but I thought, "no big deal." The runner wasn't stealing our signs. I was his teammate once, and I knew he couldn't tell you the name of the dog in a Lassie movie. The system was simple, but it gave me some options, and I felt certain my math major on the mound would be happy. I could flash one finger, then two fingers, which adds up to three, and that meant fastball. Any signals after that didn't mean a thing. On the next pitch if I wanted another fastball I could flash two fingers, then one, and that adds up to three again, and the rest of the signals still mean nothing. I should get another fastball even though my series of finger flashes looked different to the runner on second.

Remember now, all my pitcher had to do was add the first two signals I flashed. The total fingers would never get higher than five. I gave the signals, and the batter fouled off the pitch. Almost before the umpire could put a new ball in play my pitcher calls time and motions me to come to the mound. I go out and logically ask, "What's the matter?"

Here's the answer I got: "Don't give 'em so fast."

Clint "Scrap Iron" Courtney had two different formulas to keep base runners from stealing his signals. Called out to the mound because his pitcher thought they were stealing the signs, Scrap Iron had a ready answer: "Just watch my right hand. It'll be outside my leg and it'll look like I'm rubbing my hand in the dirt, but keep looking because when the runner ain't looking I'll give the sign."

The other formula was a little more complicated: "OK, we'll use the second flash you see. One finger is a fastball, two fingers a curve, and three fingers for the change of pace. Remember the only signal that counts is the second one you see. Got it?"

His pitcher nodded. Courtney went back behind the plate and with those mysterious fingers flashed 2-2-2.

Some people think that the position of catcher is a weird one, but it does have its rewards. Maybe I'm stretching it a bit by using the word "rewards" in the same sentence as "catcher," but what other position can get credit for a putout without handling the ball?

I wish I knew who came up with all these "catcher rewards." I've saved this newspaper clipping for years. See, it doesn't take much to make a catcher happy.

Here are some:

—When the batter strikes out with less than two outs when first base is occupied, even if the third strike is a wild pitch and gets past the catcher.

—When the umpire calls the batter out for swinging with one or both feet outside the batter's box.

—When the batter bunts a third strike foul.

—When the batter is called out for stepping from one side of the plate to the other after the pitcher is in his pitching position.

—When the batter interferes with a play at the plate on a runner who is trying to score.

—When the batter is called out for interference by a fan when the catcher is trying to catch a foul ball.

—When the batter is hit by his own batted ball near the plate but outside the batter's box.

—When the batter is hit by a pitched ball that he swings at, making for a third strike.

—When the batter throws a bat and deflects a ball he has hit.

—When the batter interferes with the catcher on a foul or fly ball.

—When a player hits out of turn and the appeal is made and the batter is called out.

That's eleven ways according to my favorite clipping. When you've spent most of your adult life getting hit with foul balls and having people run over you, and the only sympathy you get is some media expert referring to your equipment as the "tools of ignorance," you have to find your own ways to feel good about yourself.

Many great catchers have played the game. It's easy to talk about catchers like Gabby Hartnett, Mickey Cochrane, Bill Dickey, Roy Campanella, Johnny Bench, and Yogi Berra. The three catchers I want to tell you about are not household names, but they hold equal stature on my hero pedestal.

When catchers are discussed, at least in the conversations I'm in, two events are almost sure to be the hub of the conversation. The home plate collision of Pete Rose and Ray Fosse in the 1970 All Star Game and then, what these catchers did. Their record, or non-record, wasn't even set on the baseball field.

I'll list them in alphabetical order: Hank Helf, "Pop" Schriver, Joe Sprinz, Gabby Street, and Billy Sullivan. If you have a bubble gum card of any of them you own a real gem. If Cooperstown ever builds a baseball version of Mount Rushmore, I'd vote for these catchers. What they did wasn't part of a game but was reported in a book and a clipping I've saved since 1984 and will never throw away.

Hank Helf played for the Cleveland Indians and the St. Louis Browns. He played the 1938, 1940, and 1946 seasons. In those three years he batted seventy-eight times and hit six home runs.

William "Pop" Schriver played fourteen years from 1886 until 1901 and had a career batting average of .264 with sixteen home runs. I'm sure most of them were walk-off home runs, although they weren't listed that way.

Joe Sprinz played for Cleveland and the Cardinals. He played the 1930, 1931, and 1933 seasons. In those three years he batted twenty-one times with no home runs. You have to believe they were pitching around him.

Gabby Street became more famous as a radio broadcaster in St. Louis. He was the color man (now called baseball analyst) for Harry Caray. I might add that Gabby was the one who encouraged me to quit playing (he wasn't even my manager when he made that suggestion) and try broadcasting, another reason I'll always remember him. He managed in the Major Leagues for six years and was a catcher for eight years with Cincinnati, Boston, Washington, the Yankees, and the Cardinals. His lifetime average was .208 with two home runs, but you have to believe they were key home runs.

Billy Sullivan played from 1899 until 1916. He retired with a .213 batting average and a career total of twenty-one home runs. He must have hit in a lot of tough luck.

All baseball fans—and especially fellow catchers—should remember these guys. Obviously it wasn't their bat or games played that made them special. Nothing about catching is special.

Sports Illustrated first reported this story on June 22, 1984. According to Bruce Anderson, the record for a vertical catch was established at 555 feet 5 1/8 inches. It was set in 1908 by Gabby Street when he caught a ball dropped from the top of the Washington Monument. White Sox catcher Billy Sullivan tied the record in 1910. Notice no infielder or outfielder would try this. I don't know if that's because of the great confidence shown by catchers or the result of being hit with too many foul tips.

Catcher Hank Helf was in his street clothes when he stood at the base of Cleveland's fifty-two-story Terminal Tower on Saturday morning August 20, 1938. Standing with Helf were four other Cleveland Indians: catchers Frank Pytlak and Rollie Hemsley and coaches Wally Schang and Johnny Bassler. All catchers. They were hoping to catch balls thrown from the top of the Terminal Tower, 708 feet above. Ken Keltner, a rookie third baseman, was stationed atop the Tower with a dozen baseballs. The first three balls eluded both catchers and coaches. "I could barely see those balls when they left Kenny's hand," Helf says. "They looked the size of aspirin tablets when they started down, and when they got closer, they had stopped spinning and were dancing like knuckleballs. I didn't know if they were going to hit my glove or my head."

According to Anderson's story, mathematicians estimated the speed of the balls at ground level to be one hundred thirty-eight mph, about forty mph faster than Randy Johnson's best fast ball or by today's terms, his heater or dead red. The balls bounded six stories high upon hitting the pavement.

Helf caught the fourth ball. For that great play he received an overcoat that he wore once and then gave away, a trophy, and a round of applause from the crowd.

A stunt involving the manager of the Brooklyn Superbas, Wilbert Robinson, really made me laugh. According to Bruce Anderson's story, the team hired a pioneering pilot, Ruth Laws, to fly over the Daytona Beach practice field. As the plane flew at an altitude of about five hundred feet, a passenger dropped a grapefruit. Robinson, who had been expecting to catch a regulation baseball, circled under the plummeting fruit. It glanced off the heel of his mitt, then split open as it hit his chest. Robinson was knocked onto his back. "Jesus, I'm killed!" he cried. "I'm dead. My chest's split open! I'm covered with blood!" Robinson was very much alive, though his players nearly died laughing.

Catcher Joe Sprinz's try for recognition came on "Baseball Day" at the Golden Gate Exposition on Treasure Island in San Francisco Bay. "Mule" Sprinz tried to catch balls dropped about one thousand feet from a Goodyear blimp. The third one was on target. "I never did see the ball,"

They wouldn't even let me use home plate—I had to use a sewer lid. Courtesy Joe Garagiola.

Sprinz said. "It hit me on the mouth. It put twelve cracks in my jaw. I lost about half a dozen teeth, and my lips looked like hamburger." Sprinz spent two months in the hospital.

Bruce Anderson summed up his story by quoting Hank Helf. "It was a sports item for two or three days." Indeed, the Guinness Book of World Records for many years listed Sprinz as the record holder for what it called "highest catch," although his attempt had been unsuccessful. Now it lists no record at all.

In a book titled Balldom (copyright 1914), which called itself "The Britannica of Baseball," there is a section called Three Wonderful Catches. When it comes to catchers getting credit for anything I go back as far as I can into baseball history.

Here is the quote:

The statement has gone forth to the effect that Charles (Gabby) Street, of the Washington team, was the first player ever to have caught a ball thrown or dropped from the Washington Monument, which is erroneous.

On August 29, 1894, William ("Pop") Schriver, star catcher of the Chicago Baseball Club, caught a ball thrown from the top of the Washington Monument, thus performing a feat which had never before been accomplished.

After allowing one ball to bound on the ground Schriver caught the second one thrown. Schriver made a fair catch and the players and others who were there as witnesses were satisfied. (Post, Washington D.C., Sunday September 3, 1894)

It will thus be seen that Schriver caught the ball over fourteen years before Street, who made his catch in 1908, while Sullivan made his catch on August 24, 1910.

At least a catcher traveled from Balldom to the Guinness Book of World Records, but it goes with the position that in the final analysis, nobody really cared, not even the Guinness people.

So "Pop," Billy, Gabby, Hank, Joe, and even Uncle Wilbert, thanks for trying to make the "grunt" famous.

I think the questionnaire filled out by a Cubs catcher says it all.

QUESTION: As a Chicago Cub, what is your proudest moment?

ANSWER: I'm a catcher. I'm not proud of anything.

The King Of The Hill

CHAPTER 3

At a ball game, I'd say the pitcher jars my memory more than any other player. Maybe it's because as a catcher I spent so much time looking straight at him. In the many years I've spent as a broadcaster I've focused on the pitcher for a couple of reasons. One, nothing happens until he throws the ball. Two, the pitcher has always been the most interesting player because he is a finely tuned "apparatus" that can get out of tune in a hurry because of the slightest changes. I have heard excuses from the pitcher on the mound that would have you running to take two aspirin and hoping you feel better before the ninth inning.

But pitchers themselves never change. Today, they just use better English. In the "old days" when the pitcher threw a ball that resulted in a game-winning hit, he'd come into the clubhouse (forget the mood, you know it's bad) and tell whomever wanted to listen that it was a "horseshit pitch." Today's pitcher will tell you one of two things. One, "I missed my spot, and you have to tip your cap to him for hitting it," or "It was a quality pitch, and he hit it." It makes me wonder why so many "quality pitches" are tearing up a row of seats in the bleachers for a home run. Good hitters do hit good pitches for home runs. It's the bad pitches that are labeled quality that I can't understand. I like the old guy's version better. I know exactly what a pitcher means when he says that was "a horseshit pitch." You can put "quality pitch" in the garbage can right next to these beauties: He came to play. (Why else would a guy come to the ballpark?) And singling out a player by saying: He hates to lose. (I guess the rest of the players like losing.)

Pitchers will say things on the mound that would send Einstein to the bookcase to find an answer. The year 1952 ended with us (Pittsburgh Pirates) losing 112 out of 154. A base on balls in the bottom of any inning was considered a rally. In this Forbes Field episode I was the catcher and will use the initials JG. My genius pitcher is identified as GP.

The bases were loaded and I felt GP's best pitch was his fastball. I put down one finger for the fastball and he shook me off. I put down two fingers for the curveball and he shook me off. I put down three fingers for the change of pace and he shook me off. (Just an aside, but many teams today use the same signals. So much for modern technology.) I thought he was shaking me around to confuse the hitter, so I started the same sequence. I got the same result. So out to the mound I went.

JG: What do you want to do?

GP: I want to throw him a slider.

JG: Bases are loaded. The game is on the line, the tying run is at third, and the winning run is at second. Your best pitch is your fastball. You have to challenge him. If you're gonna get beat, get beat on your best pitch.

GP: I can get him out with a slider.

JG: You don't have a slider.

GP: That's why I can get him out. He won't be looking for it.

So there you have it, my genius was going to get the batter out with a pitch he didn't throw because the batter wouldn't be looking for it. Where was Yogi when I needed an interpreter?

When I see a pitcher call the catcher out to the mound all kinds of scenes jump into my mind. When infielders come in to talk to a pitcher I'm sure somebody will say something funny. The pitchers I knew hated when an infielder came in to say anything. A veteran infielder has some leeway and can offer a suggestion, but he knows coming to the mound that it won't do any good. Strategy is the last thing you hear in those meetings. It's more like a pep talk.

"C'mon, bear down, the bases are loaded." That's the standard pep talk from an infielder coming to the mound. The reaction from the pitcher is pretty standard too.

"No kidding! You think I'm pitching with two infields out there?"

Another great piece of advice from the infielder rarely changes.

INFIELDER: "Throw strikes...get somebody out...it's hot out here."

PITCHER: "I'll give you the ball and you can pitch because the mound is air conditioned."

A rookie infielder coming in to talk to the veteran pitcher better be asking how to play the hitter or the way to the men's room. No advice. I see a meeting and I try to put words to it. Long ago, when "old guys" were playing and listening to Glenn Miller, a wisecrack usually broke up the meeting on the mound, something like this:

The rookie comes in and says to the veteran pitcher, "Pitch him inside and I'm gonna play him to pull. Is that okay?"

"I'm only six-feet-six inches from that big gorilla with a bat in his hand and you wanna know how to play him? Let's change positions and you pitch. Don't worry too much though, I'm gonna hold the ball as long as I can, and maybe he'll leave or it'll start raining."

I once heard a pitcher almost congratulate his rookie shortstop who came in for advice before the pitch, then, after a four hundred twenty-five-foot home run landed in the upper deck, came back in to find out how he had done.

"Was I playing him okay?"

"Yeah, but next time play him higher, Dumbo."

Today the conversation might revolve around money. The rookie comes in and says, "Pitch him inside 'cuz I'm gonna play him to pull. Is that okay?"

I can see a Roger Clemens or a Randy Johnson looking at the rookie and saying something like, "Kid, you heard what they said in the meeting. Do it. Don't come in here and tell me how to pitch. I'm making twelve million and you're making three hundred thousand. What could you tell me about pitching? Get outta here or I'll buy your contract and you'll be washing my Mercedes on Thursdays."

When I was called out to the mound by the veteran pitcher I had a pretty good idea it would be about signals or setting up a defense. When the rookie pitcher called you to the mound you could expect to hear anything.

The year 1952 was the ninth of our five-year plan in Pittsburgh. You learned a player's name and the next day he was gone. Guys seemed to be coming and going between innings. I never forgot this "summit meeting" called by our latest phenom pitcher.

"What's the matter?"

"I need to take a break, my left wrist is tired."

"How the hell can your wrist be tired?"

"I'm pretty sure it got tired from squeezing the rosin bag. We never had a rosin bag on the sandlot or in high school."

Infielders can become very philosophical on the mound. With the bases loaded an infielder's advice to the pitcher was, "Throw strikes. Don't worry about it. The best thing about baseball is that you can do something about yesterday tomorrow." Figure that out, and getting a batter to pop up should be easy.

Pitchers are above everybody on the field. Officially the rule book says, "The pitcher's plate shall be 10 inches above the level of home plate. The degree of slope from a point 6 inches in front of the pitcher's plate to a point 6 feet toward home plate shall be 1 inch to 1 foot, and such degree of slope shall be uniform." No other position gets that kind of attention, so standing on the mound, the pitcher is the King of the Hill. The spotlight is always on him. Nothing happens until he throws the ball.

A good pitcher makes sure nothing happens after he throws the ball, too. The mediocre pitcher gives you a 50-50 chance to make a play or find cover. The bad pitcher might as well have a hand grenade. When he throws the ball you can expect an explosion and a change of numbers on the scoreboard. Luckily the bad pitcher doesn't last long, and you can expect him to make the same speech every time he leaves a game.

"It was still a good pitch. I only missed by a couple of inches." You really don't know if he's talking about his target or getting an infielder killed. Some pitchers must have a special way of looking at a pitch when a batter hits a tape measure home run. It's not unusual to hear a pitcher tell you, "It was a good pitch. He swung late. Hell, I got it halfway past him." As a catcher you learn fast that it's not the first half that counts but the other half of the ball that makes the difference.

The road to the pitcher's mound starts early. Every kid wants to be the pitcher. Think about who the pitcher was when you were a kid. It was either the biggest kid on the block or the kid who owned the baseball. How many times did you hear, "It's my ball, so I pitch, or you don't use my ball."

Pitchers, like most valuables, come in different sizes and shapes; but don't let the size or shape fool you. It's not what they look like on the outside but what's inside the body that tells the story.

A scout once said, "If I could just look inside and check the heart, I'd never make a mistake." Birdie Tebbetts, former big league manager, once sent in a scouting report that read, "Great arm. Arm is about ten years older than his head. Recommend head amputation."

The modern scout's file is more detailed, probably kinder, and written in better English. It may not sound as conclusive as Birdie's recommendation, but one scout saw enough in a young pitcher to send his computer-generated report that read, "Good mechanics and pitched with controlled aggression." I don't know how his general manager felt, but the scout's grade school English teacher had to be proud of his choice of words.

The two worst methods used to determine a pitcher's ability are the pitch count and the radar gun. Sitting with scouts in a spring training game, I heard one say that the gun just confirms what your eyes see. But sometimes you don't need that extra help. Like Reggie Jackson's description of Tom Seaver's fastball: "Blind people come to hear Seaver pitch." You don't need a radar gun to tell you that the Astros' Brad Lidge or Justin Verlander of the Tigers throws hard. You can watch Billy Wagner, big Jonathan Broxton, or Jose Valverde walk out of the bullpen and throw one pitch and you know you're looking at a pretty good fastball. I guess with all the money involved, that radar gun becomes an insurance policy for the scout. To say "he's got a good fastball" is not enough, but say that and back it up with "the gun got him at ninety-eight miles an hour" and you're okay.

A scout could have used a calendar to clock Hall of Famer Bob Feller yet still know that he threw hard. Luke Appling, another Hall of Famer, had the reputation of being able to foul off pitches until he got either a walk or his pitch to hit. He told a great story about one of the first times he faced a young Bob Feller: "Feller looked fast and sounded fast. I barely got the bat on his first pitch and fouled it off. I just heard the next couple of pitches." Luke smiled and then said, "He threw a fastball I know I didn't see. All I heard was the umpire say, 'Strike two.'

"I looked at the umpire and said, 'OK,' and started for the dugout. The umpire hollered, 'Where you going? It's only strike two.' I told him, 'That's okay, you can have the next one.'"

Even though the radar gun confirms the speed a pitcher has on the mound, some teams try to find out about a pitcher's potential before he gets to the mound.

One year the Dodgers had a piece of equipment called the "velocity potentio-meter." It was supposed to tell you the pitcher's leverage by measuring the distance from his fingertips to his shoulder and then from his shoulder to this thigh. The "engineers" figured the longer his levers, the greater his ability to throw hard. Sounds like a great theory, but why do I get a picture in my mind of King Kong on the mound with those long hairy arms being a cinch twenty game winner?

If the radar gun had been in use from day one I don't know how many good pitchers and eventual Hall of Famers we might have missed. I doubt that Catfish Hunter or Whitey Ford would have been tendered a contract on the strength of the radar gun, but they not only knew how to pitch, their ball had movement. It's not how hard you throw the ball, but does it move?

The radar gun would be useless with former Baltimore pitcher Mike Boddicker. He won games with the help of an off-speed pitch that I don't think made a blip on the radar gun. He even gave it a name—a fosh-ball. This was a combination of a dead fish (a term used for a change-up) and a forkball. Put the two together and add the hitter's greed to the recipe for an effective pitch called the foshball.

After giving up a home run one pitcher explained his pitch to the press. A cross between a screwball and a change up—a screw up. Pitchers have always been able to come up with names for pitches going back as far as 1908 with Christy Mathewson's fade-away to the 1946 All Star Game when Ted Williams hit Rip Sewell's eephus pitch for a home run. Today's pitcher may talk about a two-seamer, a four-seamer, a cutter, a back door slider, or a splitter.

Geoff Zahn was another pitcher who made the radar gun obsolete. He's the perfect guy to point to when you hear that to win in the big leagues you have to move the ball around and change speeds. That was a winning formula at the turn of the century, and it's still holding. The great sportswriter Jim Murray once wrote that some night Zahn is going to throw what he called his fastball, and by the time it gets to the plate, he's going to find out the batter has been waived out of the league or traded. Gene Mauch said of Geoff Zahn, "You could put a radar gun on his fastball and it didn't register. Put it on his head and it would blow the lid off it."

The discussion regarding radar guns usually revolves around which gun is being used, the fast one or the slow one. Pitchers will argue that they're throwing harder than the speed showing on the scoreboard. If a hitter's having a bad day, he'll tell you that the pitcher's throwing harder than the scoreboard says or they must be using the slow gun.

When a pitcher has good stuff he doesn't need a radar gun to tell him. Hitters will deliver that message because they can't hit him. If he doesn't have good stuff, hitters will deliver the message by playing tunes off the outfield fence.

The most famous game involving playing tunes off the fence had to be between the Phillies and Boston Braves, in the then home ballpark of the Phillies, Baker Bowl. It was also the birthplace of one of the great nicknames for a pitcher. I wish I could have been in the ballpark to see it, but here's the way I heard the story.

Walter Beck was pitching for the Phillies and getting hammered as balls ricocheted off the tin fence in right field. It sounded like a crazed mule trying to kick his way out of the barn.

No doubt fans could have checked the numbers on the outfielders' backs, as it seemed like they were in a track meet chasing down the ball. Finally, help was on the way. The right fielder saw his manager heading for the mound to make a pitching change, so he saw a chance to rest. He sat down next to the metal wall with his head in his hands trying to catch his breath. Beck didn't want to come out, so when the manager tried to grab the ball, Beck took it and tried to throw it over the right field wall but ended up throwing it up against the wall instead. Another loud bang.

Like Pavlov's dog, the right fielder heard the familiar, awful sound, jumped up, chased the ball down, and made a perfect throw to second base. He thought he had the runner. But there was no runner, no hit, and no play. After the third out the fun began. The right fielder came in and went right for his pitcher, Walter Beck.

"Listen, you boom boom bum, don't ever show me up again." It was a day of baptism for Walter Beck. On that day was born one of the great nicknames of all time, "Boom Boom" Beck.

Even now, when I'm at the ballpark and I hear (but don't see) a ball hit the wall, I think of Boom-Boom Beck. It's almost a lost sound because these days most of the walls are padded, which is the same as sound proofing them. The Giants' AT&T Park will never give birth to another Boom Boom, but it's a different kind of excitement to see which boat will get to a Barry Bonds home run ball that lands in the Bay.

Home run hitters will force a pitcher to try to come up with the pitch that will get the big out. Over the years, as a catcher and broadcaster, I've heard plenty of theories on pitching. While watching a game some of these jump into my mind:

"Throw high strikes and the batter sees the whole ball."

"Throw low strikes and the batter sees half the ball. Only a good hitter hits that half."

Theories like that always sound good, but I never understood them.

I always felt you had to be a twenty game winner to give out that kind of advice. The rookie listens and walks away thinking, "I don't know what he said but he won twenty games so it must work."

Here's a list of theories on pitching I like.

BOB VEALE: "Good pitching always stops good hitting and vice versa."

DON DRYSDALE: "Half the plate belongs to the batter and half belongs to me. That's fair. It's just that I never let the batter know which half is mine."

Good pitchers come inside and claim the inside part of the plate. Drysdale didn't like hitters to crowd the plate, so he buzzed a pitch inside to move them back. But more than one hitter thought Drysdale's feeling was that as soon as you left the on-deck circle you were crowding the plate.

BOB GIBSON: "The plate is seventeen inches wide. The middle twelve belong to the hitter. The inside and the outside two and a half inches are mine. If I hit my spots, he's not going to hit it."

TOMMY JOHN: "Challenge the hitters and hope it's your day."

TOM SEAVER: "A pitcher depends on three things: movement, location, and velocity. You can win with two of them. If you have only one you lose."

SANDY KOUFAX: "A guy who throws what he intends to throw, that's the definition of a good pitcher."

ROB FALLON: "Get ahead by throwing strikes early in the count. Get the batter out by throwing balls late in the count. Expand the strike zone and give the illusion of a strike." This is a simple theory well spoken.

JERRY KOOSMAN: "The batters haven't seen a fastball for twenty-four hours. The first time around the lineup, go after them."

The next two are my favorites.

DIZZY DEAN: "When you're in trouble you gotta play good ol' country hard ball. You just rar back and fahr that pea." Translation: rear back and fire that ball.

BROOKS LAWRENCE: "What does a pitcher need to be most successful? Easy—a lot of runs." That one's easy to understand and says it all.

Sandy Koufax was the perfect definition of a good pitcher, and he had the pitches to go with it. Courtesy Los Angeles Dodgers.

Ever since Abner Doubleday or Thomas Edison invented this game, it's a cinch that good pitching makes a good manager. Today a pitching staff is run like a Fortune 500 corporation. Each pitcher has a specific duty to perform with a name for each duty.

First, the starters. This is the elite group that usually works every fifth day as the manager sets up the rotation. The starter also used to be the finisher and often gave a team its identity. Boston Braves' fans used to say they'd win because of the formula of "Spahn, Sain, and three days of rain." It was pretty accurate, too. Another catchy description was the "Big Three" of the pennant-winning 1950 Phillies. Robin Roberts "threw it through the wall." Curt Simmons, with his herky-jerky delivery, "threw it around the wall." And Jim Konstanty, with his slow stuff, "threw it up to the wall."

But today's starters don't get the chance to forge that same kind of identity because expectations have changed. In 2006, Chris Carpenter of the Cardinals and Brandon Webb of the Diamondbacks led the National League in complete games with five each. It seemed like Warren Spahn had five complete games in one weekend. Spahn didn't really have that great a weekend, but he did have three hundred eighty-two complete games in his career. From 1947 until 1963, the fewest number of complete games he had was sixteen. Don't get the idea that I'm picking on Carpenter and Webb, both good pitchers. But they'll never get the chance to complete as many games as Spahn because they pitch in the age of the specialist.

From the starter it goes to the middle man. Fans hardly recognize the middle man because his job is to chew up innings and keep the other team from scoring any more runs. He usually comes in when his team is losing, and if the team gets close to tying or winning the game the manager brings in the star of the bullpen—the closer.

The middle man is about as well known as the Unknown Soldier. He has two jobs when he comes in. He has to get out of the trouble the previous pitcher got into and hold the opposition until the closer comes in. He's baseball's answer to the bomb squad. Make a mistake and the game blows up. Up until now, his big reward was to get an "appearance" next to his name. But now there's a new statistic; the middle man can earn a "hold." A hold to a middle man is the same as a save to a closer.

Modern baseball has come up with even another specialist. Oddly enough, they're mostly left-handed pitchers. For some reason managers bring in a particular left-handed pitcher to battle a left-handed batter but leave the right-handed batters alone. Specialists like Mike Myers and Dan Plesac have more appearances next to their names than innings pitched.

The statistic is usually one third of an inning pitched. Most of the time the specialist is expected to record a strikeout. It's like the manager handing you a match and asking you to check his gas tank. Sometimes you make it out alive. But your baseball life can be short if you lose the batter you were brought in to get out.

The specialist is mostly remembered because he comes into a situation with nothing but trouble staring him in the face. Get one man and it's great. Then the closer comes in. He's the perfect solution to the problem. Whether he runs in or strolls from the bullpen, the hometown fans know that a new sheriff just came to town. We're safe now, and the bully loses. And of course, if he shuts the other team down, he's the one who gets the headlines.

To many fans the set-up man is another specialist. He's part of the baseball tag team match that shortens a game to seven innings. In the heyday of the Yankees bullpen, when Mariano Rivera was the set-up man for John Wetteland, it was virtually a seven inning game for the Yankees. The script was simple. The Yankees had the lead going into the eighth inning and in came Rivera. It was usually a one-two-three inning and then Wettland would come in.

So, as you can see, the vocabulary has definitely changed. Now you can walk out of the ballpark knowing that the starter gave you five good innings so your team had a chance, if the middle man did his job, until the specialist got his one man to give the set-up man a chance to let the closer get his save. It is almost like you were watching some other game, maybe polo.

Watching the bullpen grow into such an important factor has been an eye-opener. If pitching makes a good manager, a good bullpen makes a great manager. When jitterbugging was the dance craze and Sentimental Journey was the number one song on the Hit Parade, the bullpen was the place they sent pitchers to break the dry spell and pitch themselves back into the starting rotation. The bullpen used to be where pitchers went to erase their mistakes. Lose a couple games in a row and you were "sentenced" to the bullpen, the slums of baseball. Work out your problem and you got back into the pitching rotation.

When kids were putting bubble gum cards in their bicycle spokes to sound like a Harley Hog and adults were more interested in looking at Mae West or listening to W. C. Fields, pitching staffs had only starters and "guys out of the bullpen." Then came a wave of specialists. Pitchers like Johnny Murphy, Joe Page, Hugh Casey, Jim Konstanty, Hoyt Wilhelm, Rollie Fingers, Goose Gossage, Dennis Eckersley, and many more too numerous to mention, not only shut down rallies and saved games but gave the bullpen the respect it deserved, ultimately elevating it from urban renewal status to an elite neighborhood.

Most of the new parks have upgraded the bullpen area—big chairs instead of the hard bench. Bathroom facilities are right there instead of having to run into the dugout when nature calls. In the Phillies' new park the bullpen is two-tiered. The visiting club has the upper floor while the home team has the lower floor. The Phillies didn't want their pitchers to trip coming down the stairs, and they say that's one reason for the two tiers. I might add there's no room service on either floor.

Fans are still close in some parks, but they don't have a chance to visit one-on-one and pass peanuts or a hot dog to the bullpen inhabitants. That's how it was in Ebbets Field and might still be in Wrigley Field, to name two parks that were fan-friendly even to the enemy. Although I'm sure the bullpen crew has figured a way to get food if they want it. Call it progress, but there was more intrigue the old way. No longer do I see a pitcher come in, fold his arms across his chest, and look tough when the whole time he's just trying to cover the big mustard stain on his shirt from the bullpen hot dog he just ate.

I really miss seeing a manager or pitching coach come out of the dugout and motion to the bullpen with pre-arranged signs that look like he was the loser in a charades game. If the pitcher he wanted wore glasses the coach or manager would use his fingers to make imaginary glasses around his eyes. The plump pitcher was signaled by a motion to indicate the big belly. Certain names made it easy. We had a pitcher with the Cardinals named Clarence Beers. He was called in from the bullpen by the manager pretending to take a drink. The knuckleball pitcher was the easiest. It was just making a knuckleball motion.

I sit in the stands now and wonder how the manager would motion to his bullpen to bring in certain pitchers. What acting ability would you need to bring in Trevor Hoffman or Mariano Rivera? Eric Gagne would bring back some memories with his size and his glasses. I miss all this because now they use the telephone, and probably a cell phone at that. With some pitching staffs you wonder if maybe the manager should add 9-1-1 or Dial-A-Prayer to his speed dial.

One great addition to the ballpark routine is the excitement created when the closer comes in. A starting pitcher like Randy Johnson creates excitement as soon as it's announced that he'll pitch. The great pitchers are unique because a fan can expect something special, maybe even a no hitter or a perfect game. Strikeouts are guaranteed and the walk from the bullpen after warming up can take on the appearance of a victory parade. The game hasn't even started but a subdued, quiet excitement is built-in.

A home run hitter puts excitement in the air during batting practice. I'm sure that was true for Babe Ruth and has carried on through to Hank Aaron, Mark McGwire, and Barry Bonds. During the game the excitement level rises depending on the situation. These sluggers give the feeling that they're in scoring position as soon as they leave the dugout. Watching them walk from the on-deck circle to the batter's box is an event with a bigger event expected—the five hundred-foot home run. You know Barry Bonds has star power when the hometown fans boo when their team walks him. It's strategy for the manager, but disappointment for the fans.

But the closer's appearance now surpasses all this excitement. The marquee closer may be one of the few guys on the team who inspires a nickname or slogan. In my day, Cardinals reliever Ted Wilks was "The Cork." Today, Trevor Hoffman has fans immediately saying, "Game over."

When the closer comes in, the excitement reaches beyond the ballpark. He doesn't put out the small flame; he's called on to put out the forest fire. Fans know this, and teams satisfy them with a show biz production when the closer enters the game.

I saw one of the best productions during a game at San Diego's Petco Park during a Padres-Cardinals game. The Colorado Rockies had just swept a series from the Padres and the Cardinals were on a nine-game winning streak. So it looked like a great night for Padres fans as they went into the ninth inning leading seven to three. With a four run lead, reliever Otsuka took his warm-up pitches with thirty-five thousand fans cheering, clapping, and doing anything the JumboTron told them to do. When the catcher threw to second after the warm-up pitches, you could almost hear fans telling each other, "We've got this one." Then the unpredictability of baseball showed up.

Otsuka walked the lead-off man, always a bad sign. Not too bad, though, with a four run lead, but then the next batter singled and the Cardinals had two runners on base. With three players in their lineup—Rolen, Pujols, and Edmonds—who each had at least forty home runs, the crowd quieted down, and you could feel the uneasiness.

Padres Manager Bruce Bochy walked to the mound and motioned to the bullpen for his closer, Trevor Hoffman. With that right hand signal for Hoffman it was show time, the start of a beyond-Broadway production. The JumboTron lit up with flames, as a backdrop with giant-size letters announced it was Trevor Time. The auxiliary scoreboard joined in with signs of Trevor Time and the ballpark was alive. With ACDC's *Hells Bells* blasting from the speakers, Hoffman made his way from the bullpen to the mound. Thirty-five thousand fans were on their feet when the death knell sounded: three loud, distinct, perfectly spaced gongs. Any minute you expected Quasimodo to make a guest appearance. Hoffman took his warm-up pitches like he was throwing at milk bottles at a carnival. The music seemed to get louder with each pitch. Hoffman was methodical, oozing confidence, and the crowd sensed it.

The first batter was Tony Womack and Hoffman struck him out. The crowd got louder and the Trevor Time signs and flames seemed to get brighter. The next batter, Roger Cedeno, hit an easy pop fly to the second baseman and the runners stayed at first and third.

Now the batter was Albert Pujols, the first of the forty-plus home run hitters. The crowd knew that a home run would make it seven to six with another home run hitter, Scott Rolen, coming up next. They were on their feet. The music was louder and the flames brighter. The Padres' closer was facing one of the Cardinals' best hitters. It was a shootout.

A situation like this couldn't be produced by any outside source. It had to just happen. Trevor Time flames rimmed the ballpark as the count got to three balls and two strikes. Thirty-five thousand fans went wild as Hoffman went into his wind-up, and, looking like they were frozen in time, watched Hoffman throw a strike past Pujols to end the game. The new sheriff had done the job. The Padres won, and the death knell gong delivered the message. This night was Emmy, Oscar, and MTV awards all rolled into one and blasting out of the JumboTron. What a contrast to the days when the only music played during the game was by the organist between innings or maybe during a pitching change.

So, it's no wonder that in the old days, some pitchers came up with their own routines to deliver their message before making a pitch—like Ryne Duren, who'd have to be a closer today. With only the great voice of Yankee P.A. announcer Bob Sheppard ringing throughout the ballpark, Duren made his entrance a performance. Duren wore thick glasses, and that's always an advantage for a pitcher. Climbing over the short fence in right field, Duren made certain he had trouble getting over it like he didn't or couldn't see it. Watching all this, the hitter is doing everything but taking notes. Upon getting to the mound he'd get set to throw, and his first pitch would sail over the catcher's head and hit the screen on the fly.

The first time it happened was an accident, but after that it was well thought out before Duren even got to the mound, as much a part of his pitching routine as his fastball. Duren explained it like this:

"When I was with the Yankees, Bob Turley was the ace and he liked the mound flat. I liked the drop-off, but Turley didn't. So you know the ground crew was going to take care of him. But nobody told me that the mound was flat. One day I came in and I let the first pitch fly. I always threw the first pitch hard. Well, the mound was flat and my knee almost hit my chin. So I ended up throwing the ball back to the screen. It was an honest mistake. The crowd went wild. The next time I came in to pitch, one of our coaches, Frank Crosetti, said to me, 'Do what you did last time. That'll really shake the crowd up.' So I did it intentionally every time I came into a game."

Pitchers will do anything to get an edge on the hitter. Duren still wasn't finished with his routine. After throwing the last warm-up pitch, Duren took off his glasses and wiped them vigorously. The hitter was ready to holler, "I'm over here…if you can't see me maybe you can hear me. Over here." You have to believe he was asking himself, "Am I in the right business?"

After wiping his glasses, Duren had one more step before he made a pitch. He'd rub the pitching slab with his foot to remove any dirt. After watching all this action from the bullpen to the mound, if the batter made the fatal mistake of asking what Duren was doing, Yogi Berra, Duren's catcher, had the answer. "He's looking for the rubber."

Glasses were a rarity in my day. The first time I saw Clint Courtney, a catcher, wearing glasses I wondered how tough that made his job. Would they fog up on those humid days? Would one of those straight back foul tips break them even though he wore a mask? Courtney wearing glasses surprised me, but I had to look twice when I saw Pudge Rodriguez wearing sunglasses not only to catch but also to hit. It's no longer a rarity.

Coming in from the bullpen is not the only action around the reliever. In an effort to speed up the game a wrinkle has been added. When the reliever takes his warm-up pitches the umpire stands off to the side and counts them. It's like the umpire is the class monitor during recess and lets the fans know when one or two warm-up pitches are left.

Another change comes when the pitcher finishes his warm up. He walks toward home plate and meets his catcher halfway. The new trend is for the pitcher to cover his mouth with his glove so the opposition can't read his lips. The next thing I'm looking for is a team to hire a Navajo code talker, who baffled the Japanese in WWII, to be a linguistic coach.

To see Ryne Duren, the pitcher, and Clint Courtney, the catcher, wearing glasses might have been unheard of but they made it part of the strategy. What did they do? They might have invented the "halfway between home plate and the mound" meeting. There was a good reason, too.

Duren comes in with all his gyrations and finishes rubbing the pitching slab. Off come his glasses and as he's wiping them he starts to walk toward home plate while motioning for Courtney to come out to meet him. Courtney takes off his mask, takes off his glasses, and starts to wipe them as he walks toward the mound. The fans think they'll stop halfway and have their meeting. Picture yourself as the hitter watching all this. The pitcher comes off the mound and walks toward you wiping his glasses. The catcher walks away from you toward his pitcher wiping his glasses, and then *they pass each other.*

Pitchers who wear glasses already have an edge because as a batter you wonder how good their eyesight is and when they last had it checked. The worst feeling for a hitter is to see the pitcher looking in for a signal, really staring down his catcher, then backing off the mound and rubbing his eyes so he can see the signals. At that point you're not worrying about his health as much as your own. The primary question in your mind is, "Can he see me?" During night games you'd consider lighting a match so he could find you. During day games you'd want to wave your arms to make sure he saw you. Hot humid days are the worst since the glasses fog up. I always thought the bright red handkerchief some pitchers used was to make sure the batter noticed he was not seeing too well and doing his best to get a good look. So, the simple act of wiping eye glasses sends a clear message.

Former Pirate Bob Veale, a hard throwing left-hander, developed a special routine for Cardinals star Lou Brock. Unknown to Brock, Veale bought a cheap pair of glasses that, from the batter's box, looked exactly like the pair he always wore. Keep in mind that left-handed batters didn't particularly like to hit against Veale. He had a great fastball, but when he got wild it was wild high and inside.

Lou Brock comes up to hit, and Veale looks for the signal but seems to have trouble reading it. Veale backs off the mound a few times then off come the glasses and he wipes. On they go, but Veale still seems to be having trouble. Again the glasses come off and more wiping. Brock, the hitter, is watching all this as Veale continues his act. Veale wipes three or four times and then in disgust throws the glasses to the ground, steps on them, and hollers to the umpire, "Never mind the glasses, let's go."

Brock backs out of the box, turns to the umpire and says, "No way am I going to hit now." He wouldn't get back in until Bob Veale put on another pair of glasses.

A reliever needs something to give him an edge, even if it's a mental advantage. Tom Ferrick, who ended his career as a top reliever, described the ideal relief pitcher: "You want a guy with no imagination. The trouble is already there or he wouldn't be in the game. You don't want him thinking. You want him throwing. A good reliever is a comic book reader with his brains beat out."

A psychologist described relief pitching as "like learning to swim by being thrown into the deep water. There's nothing fancy about it, the trouble is there. Good bullpen men are totally 'unembarassable.' They have positive denial." Not only are good relief pitchers "unembarassable," they'll put their own spin on a bad outing and usually it's good for a laugh.

Specialist Dan Plesac had just been bombed, giving up seven hits and seven runs in an inning and a third. Not exactly MVP numbers. When asked if he could remember the last time he was hit so hard, Plesac said, "Sure I remember. I was twelve years old and stole twenty dollars out of my father's wallet."

I caught a relief pitcher who had a great reputation and rightly so, as his record was a good one. I can honestly tell you that most of the time he didn't know who was batting. He just felt he could get anybody out.

Bill Rigney, then the Giants shortstop, had been in the league a couple of years. Rigs was such a friendly guy I felt certain every player in the league knew him, and so did most of the fans as he'd visit with anyone. Rigney was the batter when my "stopper" relief pitcher called me out to the mound and asked, "Who is this guy batting with the glasses on?" Do you get the feeling he had the perfect makeup for a relief pitcher?

Several clues tell a manager if it's going to be a smooth or bumpy ride to the end of the game. Managers depend heavily on a pitcher's body language. The relief pitcher is an easy read because you get used to "the look." As a catcher you stand there and look and listen. The manager does the same thing except he has the ball. As he hands the ball over he is checking the look. The relief pitcher's eyes give the answer. According to former big league manager Dick Howser, "He has to have fighter pilot's eyes." The look has to have plenty of determination in it. If your relief pitcher has the Bambi-in-the-headlights look the best thing you can do is check to see if the water in the shower is hot because that's where he's headed.

Tug McGraw, a stopper for the Phillies and the Mets said, "I know what the manager is looking for. He wants to know that the lights are all on but nobody is home." Use your own translation but to me it says, "I'm here to pitch us out of trouble and not try to think us out of it." Tug had his theories. I liked his simple Problem-Solution Theory. The situation is the problem. The hitter is the solution. An out or a hit by the batter solves the problem.

Al Holland was an intimidating relief pitcher for the Phillies. He had that mean, primitive "take no prisoners" look. I still remember him saying, "You gotta want the ball. You gottta feel that no matter who the batter is you can get him. If he gets you then you gotta forget about it." To give you a word picture he'd say, "You grab the tiger by the tail and give it a yank. If he bites you, and he's gonna get you some days, you come back the next day and give it a bigger yank. You gotta let 'em know who's the boss."

Reliever John Wetteland said, "It takes a certain mentality to be a reliever. Starters have a much more even keel. They treat the game as an opera. We treat it as punk rock, fast and furious, right now."

Like Ryne Duren, modern relief pitchers send a message before they make the first pitch. Trevor Hoffman wears his cap so low it appears he's staring from under the bill. It's like he's wearing the black hat of the bad gunfighter arriving for the shootout. Mariano Rivera is so calm taking his warm-up pitches that he sends a message to his Yankee teammates saying, "Have no fear, Mariano is here."

Like fingerprints, descriptions of relief pitchers are each a little different. George Frazier, who did some good work out of the bullpen said, "It's like being a plumber. Some days it's okay but when thirty septic tanks back up, it's no fun."

Some relievers come out of the bullpen proud and ready to save the game when they get to the mound. It may take only one pitch to know if you have a fireman putting out the fire or an arsonist who will set another one. Chuck Estrada, a good pitcher with the Baltimore Orioles, later became the pitching coach for the Texas Rangers. During a bad stretch for his pitching staff, Estrada developed what he called a simple scientific system for bringing in relief pitchers. "Whoever answers the phone is in the game." When it gets that bad all you can do is watch and hope your general manager signs the pitching machine to a multi-year contract.

I love relief pitchers, especially today's closer. If he gives up the run that causes his team to lose the game, I can't wait for his quote. He won't admit to the bad pitch, like Mike Koplove, the Diamondbacks pitcher, after giving up home run number six hundred ninety-nine to Barry Bonds. "To be honest, I thought it was a perfect pitch, but I guess he was standing a little too close to the JumboTron when he hit it." Now that's the making of a good closer. No imagination, no regrets, and tomorrow is another day. A good closer never gets beat; he just loses.

Dazzy Vance pitched before my day, but he said something that all good relievers believe whenever they lose a game: "He's a great hitter because he doesn't think, so how can a pitcher out-think a guy who isn't thinking?"

One of the best situations where you'll see that kind of game-within-in-the-game thinking is between the rookie hitter and the veteran pitcher or vice versa: the rookie pitcher with the raw ability against the veteran hitter who can rely only on a scouting report until he probes from the batter's box.

Casey Daigle, a Diamondbacks rookie pitching against Sammy Sosa, was classic. Daigle won the battle, although I have to side with Sosa on this one. The count was two strikes and no balls. It seemed the perfect time to try to make Sosa chase a bad ball. Feed off the hitter's greed is what pitching coaches teach. Here came Daigle's pitch, right down the middle for strike three. Sosa had a scouting report, but usually a rookie pitcher tries to get the big hitter out by going outside the strike zone. If he misses, it sets up the next pitch. Instead, Sosa got a fastball right down the middle that couldn't have been a better ball to hit if he had called room service. Sammy took the pitch, and you know he went back to the bench mumbling something like, "The rookie doesn't even know how to pitch. He should have at least thrown one pitch to work on me." Maybe Daigle didn't know how to pitch in that at bat, but Sosa was walking back to the dugout with his bat in his hand having just been called out on strikes.

The veteran pitcher against the rookie is always interesting to watch because the rookie usually doesn't care who throws it; he's just looking for the ball. Forget looking for a pitch. Forget the rookie thinking he's being set up for a particular pitch. It's always pretty basic. "The pitcher throws it, and I hit it."

Hall of Famer Whitey Ford said he always hated to play against the young minor leaguers because they didn't know about all these pitches and they hit them. "Most of them think a slider is a curveball that didn't break or a change up is a fastball without too much stuff, and they kill you. They don't know enough to be fooled."

Today, computers do a lot of the thinking, and pitching charts are taking over the starting pitcher's pre-game meeting. It gets so detailed it sounds like an IRS audit. Every team I played on had coaches whose instructions were easy to understand because they were using English words, but the instructions were impossible to follow. "Bear down, get ahead of the hitter. Don't give him anything good to hit, but don't walk him." Let's break it down: "Don't give him anything good to hit" meant don't throw him strikes. But in the same sentence came the instruction, "Don't walk him." How could you keep from walking the batter if you threw bad pitches? I'm convinced that the only pitcher who could follow these instructions is the pitcher who turned to broadcasting.

Scouting reports on the opposing pitcher had little variations, but for the most part they were the same. "He's got good stuff. Best pitch is a curveball, but make him bring it up. His fastball moves." Going over the opposing lineup and trying to set up defenses was more like ten ways to say, "pitch him high and tight and then low and away."

The first pitching charts I ever saw were done by a Brooklyn Dodgers statistician, Allan Roth, whom I later worked with on NBC's Game of the Week. He charted every pitch, showing what pitch the batter hit and to which field.

Now with some teams it looks like a convention of accountants as pitching coaches walk in with big books filled with computer printouts. The advance scout has reported the results from his trusty radar gun. Base stealers are told the speed with which the pitcher delivers the ball to the plate. They're told the speed of the catcher's release to second and anything else that might help. The player has all the information he needs, except how to get to first base safely.

Tim Hudson is one of the better pitchers in the National League. A pitcher profile scouting report (figure 5) against left-handed hitters reported, everything about him except the color of his shorts.

In the pre-four-seamer and two-seamer days the pitching coach might have gotten the job because he was the manager's roommate. Not any more. Today's pitching coach does his job with videotape and charts. He oversees what a pitcher does between starts and knows the mannerisms of all his pitchers so he can pick up the smallest change in a routine or delivery to get his pitcher back on track.

Both the manager and the pitching coach deal with everything with a lot more politically-correct sensitivity now. Take an expression that we've all heard either from the pitching coach, the manager, the trainer, or the pitcher himself. "His arm is tired. If missing a turn doesn't strengthen it then we'll do an MRI."

When I hear something like that I think of two former managers, George Bamberger and Charley Dressen. When Bamberger heard a pitcher had tendonitis he had an old school reaction: "I think tendonitis means you got smoked the last time out. That's all it means." So much for sympathy.

Charley Dressen was sure he was right about everything. One of his famous Dressenisms: "The trouble with pitchers these days is they don't know the difference between an ache and a pain. One needs work. The other needs rest."

When Dodgers pitcher Don Newcombe said his arm was sore he was told it was his imagination. The next time Newcombe pitched he called the trainer out and told him, "My arm is fine but my imagination is sore." Tom Lasorda loves to tell the story about the time he was pitching in the

Inside Edge
SCOUTING SERVICES

Pitcher Profile

Hudson, Tim

Braves   **vs. LHBs**

Throws:	Right	**# Pitches Charted:**	244
Ahead in the count %:	31%	**Pitches per Pl. App.**	3.08

EDGE NOTES

Covering Scouted Games from 2006 Season

Pitches
- Fastballs (72%): 4-seam straight (90-94); 2-seam sinker (86-90)
- Curves (occasional): 12/6 break (74-81)
- Sliders (12%): Not a lot of break (82-88)
- Changeups (7%): Straight (77-85)
- Splitters (7%): Hard downward movement (83-89)

Moves
- •

Notes
- Times to plate: 1.25 to 1.31

Strengths
- •

Weaknesses
- •

Tendencies
- More Sliders to RHBs (28%) than LHBs (12%)
- Throws more Fastballs 1st pitch (81%) & with runners on base (80%)
- Throws more Splitters with 2 strikes (18%)

PITCH TIPS

Pitch	% of pitches	All Counts	First Pitch	Early Counts	Two Strikes	Pitcher Ahead	Pitcher Behind	With RISP	Strike Zone %	Chase %	Opponents' Scouted BA	
	Fastballs	72%	81%	73%	69%	68%	72%	80%	61%	9%	.319 (15/47)	Very High
	Curves											High
	Sliders	12%	11%	13%	10%	15%	10%	9%	50%	33%	.250 (3/12)	Avg. or unsure
	Changeups	7%	4%	8%		3%	13%	2%	65%	17%	.286 (2/7)	
	Splitters	7%	4%	5%	18%	13%	3%	7%	22%	21%	.333 (2/6)	Low
	Total Scouted Pitches	244	79	161	49	75	61	82	57%	15%	.306 (22/72)	Very Low

---

PITCH ZONES

LEGEND:

Number of pitches   *1*

Very Favorite Zones

Favorite Zones

vs. Fastballs

8	3	14
8	10	18
8	19	20

5   1   18
12   4
14   4   10

vs. Other Pitches

3	0	2
7	3	8
1	1	5

1   0   7
1   2
20   2   5

Figure 5.

minors with a sore arm. He asked the trainer if there was a whirlpool where he could soak it. "Know what the trainer said? Go find a toilet bowl, put your arm in it then flush it three times and pretend it's the whirlpool."

Today's pitching coach also needs to know a new language. He might tell you that his starting pitcher "has a sailer (sailing fastball) and it's a runner and he can make it tail or sink. Not all tailers sink, but all sinkers tail, and when he cuts his fastball it's really a slider without a spin. The curveball? He's got a good one because the curveball will not affect your slider like the slider affects the curveball. And the best sinkers are from the eleven o'clock position, so they will bite and go down." So much for good ol' country hardball.

It's a far cry from the day I saw Chuck Tanner, then the manager of the Pittsburgh Pirates, pull a little twenty-five-cent notebook filled with notes out of his back pocket.

"What is that," I asked, "your secret weapon?"

"This is all I need; it's all in here."

"You gotta be kidding. That's all you need?"

"Joe, all I need to know is what they did the last time we played against them."

How can you argue with that system when you think about Tanner managing in the World Series? But then I've also seen the Cardinals' pitching coach Dave Duncan in a World Series with his faithful "Big Scouting Book." You can't argue with either one's success.

What both of these guys know is that in spite of all the high tech ability to punch up a picture on a computer that tells you what your pitcher did against a particular batter, the basic rules still determine the great pitchers. Managers still holler to "get ahead of the hitter." Translated that means throw strikes, especially first pitch strikes.

Failing to do that can run a manager crazy and sometimes brings him out for a pitching change. As a catcher I was usually on the mound then, and that's why today, when I'm in the stands watching a game, I really focus on those meetings. Some of the greatest lines have been delivered while making pitching changes.

Bill Meyer, our manager at Pittsburgh, came out to mercifully take a pitcher out of the game. I'd name him, but maybe he's been telling his

Dave Duncan's "Big Scouting Book" has a record of what other teams have done against his pitchers. Courtesy St. Louis Cardinals Hall of Fame Museum.

grandkids how he never came out of a game, so as a fellow grandpa I'll let him have those glorious moments that are a reward for growing old. To tell the truth, with the stuff he had I wasn't sure he'd see old age the way line drives buzzed by him.

On the mound the conversation went like this:

MEYER: Give me the ball.

PITCHER: No.

MEYER: Give me the damn ball.

PITCHER: No.

MEYER: Give me the ball, or it's gonna cost you.

PITCHER: No, I can get this guy out.

MEYER: I know you can. You proved it when he led off the inning.

A conversation between Meyer and another pitcher was even shorter than that one.

PITCHER: I can get 'em out. Let me stay in. I'm better than what you got in the bullpen.

MEYER: You're probably right, but I don't want anybody better. I just want somebody different.

One of the bright spots for pitching coach Billy Connor happened when he walked out after his pitcher had given up more than the normal quota of home runs. It happened in the one of the many parks where they shoot off fireworks when the home team hits a home run. The conversation was short but to the point.

PITCHER: What the hell do you want?

CONNOR: Nothing.

PITCHER: Then why are you out here?

CONNOR: I just came out to give the fireworks guy time to reload.

The rule, unwritten on some teams, is that you wait for your replacement before you head for the dugout. I've been on teams where pitchers were so mad that they started for the dugout before the replacement got to the mound. Two steps later, and remembering the rule and the fine that went with it, they stopped and made a quick U-turn. You would have thought they were wearing shoes with four wheel drive.

Sparky Anderson, Hall of Fame manager, made it easy for his pitchers: "When I go to take out a pitcher, I take him out. I've had pitchers tell me, 'I still got good stuff.' I tell them, 'Hand me the ball, go to the dugout, and your stuff will improve.' I've told my pitchers, 'If I ask you a question, you answer me. If not, don't open your mouth.'" It was always fun to see that act. Sometimes Sparky's head bobbed up and down like a sewing machine while his pitcher was so rigid you could use him as a foul pole.

One of the greatest catches ever made was on the mound. How can that be as it's only sixty feet, six inches from home plate? Picture this scene between the pitcher who's getting yanked and the manager who's doing the yanking. The ever-present short argument happens and in disgust the pitcher gives the innocent rosin bag a major league kick. As the rosin bag heads skyward the manager tells the pitcher that if it hits the ground it will cost him dearly. So the pitcher makes a diving, shoe-string catch of the rosin bag just before it hits the ground. What would you pay to see that play?

Pitchers no longer kick rosin bags, but sometimes a guy walks off the mound giving me the feeling he'll go straight to his cell phone and call his agent with instructions to call the general manager tomorrow to ask why he was taken out of the game. He forgets the fact that he made the field a war zone.

One of the most frequently fought battles on the field is the bean ball war. Pitchers have to pitch inside to win. Batters crowd the plate to take away the inside part of the plate from the pitcher, and then see if he'll reclaim it. The good pitchers do. Roger Clemens is one pitcher who immediately comes to mind.

This turf war sparks the bean ball war. If a pitcher comes too far inside and upends a hitter it could be interpreted as a bean ball. Today it's almost reached the point where if a batter has to move back he charges the mound and both benches empty. The result is as predictable as a WWE wrestling match. Lots of chirping, some pushing, shoving, and maybe even some dancing. Most players look for a particular friend so they can look like they're going at it. One player, six-foot-five-inch, two hundred thirty-five-pound Dick Radatz, told five-foot-five-inch, one hundred forty-eight-pound Fred Patek, "In this fight I want you and a player to be named later."

When the Red Sox and Yankees met in the 2003 American League Champion Series (ACLS), they weren't so friendly. The excitement came when seventy-four-year-old coach Don Zimmer charged the mound to get to Pedro Martinez, who did his best bullfighter's maneuver, dodged the charging Zimmer, and then pushed him to the ground.

Joe Torre, the Yankees' manager, remembers an incident with one of his players. He's quick to point out it wasn't a Yankee, but it did happen in the big leagues. "I once had a player who went after the pitcher when he was hit with the bases loaded. Did he really think a pitcher would throw at him with the bases loaded?"

The unwritten rule used to be that if they hit your star player you'd retaliate. You had to make a decision. Who's gonna get it? You either threw at the first hitter who came up or you waited for the pitcher or the catcher, whoever came up first. If your star was hit hard enough then you waited until their star came up. We even had a signal for the pitch.

With the thumb and the index finger, like you were shooting marbles, you gave the "flip him" signal.

St. Louis Cardinals Hall of Fame pitcher Bob Gibson said he used nine pitches to get hitters out. Two different fastballs, two sliders, a curve, a change up, knockdown, brush back, and a hit batsman. To make sure the hitters understood where he was coming from, Bob always said with a smile, "The knockdown is a brush back pitch with an attitude."

The Dodgers' great Don Drysdale had a reputation for letting hitters know who was boss. His mentor was Sal Maglie, nicknamed "The Barber," because when Maglie wanted to, he'd give you a close shave—his purpose pitch. Maglie told Drysdale to throw two knockdown pitches because the second one tells the hitter you were serious about the first one.

One part of this retaliation strategy I never understood. If you were the unlucky guy to hit behind the star you were vulnerable. With the Pirates, I had the distinction of batting behind Gus Bell and Ralph Kiner. Hitting back-to-back home runs was not unusual for those two. The pitcher would be so upset he'd knock me down. I could never understand it since I rarely hurt a pitcher with a bat in my hands. On the rare occasion when I joined the parade and it was back-to-back-to-back home runs, I really felt sorry for the batter that was following me.

Most pitchers don't like the trend of batters standing at home plate watching their home runs land in the seats. The first player I ever saw hit a home run and wait for the instant press conference was Reggie Jackson. Oddly enough, Reggie said he got the idea from mild mannered nice guy Harmon Killebrew. Now you see players hitting ten points lower than their weight, with six home runs for the year, standing at home plate to admire their occasional home run and then going into their home run trot. Catcher Jim Essian was honest about the method he used when he hit a rare home run: "I'd go into my home run trot except I don't have one."

Has the practice of standing at the plate to admire your blast caught on? Little leaguers certainly imitate the big leaguers. When my twelve-year-old grandson, Chris, hit a home run over the fence I asked him to tell me about it after the game. "I crushed it. I gave it the Barry Bonds

Bob Gibson had nine pitches; one pitch had an attitude. Courtesy St. Louis Cardinals Hall of Fame Museum.

watch, the Ken Griffey Jr. flip of the bat, and the Sammy Sosa skip at the plate." He had the actions and the words. Not much left after that.

When Hank Aaron, who knows something about hitting home runs, hit one out of the park, he ran the bases like you're supposed to. Hank talked about the habit of players watching their home runs, remembering what a pitcher like Sad Sam Jones would do. "He'd knock you down for a week if you did something like that. He'd probably wait for you in the parking lot and try to run over you with his car."

Another signal that can be a red flag to the pitcher is holding up your hand asking the umpire for time out while you do your landscaping in the batter's box. It's really a message from the batter to the pitcher saying, "I'm not quite ready." The hand is up, the feet are working to make a custom fit batter's box, and then the hand comes down to tell the pitcher, "Okay, I'm ready now." Some pitchers have their own way of answering that message.

In my day, one pitcher who didn't like to be told by a batter when to pitch was Cincinnati Reds great Ewell "The Whip" Blackwell. Dino Restelli, a Pirates outfielder, had the annoying habit of standing outside the batter's box with his bat leaning against his body and putting up his hand to hold up play while he pulled out a bright red handkerchief to wipe his glasses. "Get in and hit," Blackwell hollered from the mound.

Looking right back at him, not even touching his bat, Restelli kept wiping his glasses while still outside the batter's box. It was this move (or non-move) that sent Blackwell into orbit.

Finally, with his hand held high to keep the time out going, Restelli stepped into the batter's box. Down came the hand and that was Restelli's sign to Blackwell. Now he was ready to hit.

The first pitch Blackwell threw is how legends start. It was The Whip's best sinking fastball, and those who saw it said it hit Restelli in the middle of the back and stayed there for five minutes just gnawing. It must have taken at least a five hundred calorie bite.

I'm convinced the cliché is accurate—the more things change the more they stay the same. If Abner Doubleday came back, or Ty Cobb, or even Rip Van Winkle (if he was a baseball fan), they'd say the same thing. "Yep, I saw that play," and then go on to describe it.

I was the catcher in a game involving Dino Restelli that goes into the category of, "you had to be there to believe it." I wonder what kind of results Mark McGwire or Barry Bonds would have gotten if they were in the same situation.

The Cardinals were playing the Pirates in Forbes Field. Gerry Staley was our pitcher. The unflappable Larry Goetz was the umpire. When Goetz was behind the plate he had the personality of an oak tree. He was more than all business during a game.

Restelli had just come up to the Pirates and was getting a lot of publicity because he was on a home run streak. He was a home run hitter in the Pacific Coast League, and he was sending the message that he was going to do the same thing for the Pirates. He made every at-bat a command performance.

Up he comes to hit with a man on first. Immediately, he goes into his routine. First, a slow walk to the plate. Then his stop outside the batter's box with the bat leaning against his body. He surveys the field and then off come the glasses. Everybody knows the next move is the bright red handkerchief, and out it comes. Restelli starts to wipe, and he must have thought the glasses were caked with mud because he just kept wiping and wiping.

Finally, Goetz had seen enough. "Get in and hit," he said. Dino didn't know how tough Larry could be. He just looked at him. Again Goetz said, "Get in and hit." Restelli, still outside the box, said, "When I'm ready."

Larry Goetz got red as a thermometer and pulled the mask over his face so hard I thought he would break the strap. He motioned to Staley to throw the ball. Larry was going to call any ball thrown by Staley a strike regardless of where it was and regardless of where Restelli was. Staley didn't understand what Goetz was doing. He looked confused and didn't react right away. Then both Goetz and I hollered, "Throw it!" Staley thought that Goetz wanted to see the ball and maybe put a different one in play, so he just lobbed it to me. Restelli saw this, and I don't know if he ever got the glasses wiped or if he even put them on, but I do know he got a running start into the batter's box. He hit that lob-toss a mile. It was one of those high and far home runs that would make today's player say, "They ought to show a movie on flights that long." We lost the game by the margin of that home run—another reason Restelli didn't get the Good Guy Award from the St. Louis Cardinals.

Some pitchers build and live up to the reputation that they are mean, don't forget, and get even. It becomes part of the scouting report. Stan Williams, a good pitcher with the Dodgers, was known as an intimidator, and he came by that reputation honestly. I laughed out loud when he told me what he did.

"Every time I got hit with a pitch I wrote in a book who I owed one to. Well, one season I got even with everybody except one guy, but I kept his name on the list. Now a couple of years later I'm thinking I probably will never get even. Then I get a job as pitching coach with the team he's on. Well, during batting practice one day this pitcher came up for his practice swings, and I was throwing batting practice. The first pitch I threw drilled him right in the ass. He screamed. 'What the hell are you doing?' I laughed and told him, 'You were the last name in my 'get even' book. Now I can close it.'"

The pitching mound is a place like no other. It's populated with one-of-a-kind guys. I've gotten many laughs there, but I've also seen tears when a pitcher realized his arm was gone and his career was over. Like all catchers, I never knew what I might hear when I walked out to that mound of dirt, but I always felt lucky to be able to make the trip.

Stan Musial. Some said he would never hit with that peek-a-boo stance.
Courtesy St. Louis Cardinals Hall of Fame Museum.

Hitting, Slumps, and Red Peppers

CHAPTER 4

Hitting, like pitching, will never be an exact science. Theories have been around since day one. You can go back to Wee Willie Keeler's theory of "Hit 'em where they ain't," or to the Charlie Lau and Walt Hriniak theories of letting go of the top hand, shifting your weight on your front toe, and on it goes. Every good hitter has his theory. But every good hitter is not necessarily a good teacher.

Wee Willie Keeler had the right idea. Stan Musial once gave Curt Flood some hitting advice, and all it did was leave Flood speechless.

FLOOD: "Stan, I'm really having problems at the plate. What's your secret? What do you do at the plate?"

MUSIAL: "Curt, all you do is when you see the ball just hit the hell out of it."

Was he serious, or was he joking? Sometimes with Stan it was hard to tell. Here's Stan answering another player's question about his secret of hitting. I called it his ballpark theory:

"It depends on the park. If it's a big ballpark I hit the top half of the ball to get it through the infield and maybe in the gaps. If it's a small ballpark I try to hit the bottom half of the ball so I can lift it over the fence." You have to take that theory with a bag of salt, not a grain, but since Stan Musial said it some players believed it.

I attended many banquets with Stan. He always had a question and answer session after his speech, especially at a young people's banquet. One of the questions was always about his secret to hitting. His answer was either the ballpark theory or what I called his zone theory. It sounded like something from a Harry Potter book:

When I'm in the batter's box, I really concentrate. I have a zone about thirty feet from me towards the pitcher, and when I see the ball in that zone I know it's going to be a strike. I can tell by the spin whether it's a fastball or a breaking ball. If it's inside I pull it to right field, but if it's outside I hit it the other way.

The first couple of times Stan explained his zone theory I thought, is it possible he can really do that? Then I thought, *now* I hear about this zone when it can't help me. I'm not even playing any more.

Sometimes after Stan finished explaining his hitting secret, I was asked about my hitting secret. I followed Stan's theory and said the same thing except that my zone was only twenty feet from me, and when the ball got into that zone I knew the pitcher had thrown it.

The more I listened to good hitters the more I felt they were running on confidence. Some said it better than others. Ralph Garr led the National League in hitting one year. His hitting style was described by his manager Clyde King. "Most good hitters try to hit the ball where it's pitched: outside part of the plate hit to the opposite field, inside part of the plate pull the ball. Garr hits the ball *if* it is pitched." When Ralph Garr was asked what kind of a hitter he was in the big leagues he said, "I was a ball hitter. If I saw the ball, I hit it. If I didn't see it, I didn't hit it." Maybe because it's so simple, the great hitters all seem to have a variation on that theory.

ROBERTO CLEMENTE: "I see it, I hit it." Clemente was described as a good bad ball hitter but a better good ball hitter. Like Yogi, he hit many a ball that was out of the strike zone. A scouting report on Clemente read that "With one foot off the ground he'd hit a single, both feet off the ground, an extra base hit."

YOGI BERRA: "You can't hit and think at the same time. They say I'm a bad ball hitter, but it ain't bad if I hit it."

Roberto Clemente. He had a simple theory: "I see it, I hit it." Courtesy Pittsburgh Pirates.

Good hitters like Yogi get right to the point. The Yankees' Derek Jeter doesn't have much trouble in the batter's box. His batting average tells you that. But in one stretch he was having trouble with the high fastball. Yogi told him, "Don't swing at it." Jeter came back with, "But you swung at it." "Yeah, but I hit it," Yogi said.

Confidence should have been Reggie Jackson's first name. "Some players put the ball in play. I put it out of play," he said. Mention the word confidence to me, and Hall of Famer Rogers Hornsby comes to mind. How great a hitter was he? Just look at his numbers. He had a .358 life-time batting average and hit over .400 three times. His best year he hit .424, and his on-base percentage was .507. He liked to talk hitting, but really he'd rather show you his hitting theories than talk about them.

In 1952, I was at spring training in San Bernardino, California, with the Pittsburgh Pirates. Rogers Hornsby was the manager of the St. Louis Browns. Before a game, Hornsby had his favorite spot behind the batting cage, and he would talk hitting. He explained why he took a stance deep in the batter's box and where he tried to hit the ball. His lecture

Rogers Hornsby. I saw him hit a line drive that almost took a pitcher's head off—not bad for a fifty-six-year-old. Courtesy St. Louis Cardinals Hall of Fame Museum.

was mostly about hitting the ball through the middle because if you hit through the middle past the pitcher it was a hit; if you swung early you pulled the ball into left center; if you were late you hit the ball into right center. If you wanted a storyteller on hitting, Rogers Hornsby was your man. This day also turned out to be show and tell or, more accurately, tell and show.

Hornsby was trying to get outfielder Jungle Jim Rivera to hit the ball up the middle. As hard as Rivera tried it wasn't working. Finally, disgusted, Rivera turned to Hornsby and yelled, "I can't do it."

Hornsby looked at him, almost snorted, and not saying a word, grabbed the first bat he saw. To give emphasis to this story let me tell you that Hornsby was born on April 4, 1896. This was March of 1952. If you do the math it comes out that he was just a month shy of fifty-six years old.

Cliff Fannin was pitching batting practice and had a pretty good fastball. It was well known that Hornsby wasn't too popular with his players, so Fannin's first pitch might have been a message from the whole team. A fastball up and in and, as all great hitters do, Hornsby just turned his head away from the pitch. This alone was amazing to see. Here was a fifty-six-year-old man looking at a fastball and almost showing disgust as it whizzed by.

The next pitch Fannin threw reminds me of those balls hit at Charlie Brown that upend him. Rogers Hornsby hit a line drive up the middle past Fannin, and he didn't even have time to get his glove up. As he walked out of the batting cage, Hornsby looked at Rivera and said, "That's what I mean," and put the bat on the ground. Is it any wonder I remember that incident so vividly?

You don't have to be an MIT graduate to understand any of these theories. They simply make sense, and they have obviously worked for some of baseball's best hitters.

HARMON KILLEBREW: "To hit under pressure, you have to learn to relax your body completely while concentrating completely at the same time."

HANK AARON: asked if he was ever scared in the batter's box: "Yes, only scared that the pitcher ain't gonna throw it."

DON BAYLOR: "When I walk to the plate I'm in scoring position."

JOE TORRE: "You have to be intense but not tense."

LOU BROCK: "When you go up to hit, there are only three factors involved: you, the pitcher, and the ball. Once it's released, it's only you and the ball. It's a question of who's better, you or the ball."

TONY GWYNN: "I'm a knowledgeable hitter. I don't call it guessing. I know what I like to do. As a knowledgeable hitter, you're able to realize what's happening around you every time at bat instead of waiting until after you're heading back to the dugout."

Those are some great theories by great hitters. A few I've played against, and others I've watched. Regardless of the era, they all express confidence. Ted Williams was often quoted as saying that the toughest thing to do in sports was to hit a baseball. He wouldn't get an argument from me. Still, Ted Kluszewski gave the best word picture of the art of hitting when he said, "How hard is hitting? You ever walk into a pitch-black room that you've never been in before, full of furniture, and try to walk through it without bumping into anything? Well, it's harder than that."

I agree, and my numbers back that up. In a conversation with one of my favorite people, Casey Stengel, he said something like, "My boy, I know you grew up with Mr. Berra who is a fine hitter even when he don't hit strikes, but I saw you play, and if I had you on my team I could tell by the way you hit that I gotta play you only when the wind is blowing out."

Of course, even the greatest hitters have been afflicted with that "disease" called the hitting slump. It leads you to believe you should have listened to your mother and gone to law school or listened to your father and gotten a union card and become a plumber. When a player's in a slump, the hitting coach works to find the key to get him hitting again. He needs to get inside the player's head but at the same time make the player feel that he discovered the secret by himself.

Next time you're at the ballpark, try to find the hitting coach. It's a kind of *Where's Waldo* game you can play if you get there during batting practice. He's the one watching everything trying to find the clue to make his guy a better hitter. Or he might be Dr. Phil, listening to a player who didn't get a hit the night before tell him why he should have gotten four. You can find a hitting coach in one of three spots if he's on the field for batting practice. His number one position is usually behind the batting cage watching hitters. Number two is seated on a stool near the stands tossing a ball underhanded to a batter hitting it into a net. Number three is off to the side with a fungo bat in his hand hitting ground balls. If you can't find him, he's probably working with a player in the batting cage under the stands or studying tapes of previous at-bats that could be as recent as his last one or as far back as the player's rookie year.

Ted Kluszewski. I agree with his explanation of how tough hitting really is.
Courtesy National Baseball Hall of Fame Library, Cooperstown, N.Y.

Maybe it surprises you to know that when a slump happens, hitting coaches don't usually tweak the batting stance. If hitting coaches were hired to change stances we would never have seen the likes of Mel Ott with the high leg kick, Stan Musial with his look around the corner, or Craig Counsell, a chiropractor's delight with his pretzel-like stance. All batters will tell you the same thing: "I feel comfortable with my stance." Add to that the fact that all good hitters regardless of the stance hit the ball hard most of the time when it's in the strike zone.

Still, none of that explains the dreaded slump, an ugly sounding word that fits an ugly condition. Some players consider it a voodoo word and will not even say it. Hall of Famer Dave Winfield was never in a slump. He would emphatically say, "I'm going through a statistically acceptable variation."

Wade Boggs, who knew something about hitting, would never admit to a slump. He referred to it as a "readjustment period." I might add that if that readjustment period lasts too long you might make a decision to change careers before your manager makes that decision for you.

Players may not like to say the word, but they will tell you what a slump feels like, and some of the descriptions are colorful. Like this one from a player from the Deep South. I wrote it on the back of a gum wrapper and I have no idea what it means, but it sounds right: "Damn, this is enough to make a monkey eat red peppers." I don't remember how many at bats he had without a hit, but his explanation makes a great word picture.

A player will do everything to avoid a slump, but once he's in it he'll do anything to get out of it. Red Schoendienst put eye drops all over his bat because he wanted the bat to see the ball better. He thought maybe he'd get some "seeing eye" hits, those welcomed beauties that take fifteen hops, seem to crawl through the infield, and make it successfully for a hit.

I've seen batters draw a pair of eyes on the bat, then go maybe another six or eight times without a hit and draw glasses around the eyes. Players have used everything from Mercurochrome to iodine to Pepto Bismol and Bengay in order to cure a "sick" bat. Hall of Famer Willie Stargell would only use a bat with someone else's name on it. Some players like a thick grain spaced widely apart while others like a tighter grain, and still others will tell you that knots in the barrel mean a better bat. Harry Walker, who led the league in hitting for the Phillies, used a two-tone bat. The bottom part was untouched, but the barrel of the bat looked like it was dipped in chocolate. He claimed that balls hit off a dark bat are harder for the defense to read.

Slumps have never been explained to my satisfaction, but the most common explanation is that you have enlarged your strike zone and you're swinging at bad pitches. When this happens pitchers jump all over it, and they keep expanding the strike zone as they feed off your anxiety and desperate attempt to get a hit.

With this in mind the great philosopher Yogi Berra had his own answer. "I ain't in no slump. I just ain't hitting." As the hits took longer to come and the pitchers had him chasing worse pitches than usual he added his other observation: "How can a pitcher that wild stay in the league." That's the power of positive thinking.

My two favorite definitions of a slump came from two catchers.

Johnny Bench said, "Slumps are like soft beds; they're easy to get into but hard to get out of." Roy Campanella said, "It starts with your swing, goes to your head, and ends up in your belly."

Players will blame a slump on anything. The bat either takes the biggest beating or gets the best of care. Phillies star Richie Ashburn freely admitted that he took his favorite bat to bed with him because it had been treating him so well. I don't know what today's players do, but over the years players have done some interesting things to get their bats ready for the season and to break out of slumps.

The Gas House Gang manager Frankie Frisch hung his bats in a barn to cure like they were sausages. Home Run Baker supposedly used a magical potion made of ingredients so secret that he wouldn't even tell his teammates what they were. I once read that Honus Wagner boiled his bats in creosote, an oily liquid from Beachwood tar that's used as an antiseptic. Eddie Collins was supposed to have buried his bats in a dunghill to keep them alive. In one clubhouse, I remember seeing a large bone fastened to a board. Players rubbed their bats on it supposedly to seal the pores and toughen the wood. Some players used to "bone" their bats by using a Coke bottle. Jim Frey soaked his bat in motor oil. I've seen players wipe their bats with alcohol after every game so they could see exactly what part of the bat they hit the ball with. Cardinals infielder Solly Hemus carved grooves into the barrel with an ice pick to roughen it up, explaining that it created a pocket of air to help push the ball off the bat. Players will try anything when a slump is involved. Desperate times need desperate measures.

One question I hear a lot is, why do bats break so often? Bats used to look the same. Now they can be two-tone or a shade of orange, and they can be hollowed out on the end—or whatever. Bats used to crack, splinter, or just break. One of the big surprises while watching a game now is how far the pieces go when the hitter breaks a bat. Today it's not unusual to see a bat break in half and the broken end go farther than the ball. I've seen pitchers not worry about fielding the dribbler but instead worry about the broken end of the bat heading toward the mound.

Embarrassing? Yes. But unusual? No. Blame the pitcher with a good slider for breaking plenty of bats. The slider looks like a fastball, so the batter swings, and then at the last minute it breaks inside. So instead of hitting it on the fat part of the bat, the sweet spot, the batter hits it on the handle and he has an instant toothpick factory. The explanation I hear from most players about broken bats is the thin handle. You really don't see too many thick handle bats because the players want that whip action they believe translates into home runs, which translates into more money. Most players live by the philosophy of a teammate of mine, Ralph Kiner. His belief was that "Home run hitters drive Cadillacs." Roy Campanella tried to offset that philosophy by coming back with, "True, but singles hitters buy the gas." The best explanation I've heard for the epidemic of broken bats comes from Hall of Famer Lou Brock. "I guess they must be using wood from trees that grow on the shady side of the mountain," he said, laughing.

Choosing bats was always a rite of passage for the rookie, but it changed as your batting average went up or in other cases went down. The clubhouse attendant (clubbie) might have had orders from the front office, but he made it sound like it was his decision as to who got new bats and who did not. I played with four teams when there were only eight in the big leagues, and it was always the same. The stars had no problems. Guys like Stan Musial with the Cardinals, Ralph Kiner with the Pirates, Ernie Banks with the Cubs, and Willie Mays with the Giants could order bats whenever they wanted.

For me, it was a little different. Many times players are asked, "When do you know it's time to quit?" One of my signs came when I asked the clubbie if I could order new bats. His answer was, "Order new bats? What for? Why don't you use the ones over Stan's locker? He doesn't like 'em, but maybe you will."

There's no doubt that in today's market, the big hitters get the big contracts. All those zeroes and guaranteed clauses have made fans ask me, "Hey, Joe, don't you wish you were playing today with all that money out there?" Sure, I'd love to be playing for that kind of money, but I'd also be a lot of years younger, and that would be even better.

The next question usually is, "Don't you think players are overpaid? Are they worth that much?" My standard reply is, "Have you ever met anyone who says, 'No, don't give me a couple million dollars because I'm only worth half that much.'" Ballplayers are no different than anyone else; you give, they take.

Ask Willie Mays if he'd like to be playing today with all that money, and he'll break into a big laugh. I once had a chance to ask Joe DiMaggio that question, and he said it best for all former players. I was playing in the Dinah Shore Nabisco Golf Tournament and as I pulled into the parking lot, Joe DiMaggio and Johnny Bench got out of the same car, and in the car next to them was Willie Mays. I must say, when I saw the three of them I immediately tried to figure how many home runs and RBIs they had between them, but I couldn't do it without a calculator and a record book.

On this particular day, the morning paper had a story about a player who had just signed a multi-year contract with plenty of zeroes on it. I said to DiMaggio, "Joe, I know you saw the sports page this morning. How would you like to walk into Steinbrenner's office to talk contract with your numbers? What would you say to him?" He pulled his clubs out of the trunk, turned to me, smiled, and said one of the funniest things I'd ever heard from him: "No problem. I'd walk in, shake hands, and say, 'Howdy, partner.'"

You read of these humongous signings with all kinds of goodies attached. A bonus to make the All-Star team (for that kind of money I would *expect* a player to make the All-Star team), a bonus for number of at-bats, innings pitched, MVP votes, and more. And the bonuses aren't just money. It's suites at the hotel, ballpark luxury suites for the family, and trips home on private jets. Roger Clemens made a deal that he doesn't have to make the road trip if he isn't scheduled to pitch in that series. My take on all this is, why not? Go Biblical; ask and you shall receive.

When I see these gold-edged perks I smile remembering a story the great home run hitter Hank Aaron tells:

When I signed, they told me I was going to Eau Claire and the scout gave me a $2.50 suitcase. I found out the first time I used it that it was made out of cardboard. When I got off the bus in Eau Claire it started to rain. I was walking down the street with my new suitcase all packed. I had to walk about three blocks in the rain. Pretty soon there I was standing on a corner in the pouring rain holding just the handle of my bonus suitcase.

Signing a major league baseball contract always gave you a great feeling, but now that's all gone. Negotiations are done by agents or representatives. To be honest with you, though, I'd gladly give up that great feeling for some of the numbers that agents are able to get into today's contracts.

So many scenes jump into my mind because players and owners did some funny things when it came to holding out for a better contract. One player signed his name in blood to emphasize that he was bleeding to death. Joe Engel, a minor league team owner, answered a player's request to "double my salary or count me out" by writing back, "Okay. 1,2,3,4,5,6,7,8,9,10, you're out."

In 2006, the minimum salary stood at three hundred thirty thousand dollars. How can I not smile when I think of the great Joe DiMaggio, Ted Williams, and Stan Musial racing to see who would be the first one hundred thousand dollar a year player? I smile because in 2006 you only had to get a uniform and be in the team picture and your salary was three hundred thirty thousand dollars.

Hank Greenberg was a big star for the Detroit Tigers, a powerful home run hitter who in 1938 looked like he was going to break Babe Ruth's single-season home run record of sixty. Greenberg hit fifty-eight. He went on to become an owner of the Cleveland Indians and later, with Bill Veeck, the Chicago White Sox. You can only imagine how Hank Greenberg felt about high salaries when he remembered his numbers.

Steve Greenberg, his son, was an agent for a time and remembered going to his father to ask for advice about an upcoming negotiation. After going through all the details Steve said, "My player hit .238. What should I ask for?" Hank didn't hesitate and went right to the point. "Ask for a uniform."

Contracts, money, and hitting are the most popular conversation topics in the stands. Sitting in the stands is like playing *Jeopardy* without the categories, just questions:

   —*Why and when did they start to use K's for strikeouts?*
   —*Why do they call it a foul pole when it's fair if the ball hits it?*
   —*If a left-hander is a southpaw, why isn't a right-hander a northpaw?*
   —*Why doesn't anybody choke up on the bat any more?*

Fans also like to talk about their own playing experiences. I took this one to the umpires to get an explanation, and all I got was a laugh. Here's the fan's story:

   I was born in a little coal mining town in Illinois, and we had a town team. One day we played the team from the next town, and the game went to the bottom of the ninth inning. The score was tied. There were two outs and a man on second base, and I was at bat. The count went to three balls and two strikes, and I expected a fastball, but the pitcher threw a slow ball, and I swung at it. I was anxious and swung with all my might and missed it but went around and hit the ball for a single on the second time around. The man on second scored so we won. I want to ask you, was it a hit or a strikeout?

What do you think?

   That's the beauty of sitting in the stands, where I don't have to think or worry about slumps. Let the hitters figure it out any way they want. All I have to do is follow the ball and enjoy the game.

Bill Klem, "I never missed one in my heart." Courtesy National Baseball Hall of Fame Library, Cooperstown, N.Y.

Honest, They're My Best Friends

CHAPTER 5

*Any umpire who does not think he is the best umpire
in the world is not a good umpire.* — BILL KLEM

A great book by James M. Kahn simply called *The Umpire Story* gives a really good explanation of umpires, especially Bill Klem. A line on page eighty-seven tells you everything you need to know: "Also for sixteen straight years Klem umpired behind the plate in every game." Even now I have a hard time comprehending sixteen years of calling balls and strikes. That kind of dedication explains Klem's own summing up of his career. "I never missed one in my heart," he said.

I respect that, although when I'm watching a game I fall back into old habits. I know the umpires can't hear me, but that doesn't keep me from saying, "Where was that pitch?" or "Don't be afraid to put the right hand up." My favorite expression, Bucket Head, was one much used as a player, mostly from the bench where I could hide.

Umpires, my "best friends," were very friendly mostly between calls and pitches. Today, almost anything an umpire does reminds me of the ones I knew. Even dusting off home plate with a whisk broom triggers a memory.

Bill Stewart wasn't tall but fit the description of strong and stocky. His whisk broom was just about worn to the handle, and he was always telling catchers how long he had used that broom and how it was going to the Hall of Fame when he retired. His other favorite subject was his hockey-playing days and how tough you had to be to play that game. Sometimes walking back to his position he'd give me a modified body check saying, "That was just a love tap. I could send you into the second row if I wanted to. You gotta have guts to play hockey, and I got more guts in my little finger than you see on this field." I always looked forward to a fun time with Stewie.

A crease on an umpire's pants immediately reminds me of Babe Pinelli. He always looked like he just fell off the cover of a fashion magazine. Babe loved New York, and when you saw him in the hotel lobby you knew he had been out clothes shopping. If he was working the plate, all you had to do was ask what he had bought and you would get a rundown of his entire new wardrobe.

Beans Reardon owned a Budweiser beer distributorship in California, and that was his main topic behind the plate. How good a cold Budweiser would taste lasted for about six innings. Beansie spent the other three telling you he didn't need the job, and that's why he didn't take any guff from anybody. He umpired like he really had money in the bank.

The umpires I knew were no different than you and I in that they liked some of their fellow workers and couldn't stand others. The fun part was to find out who got along with whom. For example, when I got the umpire who was not a member of the Bill Stewart Fan Club all I had to say was, "Man, I get tired of hearing how tough Stewie says he is." Then for nine innings it was Stewart-shredding time. Or I would tell the right guy that Pinelli can wear you out with how much his shirts cost. There's not much fun back there, so you have to make your own, especially if you're on a losing team.

When I see a catcher walk back to his position, I always wonder if he's going to use one of the better triggers to get the umpire going. You had to pick your man carefully, but with certain umpires all you had to say was, "Did you hear what he just said?" Of course you were always referring to the opposition's bench.

"No, what did he say?"

The casual answer was, "Well, if you didn't hear him then it's OK." You knew that the rest of the game he'd have one ear tuned to their bench.

Dodger Roy Campanella was one of the best at walking back to his position and getting his point across. If he thought a pitch was a strike and didn't get the call, he'd walk out about ten feet in front of home plate, throw the ball back to his pitcher, put his glove under his arm, rub his hands, and with a big smile and a soft voice say to the plate umpire, "We in the same ballgame, baby?"

Ed Bailey was a forgiving catcher when it came to the umpires. He had the needle out, but it was a soft sting. More than once I heard him say, "Aw, don't tell me you missed that pitch and take all the blame. Let the other umpires share. Let's spread the mistakes around." Or how about this little zinger to a rookie umpire as Bailey walked back from the mound, "Well, if that's a sample of your work, you ain't gonna be around very long."

Umpires and catchers were friends even though sometimes an argument was the main topic of the day. Most married couples know what I'm talking about. But today, the climate around home plate has changed. Even the position the umpire works from has changed. It used to be that the National League umpire worked inside and was lined up over the catcher's left shoulder with a right-handed batter. Vice versa with a left-handed batter. The American League umpire worked standing directly behind the catcher. The argument used to be that the National League umpire's position didn't let him get a good read on the outside corner, while the American League umpire couldn't get a good read on the low pitch. So the umpires went to a comfortable position that allows them to see the strike zone. Their positions went from inside to behind the catcher to holding on to the catcher to kneeling. The rule book defines the strike zone, but the home plate umpire tells you his strike zone with his calls, and you better learn it fast. It's the only one that counts, but he has to be consistent.

Since all umpires now work for the same boss—the commissioner—baseball seems to be on a crusade to get the umpires to look like they're all on the same page when calling a game. The object is to have the same strike zone. It's striving for a perfection that can't be reached. Now most plate umpires take a position right behind the catcher. Some still lean on the catcher, but kneeling has mostly gone the route of the inflated chest protector.

To many, and that includes me, it's the position that has become uniform not the strike zone. As long as human beings are making the decisions you will have differences, and I hope that never changes. No mechanical or high tech devices to call pitches or plays. I want the umpire. A camera called QuesTec records balls and strikes to try to get a uniform strike zone. At the end of the game the umpire gets the tape so he has a record of how many times his decision agreed with the camera. According to what I hear, it behooves an umpire to work toward agreeing with QuesTec as the reward may be working post-season games.

Players, especially pitchers and catchers, feel that some umpires make calls based on how they think the camera recorded the pitch and not by what they saw. QuesTec is not used in every park, but it got a lot of publicity when pitcher Curt Schilling, while with the Arizona Diamondbacks, got so upset with the inconsistency that one night before walking into the batter's box, he took his bat and knocked the camera out of commission. Schilling was fined, another camera was installed, and the beat went on.

In today's game umpires have a new duty. The plate umpire and the first base umpire are usually too busy to handle it, so the job of clock-watcher goes to the second base umpire. As soon as the third out is made he clicks his stopwatch and makes sure the next inning doesn't start while the telecast is showing a commercial. Only when the time is up does he give the sign. Stream of revenue strikes again.

During the NBC *Game of the Week* days this was done on the sly as much as possible. We were told that someone was sitting near the dugout with a towel wrapped around his neck. Once the commercial was over he'd remove the towel, which was the umpire's signal to start the inning. If the pitcher was ready but the commercial was still running, umpires stalled by dusting the plate or getting a new supply of baseballs. Today the umpire just stands alongside home plate and gets the direct signal from Big Ben dressed in blue. During the World Series that duty goes to a person hired especially to make sure the clock starts and stops when he gives the signal. I'm basically trying to paraphrase a comment made by Grantland Rice who wrote, "Remember when the Great Scorer comes to write beside your name, it's not who won or lost the game but if the commercials got on and off in time."

Today it's rare to actually hear an umpire call a strike. Most of the umpires I see are what I refer to as closet callers, no booming it out and barely moving the right arm. Even though the diction was bad and Dusty Boggess would call a strike something that sounded like "Axxxxxxxxx" and call a ball a "ballwell," at least you heard it. When Al Barlick called a strike you heard him in the next area code, and if you were catching right next to him he cleared your sinuses at the same time. Dutch Rennert was another umpire who let everyone in the park and anyone driving by on the Interstate know what he had called. That was great with a three-two count and less than two outs when you felt the runner on first was going. Today, some umpires could call a pitch at High Mass and not disturb anyone. My friend Doug Harvey says, "An umpire has to sell the call. You make it in such a way that everybody, especially the players, knows you are not only sure of your call but positive you are right."

Here's the answer I got from an umpire when I asked why they call strikes, balls, and outs as if they have lockjaw. "They (I think he meant the people in charge of umpires) don't want us to holler too loud because the players feel like we're showing them up, especially on the third strike." I don't know what you just did, but I laughed out loud when he told me that.

I like to think all umpires know the rules better than their own name, but something Al Barlick said should be the testing yardstick. "If you're gonna preach the game you better know the bible." I'm sure he wasn't talking about Matthew, Mark, Luke, or John.

I've gotten to know Doug Harvey pretty well since we are now on the same team fighting the enemy, smokeless tobacco (chew, leaf, or dip), or as I call it, "spit tobacco." When you travel with Harvey you get the good umpire's mantra. "When I walked on the field, it was my field. I was in charge," is the simple way Doug says it. Lenny Dykstra, Philadelphia outfielder, walked up to home plate one day, looked at Harvey and said, "Hello, God." That's respect, and that's what an umpire wants and needs. Doug Harvey says you don't just get it, you earn it. In my day umpires didn't care whether you liked them, talked to them, or even said hello, but you better have respected them.

Now when I see an umpire rip off his mask and go face-to-face with a catcher who's chirping while looking straight ahead I think about some of my guys. Fans might guess the catcher is chirping, but they aren't sure because both player and umpire keep looking straight ahead. I remember both Jocko Conlan and Beans Reardon listening for awhile and then going around me to dust off the plate. It might as well have been a podium. Jocko's speech varied but was pretty much the same theme.

"You've had your say, so just shut up and *try* to catch. I got a headache and I don't wanna hear you moaning. The plate's clean, let's play ball."

Beans Reardon was as subtle as a chain saw. "Listen, Dago, it's hot and I'm tired. You know what I'm thinking about now is a cold beer. You're lucky you're here instead of behind some push cart selling cantaloupes like the rest of your *paisanos*. So shut up and catch because you wouldn't know a strike if you saw one whether you had a bat in your hand or a glove. Let's go." Beansie really didn't care that he wasn't politically correct. First came the order, and then came the insult.

Larry Goetz had a great sense of humor, but he always left it in the dressing room and picked it up after the game. He'd brush off the plate and simply say, "That's enough." And you better not bring it up the next day either.

I was catching a game when Goetz kicked out then manager of the St. Louis Cardinals, Eddie Stanky. The next day we were all around home plate and they were exchanging lineup cards when Stanky made a costly mistake. After handing in the card he looked at Goetz and said, "And Larry, I want you to know that what I said yesterday still goes."

Goetz looked at him and said, "Are you sure?"

"Yeah," said Stanky, "what I said yesterday still goes."

"Okay," said Goetz. "And what I said yesterday still goes. Get outta here." So before a pitch was even made Stanky was gone. Now how can I sit in the stands and not think of times like that?

After the third out, umpires used to walk to the opposite side of the field from the dugout of the team that just batted. For example, the home team dugout is usually on the third base side. The third out is made and the umpire walks to the first base line with his cap on. Today I notice that many times the umpire walks to the side that just made the third out so he's in a convenient spot should there be an argument on a decision, whether it be about a called strike or a play on the bases. Usually his cap is off. I'm not referring to those umpires who wear the one piece heavy helmet with the built-in mask. I don't blame them for taking that off, but the little cloth cap can't be too uncomfortable.

Some people may think I notice this because I'm bald. Not really; although I have noticed a few bald umpires who spend the half inning wiping or shining their heads. Then there are the "hairy" guys who keep their hats off and spend the time pushing their hair back as if auditioning for a shampoo commercial. All the while they're doing this, both baldy and hairy are usually working their way toward the stands. This was also a no-no in the "good old days."

Today, between innings, some umpires look into the stands so intently it seems like they're counting the fans because they have an attendance clause in their contracts. Every time I see this, one of the scenes that jumps to my mind is of Larry Goetz, plate umpire in game four of the 1947 Yankees-Dodgers World Series. Yankees pitcher Floyd Bevens was pitching a no-hitter until the ninth inning when Dodgers pinch-hitter Cookie Lavagetto hit a double off the scoreboard in right field to drive in pinch-runner Eddie Miksis with the winning run. When Miksis scored, Ebbets Field became a madhouse and home plate was crowded with happy Dodgers jumping on one another and slapping backs. Everybody was celebrating except Goetz. His concentration was so great that he walked around the crowd and was sweeping off home plate getting ready for the next batter. The problem was that the next batter wouldn't show up for twenty-four hours. Goetz didn't know whether any fans were even in the park. When I see today's umpire prancing and preening between innings I have a pretty good idea what Larry would say.

My memory kicks into gear when I see some of the arguments now. An umpire will whip off his mask and challenge a hitter, pitcher, or the bench. A couple of stock answers umpires give you almost make you believe they learn them at umpire's school. I've heard other players, mostly catchers, tell their version of these two discussions with the umpire. It's a squelch that leaves you speechless, and for most catchers that's almost impossible.

Answer number one:

BATTER: "That wasn't a strike. You missed that one."

UMPIRE: "Maybe I did, but if I would have had a bat in my hand like you I wouldn't have missed it."

Answer number two: (This usually happens after you've been nagging the umpire about a pitch that you think is a strike.)

CATCHER: "That's a strike. You missed it."

UMPIRE: "It's not a strike and I didn't miss it." This short discussion is a booby trap. If you use the "you missed it" line more than once, get ready for the next squelch.

CATCHER: (Takes a pitch he thinks is the same one he was griping about when he was catching.) "That's the same pitch I'm talking about, how come when I'm hitting you call it a strike?"

UMPIRE: "You're a decent guy and I know you don't lie, so between innings I was thinking about that pitch and I think you're right. I'm not calling it a ball anymore, it's a strike."

The ump wins again, as you lose the argument and find yourself with a bat in your hand and behind in the count.

One of the better lines I ever heard came from umpire Tom Gorman, who stopped a rookie by telling him, "Turn around and hit. You haven't been up here long enough to use the hot water in the shower." Umpires had quick answers when you asked for a strike. As a hitter I was often asked, "How would you know with your batting average?" As a catcher with Musial hitting I would hear, "Don't worry about it, Stan's bat will let you know if it's a strike."

I can't remember Bill Meyer, my manager at Pittsburgh, ever getting kicked out of a game. Every time he came back from arguing he'd have a pixie look in his eye and a smile on his face. The umpire always let him have his say.

Umpire Bill Engeln went way back with Bill Meyer, and I think Meyer took advantage of that relationship. I know of two visits that should have gotten him kicked out of a game, yet he came back with a big silly grin. Engeln, behind the plate, had made a call that went against us in Boston. Bill Meyer strolled out to home plate. The conversation was short and went something like this.

MEYER: "Bill, we go back a long time don't we?"

ENGELN: "Yeah, what's that got to do with it?"

MEYER: "You know I like you as a guy but I'm out here because I think you missed the play."

ENGELN: "I didn't miss it, and that's it. You said enough."

MEYER: "OK, Bill, I'm leaving. Now you know I'm quitting after this season, so why don't you think about quitting with me?"

I'm certain that today Meyer would be ejected, yet all Engeln could do was laugh and call him an expletive that has been deleted.

The argument I always liked was when the umpire and the arguer used the same question. Like when Bill Meyer headed for the plate and Engeln said to him, "What are you doing out here?"

"I wanna know the same thing from you. What are you doing out here?" Meyer asked.

Umpire Dusty Boggess was a big man and a real easy going guy behind the plate. He was from Texas and was always giving you that good ol' boy Texas talk. When you asked Dusty about a pitch, his answer made you feel like you were just sittin' around a campfire. It almost always put a smile on your face.

Once Phillies third baseman Willie "Puddin' Head" Jones complained that a pitch was inside. It was the top of the ninth and the Philles were losing by a couple of runs. There were two outs and the last pitch was just called strike two. Dusty listened to Pud's complaint and then gave him some good ol' down home advice.

"Mister Jones," Dusty began, "you think that last one was inside. You take the next one and we will all be inside." I thought Jones was going to start swinging as soon as our pitcher went into his windup.

Umpire Frank Dascoli called the pitch a strike, and Pud stepped out of the box, looked straight out to center field, shook his head, and said, "I dunno, I dunno." Of course, he was letting Dascoli know that it wasn't a strike, but he was doing it in such a way that the fans couldn't tell he was complaining. Another pitch and the same thing. "I dunno, I dunno," moaned Pud. Dascoli took off his mask and calmly walked around to dust home plate.

"Well, *I* know," he said. "And I'll tell you another thing—Stan Musial would know if it was a strike." Jones just looked at Dascoli and then stopped him cold. "Hell, Stan Musial can hit."

Even now, it's easy for me to picture Puddin' Head Jones at the plate. He was one of my favorite guys because he would entertain you while moaning about the umpire's call.

Another guy who could make even an umpire laugh was Jackie Brandt, an outfielder with the Giants. Brandt once took a pitch that was a perfect strike right down the middle, and Frank Dascoli called it a ball. Jackie turned to Frank and said, "How the hell could you call that pitch a ball." I miss hearing conversations like that.

Whether it's behind the plate or on the bases, most umpires will give you an answer that has squelch written all over it. Bill Haller was working the bases when the runner slid into second in a cloud of dust. It was a close play. Here's Haller's version:

"I holler safe, and the second baseman is all over me. I let him scream and then he says to me, 'Would he have been out if I'd tagged him?' I looked straight at him and then said, 'I really think you would have had a better chance.'"

When I watch those in-your-face arguments my mind turns like a kaleidoscope. I see Earl Weaver turning his cap around because he doesn't want to use the bill as a weapon. In the early days he'd use the bill of his cap like a woodpecker working on a tree.

I remember Leo Durocher using good clean words that begin with an "s" in an argument because it made the words juicy. "It wasn't a *strike*. You *said* it was a *strike*. How could you *say* it?" On and on he went with the s-words. Pretty soon the umpire, practically dripping, would say, "Are you spitting on me?" That was the signal Leo was waiting for. Now the words began at his shoes.

"Who's *spitting*?... I ain't *spitting*!...you can't *say* I'm *spitting*."

The umpire looked like he needed windshield wipers before he could continue the discussion.

Watch an umpire's reaction to those in-your-face arguments. Tommy Helms at Cincinnati always liked it when his manager, Dave Bristol, got into an argument with an umpire who had given him problems. Dave was prepared. "If he didn't like the guy behind the plate," Tommy said, "he'd eat green onions for supper." Green onion breath is unjust warfare.

Jocko Conlan was one of my favorite umpires because of his great ability to solve problems, even if he solved them his way. This problem involved Richie Ashburn. Here's Richie's version.

In a game between the Phillies and Milwaukee, Ashburn had been chirping all afternoon about the ball and strike calls. Finally, Jocko said, "OK, you call 'em. Call your own pitches."

Ashburn couldn't believe what he'd just heard. Neither could Braves catcher Del Crandall. Richie said, "I stepped out of the batter's box and asked, 'Are you serious?'"

"Yes, I'm serious," Jocko told him. "I'm tired of hearing you complain. You call 'em."

According to Richie, Crandall was laughing and said, "That's OK with me. Let's go."

"I'm thinking I want to be fair, so I'm going to bear down. I don't want to take advantage of what Jocko is doing. Burdette was the pitcher and he had a good sinker but a better spitter. He wound up and threw a ball that looked like it would cross the plate about knee high. I didn't want to look like I didn't know what I was doing so I called it a strike right away. I'm sure the pitch was a spitball. The bottom dropped out, and by the time the ball got to Crandall he had to block it in the dirt."

"You're brutal," Jocko yelled. "I never missed one that bad. You had your chance to be an umpire, and you blew it. Now get in and hit and shut up."

Ron Luciano was an umpire who let catchers umpire pitches. He had his own system. John Roseboro was one of his favorite catcher-umpires. If Roseboro thought it was a ball, he then threw it back quickly. If he thought it was a strike, he held onto the ball a little longer. Watching a game now, when I see a catcher hold the ball, how can I not think he was the umpire on that pitch?

Ask Luciano if he ever missed a call, and he would give a speech. "Sure, I missed calls, but I didn't try to miss them. I gave a lot of 'strikall' and 'ballike' calls, too. Sometimes my arm gave me away, though."

A pitcher asking for a new baseball also triggers a thought. I especially like it when the pitcher throws the ball, the hitter takes it, the umpire calls it a strike, the catcher throws it back, and then the pitcher wants a new ball. I have to figure that the pollution between the mound and home plate must be bad.

How would you like to have been in Wrigley Field when pitcher Jack Sanford kept asking for a new ball? None felt right to him, and it seemed like he had rejected about ten of them. Jocko got so disgusted that he reached into his pocket, grabbed all the balls he had, and rolled them toward the mound. "Take your pick," he said.

One non-event I look for at a game is what happens to the ball that was just used to end the inning. Sometimes a player will try switching the infield practice ball with the game ball at the start of an inning. If you give some pitchers a dirty ball, like the infield ball, they can make the pitch dance up to home plate. Clete Boyer, then with the Yankees, got caught switching balls but Umpire Ed Hurley got even with him. He kept the infield ball until it was Boyer's turn to hit and then gave it to the opposing pitcher to use.

The next time you see a play that forces all the umpires to have a meeting, don't think they're studying the rules. Umpires have their own language when they have to interpret a play—their own system of questions.

Bobby Bragan, famous for his discussions with umpires, was once stumped by Durwood Merrill in a Texas League game. A ball was lined to third and it was a tough call because you couldn't tell if the third baseman had caught the ball or trapped it. Merrill, the home plate umpire, called the batter out. Bragan ran out to protest the call. After arguing for some five minutes Bragan said to Merrill, "Would you ask the other umpire for help on this play?"

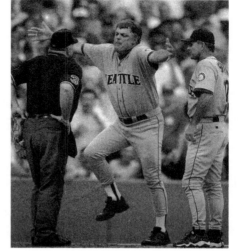

Lou Piniella never had trouble expressing himself to an umpire.
Courtesy Sports Illustrated.

"Sure," said Merrill, turning to yell to his partner umpiring on the bases. "Did you see what I saw?"

"Yes!" the base umpire hollered back.

Durwood turned to Bragan and said, "See, I was right." All Bragan could do was walk back to the bench.

Joe Morgan, not the second baseman from the Big Red Machine but the former Boston Red Sox coach and manager, had a great sense of humor when dealing with umpires. A lot of managers have signals with their infielders and catchers as to whether the play was called correctly. It's a good system because sometimes the manager has a bad view from the dugout but comes busting out to argue anyway, and then has to save face if he's wrong.

Morgan came charging out to argue a close play at first base. He then looked at his first baseman who gave him the "runner-was-safe" sign. Joe had gone too far, so he had to go down the line to argue with the first base umpire. It was a quick discussion and a quicker U-turn for Morgan, one of those scenes that really make you wonder what went on out there.

"What was he?" Morgan asked when he reached the umpire.

"Safe," the umpire answered. Morgan looked him right in the eye and said, "You're damn right he was," and then he immediately headed back to the dugout.

This even happens in a World Series. Former Yankee Tommy Henrich used to tell this story on the banquet circuit. "I got picked off second base in a World Series game. I was out, but I looked foolish getting picked off, so I jumped up and rushed over to the second base umpire, Beans Reardon. I said to him, 'Help me. I looked pretty silly on that play. Give me a couple minutes of arguing time so I won't look too bad.' Reardon looked at me and said, 'Okay but don't stay too long.' Beansie took the heat, and since it looked like a good argument from the stands I got an ovation for a dumb play. And that's why I think umpires are great guys."

One question I've heard at least two million times is, "Why do players argue with the umpire since they never win?" Leo Durocher's answer was, "You argue with an umpire because there's nothing else you can do." The umpire always wins—and in more ways than one.

Leo was in one of the most famous arguments of all time, a kicking contest with Jocko Conlan. Leo loved telling the story even though he was the loser:

I'm already out of the game. Jocko got rid of me in a hurry, and I was mad. I walked by him and tried to kick dirt on him. I kicked, and he kicked dirt back at me. I forgot that umpires didn't have spikes on their shoes like we had, so when he kicked the dirt he slipped a little bit and kicked me right in the shins. A beauty. I kicked him back. He kicked me back. We must have looked like two untalented Radio City Rockettes. He kept kicking me, and I kept kicking him. Another thing I forgot was that umpires wear shin guards and they have iron plates in their shoes to protect their toes. So he's blocking my kicks with shin guards and nailing me with steel toes that were raising lumps on my shins. Even I figured out that wasn't good, so I stopped.

When umpires eject a player or manager, they have to make a report to the league office. Sometimes when I see a guy get ejected I really wish I could read that report.

One of the most creative reports I've ever heard about involved umpire Stan Landes and Pirates pitcher Vernon Law. Vernon's nickname was Deacon because of his affiliation with his church. If ever a player had a Good Housekeeping Seal of Approval it was Vernon Law. This was the only time in his career that he was thrown out of a game. The report read, "I threw Law out of the game because I know he's a minister and there was a lot of abusive language on the bench and I didn't want him to hear it."

It's a safe bet that if you see a play you know you'll never forget, an umpire is involved. One of mine had my friend Jocko Conlan behind the plate, and it may have cost me a trip to the World Series. In 1949, the Cardinals finished second to the Dodgers. The Cardinals' record was ninety-six wins and fifty-eight losses. The Dodgers won ninety-seven and lost fifty-seven. We finished just one game behind.

The Cardinals were playing the Giants. How well do I remember it? I was counting on the extra money from a possible World Series because I was getting married that fall. Usually I looked for a job in the winter, but I thought that maybe with a World Series check I could have a great start for my new life. That game is so burned into my memory that I still remember not only the date, August 6, 1949, but every detail.

A left-hander named Adrian Zabala was the Giants' pitcher. In the clubhouse meeting we had talked about how Zabala didn't come to a stop with men on base. "Be careful if you get on. Watch him. Don't get picked off."

It was the first inning, and Red Schoedienst was on first with two outs. Nippy Jones, our first baseman, was the batter. Zabala checked Schoendienst on first and delivered to the plate. Nippy Jones hit a screamer into the left field bleachers, and we thought we had a two-run lead. The next thing we saw was Jocko Conlan calling a balk on Zabala for not hesitating at the belt. The home run was nullified, Jones had to bat again, and this time he flew out to center to end the inning.

In spite of a lot of yelling and arguing, that was the rule. Jocko had made the right call. Zabala had made a mistake, but the Giants benefited and the Cardinals were penalized. Those two runs the Cardinals didn't get were the difference in the game; the Giants won three to one. That game really came home to haunt us when the season ended and we had lost the pennant by one game.

That balk call actually led to a rule change. The rule covering that play now is Rule 8:05, which states, "the penalty for a balk is the ball is dead and each runner advances one base unless the batter reaches first on a hit, an error, a base on balls, a hit batter, or otherwise, and all other runners advance at least one base, in which case the play proceeds without reference to the balk." In this case, Nippy Jones would have reached four bases, and we might have won the game. Unfortunately there was no change in the final standings.

The next day, Dizzy Dean sized up the situation for all of us. "Boy, it sure is great to be a pitcher these days. Shucks, you can even call back a home run ball."

I saw another strange play involving an umpire's call while broadcasting an inter-league game between the Arizona Diamondbacks and the Detroit Tigers. Curt Schilling was pitching to Wendell Magee. In the third inning with two outs and nobody on, Magee hit a ball into the right field corner. Right fielder Jose Guillen gave it a hard chase and tried for a diving catch. Mark Wegner, the first base umpire, went down the line and, the way I saw it, not at top speed. When he was about two thirds of the way there he threw up his right hand indicating that Guillen had caught the ball and the batter was out. Here's where it turned into a scene from a Marx Brothers' movie.

Magee, running hard, rounded third base but then saw the "out" sign, so he headed for the first base dugout by walking across the mound. In the meantime, umpire Wegner was alongside Guillen, who was still on the ground, when the Tigers' bullpen on the other side of the fence got into the act. One of the players pointed with his toe to the ball lying on the ground. When Wegner saw this he reversed his decision and called it a "no catch" so the ball was still in play. Technically, Magee should have been out for leaving the baseline, but he went back to touch third and scored. Wendell Magee had an inside the park home run, the Diamondbacks were upset, and the umpire had an omelet all over his face because he didn't hustle.

That wasn't even the first time I'd seen a play like that. Joe Torre was the runner and Tom Gorman was the umpire. When the throw came into second base it appeared to beat Torre and the tag was made. Gorman was in perfect position and called him out. But then Torre and Gorman had a conversation and the call was reversed.

The next day we found out why Gorman not only changed his decision but why both he and Torre were laughing about the call. When Gorman called him out, Torre, still on the ground from the slide, very calmly told Tom that he didn't think so.

"He had you, Joe. The ball beat you. I had a good look at it."

"I still don't think I'm out because he didn't tag me."

"Joe, you're wrong. He got you."

"Tom, I know I'm safe because I'm sitting on the ball."

Beans Reardon had the solution to that kind of wrong call. In a game between the Dodgers and the Phillies, Richie Ashburn hit what he thought was a triple. As he slid into third, Billy Cox, the Dodgers' third baseman, made the tag. Reardon yelled safe but raised his right hand in the "out" sign.

"What the hell does that mean?" Ashburn yelled at Reardon.

"Richie, you know you're safe. Billy knows you're safe. I know you're safe, but thirty thousand fans see my arm, so you're out!"

When I see the batter duck a pitch and the ball hits something, I know the umpire is in for a rough couple of minutes. It's a tough call because he has to decide whether it hit the bat for a foul tip (a strike) or if it hit the batter and he has to award him first base. I don't know if the umpire calls it because of the sound or if he really sees the ball all the way. Two plays come immediately to mind.

I was with the Pirates, and we were playing the Phillies. As usual, we were losing in the top of the ninth. Pete Castiglione was our hitter. Pete was a real battler and wouldn't give in to anybody. Here came the pitch,

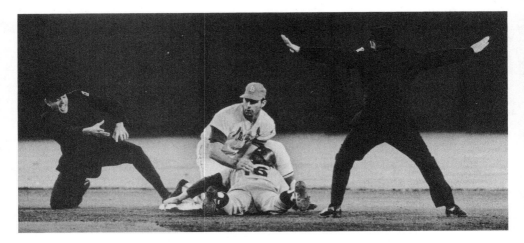

The double decision. The umpire's nightmare, but one of them was right. Umpire John Kibler (left), Dodger Bill Sudakis, and Umpire Ed Vargo (right).
Courtesy St. Louis Post-Dispatch.

and Pete, along with the rest of us, thought it hit him on the arm. He was holding his arm in pain, but Tom Gorman, the plate umpire, said it hit his bat. Pete was in so much pain he wasn't even arguing. He was just trying to show Gorman the spot on his arm where the ball hit him. It wasn't doing any good. The ball had rolled out toward the mound, so it was an easy out once the pitcher tossed the ball to first. Pete headed for the clubhouse for treatment. It turned out he had a broken arm. But here's the irony. Bob Friend, a teammate, walked up to Pete when he was lying on the rubbing table and said, "Hey, Pete, you know the worst part of it all? You got a double whammy. It's not just your broken arm but you got charged a time at bat, too."

The other play happened at Forbes Field. Lew Burdette was pitching for the Braves and was also a pretty good hitter. Lew ducked an inside pitch but claimed it had hit him on the hand. He started to go to first with his hand to his mouth when plate umpire Bill Jackowski called him back. "Get in here and hit. That ball didn't hit you."

"It did. Here look, you can see my hand is red," Burdette pleaded.

"You think I was born yesterday?" Jackowski quickly replied. "You bit that hand."

"I didn't bite it. My hand hurt; I was kissing it."

Jackowski's final argument was a beauty. "Kissing it? You know when I was a kid and I'd fall on my ass, my mother didn't kiss it. Get in and hit."

As a catcher I enjoyed the mystery—or the non-mystery—of the spitball. It seems like everyone knows it's happening. When the opposing pitcher throws a loaded one, the word on the bench spreads like the latest rumor in the *National Enquirer*. A batter may come back to the bench and mention a fastball looking extra fast or a curveball breaking bigger than ever, and the reaction is almost indifference. Nobody really pays that much attention, but the spitball alert gets center stage.

"I'm telling you he loaded one up," or "Don't tell me he doesn't throw a spitter." These are just a couple of the typical comments you hear from a batter who has just seen (not necessarily swung at or hit) a loaded pitch. It seems everybody who goes up to hit is wary of being the victim. Even the threat of the pitch works. Most hitters will take the pitch and then complain. Stan Musial had a simple answer to the complaining: "When you see it coming just hit the dry side."

It's like a political rally with a lot of hot air—plenty of accusations—but nothing is done about it. The spitball is an illegal pitch, but that fact doesn't keep pitchers from throwing it. It also doesn't keep a pitcher accused of loading one from making funny remarks about it. With the exception of Gaylord Perry, who wrote a book about it, most pitchers will keep the talk going because the threat of the pitch can work for them as much as the pitch itself. Don Sutton talked about the baseball rule book stating that no foreign substance may be applied to the ball. Sutton said he never applied any foreign substance because the Vaseline he used was made in the United States. Roger Craig complained about pitching in dry Arizona during spring training. He said his spitball dried up halfway to home plate. Don Drysdale said he didn't throw a wet one because his mother told him never to put his fingers in his mouth in public.

Some players and coaches (and broadcasters, like me) believed otherwise. I remember doing a World Series broadcast between the Yankees and the Dodgers in Dodger Stadium. Frank Crosetti was coaching at third base for the Yankees, and Drysdale was pitching for the Dodgers. After Drysdale delivered a pitch, Crosetti came charging halfway to

Sutton, trying to prove that he did not apply a foreign substance to the baseball.
Courtesy Los Angeles Dodgers.

home plate screaming at the umpire. Since the batter, Mickey Mantle, took the pitch I felt the only thing Crosetti could be complaining about was that Drysdale had thrown a spitball. After saying that, I thought I'd have some fun with the pitch and added, "It's hard to tell from up here, but I am almost certain it was a spitball because I can see the rainbow from the mound to home plate."

It's fun to hear about the spitball because of the intrigue and the different methods used to disguise it. In his book *Me and the Spitter,* Gaylord Perry wrote about the many different ways he loaded it and the hiding places where he kept "the load." Gaylord used everything from slippery elm to KY Jelly to maybe even marmalade.

Hall of Famer Robin Yount tells a story about Gaylord Perry and the spitball when Robin was with the Milwaukee Brewers and Perry was the pitcher.

"Here comes what I think is a fastball, and I take a healthy cut but foul it off. One of those foul balls that you know you just missed it and it goes straight back to the screen. I back out of the box and moan a little about just missing the pitch, and when I look at my bat there's a big glob of something that looked like Vaseline. I showed it to the umpire and told him this was proof that he was using something because I don't hit with stuff like that on my bat.

"You know what the umpire said? 'Get in there and hit. How do I know you didn't put that stuff on your bat?' End of story. I couldn't believe what I heard."

I can think immediately of three pitchers with three different methods of loading it up. One of my pitchers threw a knuckle-spitter. He'd constantly be wetting his fingers and making sure the umpire saw him wipe them on his uniform. I could always tell when he was getting ready to throw a spitball because he really worked hard to show the umpire he was drying his fingers. The ideal time to load one is immediately after a foul ball is hit. Fans, players, and umpires are all concentrating on the foul ball. That's all the time the pitcher needs to get ready. I could never signal for a spitball. The pitcher gives his catcher a signal that he is loaded and locked. My guy had a routine. He'd crease his glove to let me know it's on the launching pad and coming. Then he'd wipe his fingers extra hard. His knuckles would be almost dripping to the point that I thought they'd warp if he didn't throw it in a hurry.

George "Red" Munger, pitcher for the Cardinals, got frustrated when the opposing pitcher let fly with a spitball and nothing was done about it. He was very open about it when he was going to throw a spitball. Munger chewed tobacco, so when he wanted to throw the spitball he'd spit a big glob of chew into the pocket of his glove. He'd catch the throw from the catcher in the webbing; then it got funny. Munger would stand on the mound, take the ball out of his glove, then like chef Wolfgang Puck, dip it into the tobacco juice like he was breading a pork chop. Then he was ready to throw it. The ball came up to the plate spinning like a barber pole, and the hitter would scream "Spitter, spitter." The umpire would agree, and then the game could continue.

The third pitcher on my "most entertaining" list had a unique way of delivering this pitch. With his method you *heard* the spitball. He had a space between his two front teeth. When he took the full wind up he always paused when the glove was in front of his mouth. As a batter you'd really bear down to follow his arm to the release point of the ball. Most of the time you didn't hear anything while you were in the batter's box, but when the spitter was coming you heard it, and you were helpless. He went into his full wind up, paused, and then you heard the hiss as he was loading it up. It sounded like an angry rattlesnake, and you were trapped in the batter's box. Like the man in the electric chair you knew that you were going to get it, but there was nothing you could do. Nine out of ten times you took the pitch for a strike.

When a batter tells an umpire that a guy is throwing a spitball, the umpire usually has one of four answers: you're right; you're wrong; it was a sinker; or it was a forkball. Gil Hodges once stopped an umpire cold with his observation.

HODGES: "That ball was loaded. He just threw a spitter."

UMPIRE: Tom Gorman: "No, Gil. It was a good sinker."

HODGES: "OK, but that sinker just splashed me in the eye."

Eddie Popowski, a Red Sox coach, wanted to change the name when the pitcher would call it a forkball.

"Forkball. You oughta call it a spoonball because you can't hold spit with a fork."

I've played on teams where the infielder was able to nick the ball with his belt buckle and then walk up to the pitcher to tell him it's ready. Some catchers nicked the ball by rubbing it against their shin guard buckle. Some mashed the ball in the dirt when picking it up to put dirt in the seams because certain pitchers could skywrite with the ball when they had that kind of help. We used to joke about it and call it a "room service" spitter. Today, as soon as the ball touches the "evil" dirt, the umpire throws it out of the game. I've seen the end of the "room service" spitball era.

The times I felt badly were when the umpire was hustling and really blew a play big time. When an umpire does the unexplainable he only has three other friends to lean on, and he's not so sure they want to be there either. I've never seen another situation like this one that happened in Wrigley Field. I was in the broadcast booth working with Harry Caray. Our listeners must have thought we had lost it completely.

Bob Anderson was pitching for the Cubs, and Larry Jackson was pitching for the Cardinals. Vic Delmore was the plate umpire. It was the fourth inning with the Cardinals ahead two to one. Stan Musial was the batter with a three and one count. The next pitch was wide for ball four. Musial trotted down to first, but the pitch glanced off umpire Delmore and rolled to the backstop. When Musial reached first and turned to look at the next batter he saw that Cubs catcher Sammy Taylor hadn't chased after the ball. It was still in play. Taylor was arguing with the umpire claiming it wasn't ball four but a foul ball because it hit Musial's bat.

Here's where the fun began. Musial headed for second. While the argument was going on, the batboy picked up the ball and fliped it to Pat Pieper, the field announcer. (Pieper sat on the field alongside the ball bag since he was in charge of supplying the umpires with baseballs.) Alvin Dark, playing third base for the Cubs, saw Pieper holding the ball so he grabbed it and threw to second. While all this was going on, the catcher, Sammy Taylor, put out his mitt for a new ball. Umpire Delmore accommodated Taylor and put a new ball in his mitt. Taylor then threw it to his pitcher who turned and threw it to second trying to get Musial, but his throw went into center field. Musial was running and baseballs were flying. Now there were two balls in play. Musial saw the ball go into center field and headed for third. Meanwhile, the other ball, the one Dark had thrown, was caught by Ernie Banks, the short-stop, who tagged Musial as he went by.

The umpires had to have a meeting and make a decision. A novena couldn't have helped them, but they had to do something. It was a lose-lose situation. The ruling came down. Musial was out because he was tagged with the first ball. Cardinals manager Solly Hemus went ballistic arguing that the first ball was a dead ball because the batboy had picked it up and that Musial had been deceived by the second ball, which went into center field and should not have even been in the game. Hemus protested the game but then dropped the protest after the Cardinals won four to one.

The good official, whether an umpire or a football or basketball official, has to have certain qualities or he won't last. The easy ones to name are dedication, knowledge of the rules, and concentration. It also helps to have a quick answer and a sense of humor. The man with all these qualities was a basketball referee, Earl Strom.

During a game he was officiating, a female streaker ran across the floor. Strom said to a lady fan, "That is really disgusting."

The fan replied, "If it's so disgusting, then why are you watching so intently?"

Without missing a beat Strom said, "I just want to see how disgusting it is."

The officials win another one!

Ron Luciano was a colorful, flamboyant umpire who enjoyed what he did. When you can say that about your job you are successful. Ron was one of my favorites because he had a great sense of humor and could put most anything in perspective.

He was always telling stories about not running players out of the game. "I remember this guy—I'm not gonna tell you who—coming up to the plate and begging me to run him out of the game. 'C'mon, Ron, it's one hundred and ten degrees, I'm tired, I'm already oh-for-two and I didn't get in until four this morning. C'mon, throw me out.' You know what I told him? 'Suffer. I'm hot and I weigh three hundred pounds, and I didn't get in until five this morning. I stay, you stay.'"

Why do they want to become umpires? It's an often-asked question, and the number one answer I hear is, "I wanted to be a part of the game." Ron Luciano had a different view. "Being an umpire is a lot like being a king. It prepares you for nothing."

It's a tough job. The description has been used so much it has become a cliché. What kind of a job is it when the greatest praise you can get is silence? When nobody remembers you were there, then you've done a good job. I had one umpire tell me they were in the same class as a pickpocket. When I asked what he meant, he said, "As soon as you notice us we're done."

When you get to know some umpires it's easy to call them friends. In St. Louis, the owner of Donnelly Funeral Home struck up a great friendship with the umps and would always send a limo to their hotel to take them to the park. He even put it in his will that as long as Donnelly was in business, the umpires would go to the park in style, and that meant in a stretch limo.

Ogden Nash has made me laugh a lot of times with his writing, and I'm sure you, too, will feel his admiration for umpires here:

AN UMP'S HEART

There once was an umpire whose vision
was cause for abuse and derision.
He remarked in surprise.
Why pick on my eyes?
It's my heart that dictates my decision.

The Storytellers

CHAPTER 6

Most American Indian cultures have elders called Storytellers. His or her job is to preserve the history of the tribe. According to my friends on Arizona's Gila River Reservation, an elder gathers young people around and proceeds to do what the title says, tell stories. The stories might be history lessons, feel good stories, or just funny experiences. I have a wonderful Kachina storyteller figurine with about twenty-five young people gathered around her ready to listen or laugh. Baseball, too, has always had more than its share of Storytellers.

One I worked with for years on NBC's *Game of the Week* was Vin Scully. He would be the Storyteller for his tribe because he knows that stories are about people not numbers. Vin didn't like to listen to statistics. He said, "Statistics are like a lamppost to a drunk; something to lean on." Many times we looked at the same thing, but he'd talk about it in a way that made me reach for a pencil to get it down on paper. I was working with him at the 1988 World Series when Kirk Gibson hit his dramatic home run off Dennis Eckersley to win the first game for the Dodgers. As we watched Gibson limp around the bases Vin said, "In the year of the improbable, the impossible has happened."

To try to list all the Storytellers in my baseball life wouldn't be fair. There are so many. I'm the kind of a guy who, when I hear a story I like, writes it down and saves it. The bad part is sometimes I don't write down the name of the person who told me the story. So, guys, I'm sorry about any oversights. I've also saved stories I've seen in print and will give the names of the people involved, although I know sometimes the wrong guy gets the credit. So with all the excuses of a pitcher who hung a curveball or an outfielder who lost a ball in the moon, let me share with you some Storytellers and their stories.

At a banquet in Manchester, New Hampshire, I sat next to the great Ty Cobb and listened to him talk baseball and tell stories.

"Did you have a plan when you stole a base?" I asked him. His answer was one I'd never heard before: "When I slid I always looked into the fielder's eyes. I knew which side to slide on to get to the base. His eyes told me where the ball was coming from."

The other thing I remember about the conversation was how he made sure to let me know a base runner didn't steal a base just for that game. "You steal a base and they'll talk about it for thirty minutes in the meeting. You steal for tomorrow."

This banquet was the B'nai Brith in New York, honoring the living Hall of Fame members. The day before, as I came out of the elevator, I saw Lefty Grove and Rogers Hornsby seated in the lobby. I forgot about breakfast and walked over, trying to think of something I could ask them about the banquet. I was the emcee, and I wanted to make this visit sound official. I can't remember what I asked, but I know I was sitting next to Lefty Grove when I heard one of the greatest exchanges of confidence ever.

"Mose," as Hornsby called Grove, "when I was hitting, I gotta tell you, I felt sorry for the pitcher." I couldn't believe anybody, including Rogers Hornsby, would say this to the great Lefty Grove. But Grove just took a deep puff on his Roi-Tan cigar and made his speech.

"Rog, I gotta tell ya. Ain't that funny, 'cuz when I was pitching I really felt sorry for the hitter."

Baseball's Storytellers fall into different categories. But for the most part they all tell the funny side of the game.

Tommy Lasorda tells this story about trying to inspire one of his young minor league pitchers:

The kid had good stuff, but when he got into trouble it looked like he was scared to throw the ball. So, they got the bases loaded and we're winning by a run, so a base hit wins it for them. I walk out to the mound to have a talk, and I'm reaching for everything I got to get my message to him. 'Bobby, I want you to think about this for a minute. What if right now, before you make a pitch, you hear a voice come out of the heavens? You hear, 'Bobby, this is the last hitter you will face on Earth. Do you want to come to heaven by giving up a hit or getting the hitter out?'

'I wanna get him out.'

'Then go get him. Get that out and make God happy.'

I walked off the mound confident the kid was going to get the job done. I get about five steps from the dugout when I hear an explosion. The batter hits a grand slam home run about fifty feet over the left field fence and we lose the game. In the clubhouse I asked him, 'What happened? I thought you were pumped up to get that out?'

'I was, but after I listened to you I was afraid of dying and I wanted to get off the mound.'

One of Lasorda's favorite players was Pedro Guerrero. "I couldn't believe it when I read in the papers that he said the Dodgers treated him like a dog before we traded him," Tommy said. "So I couldn't wait to see him. When he came to Dodger Stadium I asked him about it. He said, 'It's the sportswriters. Sometimes they write what I say and not what I mean.'"

Mike Davis told the *Sporting News* that Lasorda had him playing tailback for the Dodgers. Tailback?

"Whenever I tried to run onto the field," Davis said, "Lasorda said, 'Get your tail back on the bench.'"

Here's Lasorda on control:

When I was a rookie with the Dodgers, Preacher Roe asked me one day, 'Tom, what happens if a batter hits a fair ball against the left field fence and drops dead running to first base?'

'You throw him out.'

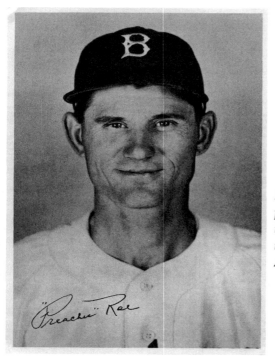

Preacher Roe used good ol' boy philosophy to convince pitchers that there is no defense against the base on balls. Courtesy Los Angeles Dodgers.

'That's right. Now, what happens when you walk a guy and he drops dead on his way to first base?'

'You put in a pinch runner.'

'Right again. The moral of the story is there is no defense against the base on balls.'

Lasorda's answer to what made Bill Buckner a good hitter would cause you to walk away mumbling. He said, "I'll tell you why he's a good hitter. Buck can read a book in the dark, that's how good his eyes are. He tries to hit the ball between the N and the L where it says National League or between the Charles and Feeney on the president's signature."

Tommy Lasorda is never dull. Maybe it's his friendship with Hollywood people, especially Don Rickles, but it's almost like a roast when he talks about some players. I admit I've written down some of his descriptions after a session with him.

Lasorda couldn't just say a player had a drinking problem: "When he blows on his hands to get warm, his breath guarantees his hands will come up numb." On an overweight player: "To him, a four bagger is lunch." Describing a prospect: "He's got all the tools and by the All-Star game he'll be a carpenter."

Baseball humor isn't just stories. A lot of players were the Hall of Famers of one-liners. Pete Ramos came from Cuba. He learned to speak English pretty well, but he was also innovative:

"I learn to say 'Come here' and the person understands."

"What do you do if you want the person to go over there?"

"I go over there and say 'Come here.'"

Don Zimmer told general manager Buzzie Bavasi to either "Play me or trade me." A week later Bavasi came back with, "Well, we played him and now we can't trade him."

Pitcher Dave Boswell was asked about a tough loss, but he didn't want to talk about it. "It's a forgotten memory," he said.

Baltimore infielder Jim Gentile had it all figured out. Upon getting his release he said, "I only went to bat thirty-nine times. I didn't even get a chance to be a failure."

Mike Epstein to Boog Powell: "How far did you go in school?"

"Oh, about two blocks."

Kurt Bevacqua played a lot of positions, so he was called a utility player. His complaint was that it wasn't a very classy title. Did he have a suggestion? "I'd rather be called a role player than a utility player. Utility sounds like I work for the electric company."

The line wouldn't have to be about baseball, either. Dodgers outfielder Gene Hermanski would come into the clubhouse and ask, "Did any of you guys see the morning paper?" Invariably somebody would ask, "Why what's in it?" Hermanski would start laughing and say, "My lunch."

Curt Flood, Cardinals center fielder, had that kind of sense of humor. Some called it corny, but I always found him good for a laugh.

If his target had put on a couple of pounds Curt would squeeze the belly and yell, "That's what they call summer muscles. Some are and some aren't."

Even players' family members can master the one-liners. Jim Leyland won a World Championship managing the Florida Marlins and was also a successful manager with the Pittsburgh Pirates and Detroit Tigers. But it wasn't always that way. At one time his own mother had to think of a new position to help her son. Jim was in the Tigers organization and wasn't moving up the ladder. He called his mother and complained about not making any progress in his career.

"I called my mom and said, 'They won't even make me a bullpen coach or give me a chance to coach at third base. I'd like to get a chance to coach, even at first base.' You know what she told me? Don't worry; maybe they'll let you coach second base.'"

Pitcher Fred Hutchinson had been knocked out of a game, and that was never good. Yogi always said you could tell if Hutch won or lost by how many light bulbs were left in the runway between the dugout and the clubhouse. He hated to lose, and his temper was well known all over the league.

Driving home after a game he kept hearing one of his boys say, "Are we gonna go back and get 'em? Are we gonna go back and get 'em?" Hutch didn't pay much attention since he was still steaming at being knocked out of the game. Finally the question got through to him. "Are we gonna go back and get 'em?" Hutch asked the little boy, "Go back and get what?" The answer he got didn't help. "Mommy said they knocked your ears off, so we ought to go back and get them."

A scouting report on Danny Gardella wouldn't put him with the Storytellers, but what he did to a teammate ranks him at the top of the list of practical jokers.

One day Gardella and his roommate, Nap Reyes, had a small argument at breakfast. While Reyes was in the bathroom Gardella went to work on the joke. The hotel was the Netherland-Hilton in Cincinnati, where the rooms were designed so that to leave you had to walk past the bathroom. Gardella wrote a suicide note blaming the argument on Reyes and left it on the bed. Reyes didn't see Gardella walk by the bathroom, and he knew there was no other way he could have left the room. When Nap came out of the bathroom, Gardella was nowhere to be seen. Reyes searched the entire room, the closet, and under the bed. No Gardella. Reyes became alarmed.

Working up enough nerve, he walked over to the window fully expecting to see a crowd below standing over the fallen body of Gardella. Instead he saw a laughing Gardella, hanging by his fingertips onto the windowsill ten floors above the sidewalk, feeling that he had pulled a "gotcha" on his roommate.

Scouts are another great source for stories. Tony Pacheco tells this one about Earl Weaver. While managing in the minor leagues, Weaver had a young pitcher who seemed to have all the qualities of a winner but was losing. It was hard to figure out. Earl Weaver ended up in the Hall of Fame, and this story is a good example of his ability to motivate.

One of his players went to him and said, "Skipper, he's just a nervous kid. Don't tell him the night before that he's going to pitch the next day. Wait until about five minutes before he has to warm up and then hand him the ball and tell him he's the starter."

Weaver was willing to try anything, so he went to this new system and it worked. The kid won ten games in a row including six shutouts. Then came the playoffs. Weaver didn't use him the first game and they lost, but right before the second game he handed him the ball and he won easily.

Later with the same system the kid won again, and the playoffs were tied at three games apiece.

The kid figured he was going to start the big game, and he was right. Nervous as a cat, he got knocked out in the third inning. Here's how Tony Pacheco tells the story: "Weaver goes into the clubhouse and he's chewing everybody upside down. The kid pitcher is scared to death, trying to hide as Weaver gets closer to him. Weaver surprises everybody as he lowers his voice, puts his arm around the kid, and thanks him for a great job. The kid smiles and takes a deep breath as Weaver walks away.

"As the youngster is enjoying this happy moment, Weaver comes back and says, 'I forgot to tell you something. I want you to know that you're going to be my starting pitcher on Opening Day next year. Here's the ball. So now go home, and I hope you don't sleep the whole damn winter.'"

The bizarre things that happen in baseball turn some players into Storytellers. One of the strangest incidents I've ever seen happened when I was with the Cardinals. We were playing the Pittsburgh Pirates in Sportsman's Park. Attached to the foul poles in both right and left field is a three-foot screen. If the batted ball hits the screen it's a home run. The screen was put up to make the foul pole home run call easier for the umpire. Nobody paid attention to this screen except maybe the umpires. The ground rule was simple and still is: if the ball hits the screen, it's a home run.

Pirates infielder Eddie Bockman was the batter, and he hit a ball down the left field line. It was going to be close, and it did hit the screen. Only then did everyone notice that the three-foot screen was put on the wrong side of the pole. It was on the foul side, so obviously it was a foul ball. Wrong! The ground rule states that if the ball hits the screen, it's a home run. Forget that the grounds crew put it on the wrong side and it extended three feet into foul territory. It was ruled a home run. Common sense did not prevail, but the ground rule did. The next day, anyone who had anything to do with the Cardinals, whether a player, manager, owner, vendor, or secretary, went out and checked the location of the screen on the foul pole.

The Yankees came close to having the same situation. A worker was asked to put up a screen on each foul pole. When a club official checked on the screens he discovered that one was in foul territory and the other one in fair territory. When the worker was asked why, his honest answer stopped everybody cold.

"I'm not a baseball fan," he said, "so I put one screen on one side of the pole and the other one on the other side. That way I knew one of them would be right."

Boston Braves infielder Sibby Sisti tells one of the weirdest stories in baseball. I still find it hard to believe, but Sibby tells it so well on the banquet circuit.

The Boston Braves are playing Brooklyn. Max West is hitting with a runner on second. He grounds out to the second baseman and the runner goes to third. As Max is walking slowly back to the bench there's a wild pitch. The ball is near him, so the catcher asks Max to throw it to him. Max does. The catcher tags the runner out, and while Max West is catching hell on the bench, Paul Waner, the next Boston batter, fouls off a pitch and hits Max in back of the head.

Sometimes you might even get a philosophy lesson from a Storyteller. During a contract session with Branch Rickey Jr., I'd try everything.

GARAGIOLA: "If I sign that contract I'll make my wife very unhappy."

RICKEY: "I guess so, but if I give you a raise that makes my father unhappy and therein lies the trouble with having families."

I'm sure only a baseball player could find humor in a death threat. When it happened to Ralph Kiner, star home run hitter with the Pittsburgh Pirates, all the precautions were taken. The authorities were notified, and Ralph was secretly moved to a hotel. In the pre-game meeting the team was told first about the threat. Then the talk came around to the usual matters like how to pitch to the opposition and how to set up the defense.

When the meeting was over, George "Catfish" Metkovich raised his hand because he had something to say. The conversation was simple but it broke everybody up.

"Yeah, Cat, what is it?"

"I can't play today."

"Why not? You're not hurt, are you?"

"No, but look at Ralph and me. He wears number four and I wear forty-four. What if this guy has double vision?"

Sam Mele took his Minnesota Twins to the World Series, which meant the following year he managed the American League All-Star team. Mele didn't play Mickey Mantle in that game, and apparently some fan was upset enough to threaten Sam's life. He got a note stating, "When you come to New York I'll blow your head off." The authorities had their way of handling it, but so did Sam: "When we got to New York I walked over to Billy Martin, one of my coaches, and said, 'You always wanted to manage this team. Let's change shirts and you manage.'"

In my day, many managers did bed checks. At a certain time, either the manager or a coach called every room to make sure the player was

*Catfish Metkovich always had
a way of breaking up a serious
clubhouse meeting.
Courtesy Pittsburgh Pirates.*

there. Stories run the gamut from a player trying to imitate the voice of his roommate to being awakened by a call only to be told it's bed check time. The big stars could get away with it, but not the second stringers who answered the phone and tried to be funny. Sometimes this answer could get you in trouble. "Bed check? Both beds are still here. They haven't stolen a bed from this hotel in years." To break the monotony the coach sometimes asked, "You got any girls in there?" The answer: "No, send a couple up."

Manager Charlie Dressen used a simple trick—he'd give the elevator operator a ball and ask him to get a player's signature on it. The only instruction was to do it after midnight. The next morning Dressen would tip the operator and get the signed ball. Then he'd check it over and know who had broken curfew.

Sometimes Dressen made his own calls to check the rooms. During bed check he called one room and told the player who he was and what he was doing. Dressen got a question that stopped even him for a minute.

DRESSEN: "Who is this? And then put your roommate on. This is your manager, Charley Dressen, and I'm checking rooms."

PLAYER: "Oh yeah? If you're Dressen, what's the bunt sign?"

Not even religion is safe from the Storytellers. Giants star pitcher, Larry Jansen, told this story on his roommate, Sal "The Barber" Maglie: "Sal and I roomed together a couple of years. We were both Catholic and in those days we were not supposed to eat meat on Fridays. Well, if Sal was to pitch a Friday night game, we usually ate about 3:30 in the afternoon, and he'd always order a steak. He said when he pitched he wanted to be as strong as possible. When they brought his food he'd make the sign of the cross over the steak and say, 'Swim, you son of a gun, swim.'"

Or how about the deeply religious player who was constantly putting himself in the hands of Jesus? He broke out of a hitting slump with a double, but as he rounded first he tripped and fell. While he was being tagged out he looked up and said, "Thanks for the help, but you didn't have to push me."

I can't remember the batter, but I do remember the pitcher in this story. Tracy Stallard was on the mound and was ready to pitch when the batter repeatedly made the sign of the cross. It could have been a league record. Stallard watched, made the sign of the cross himself and then hollered, "What's he gonna do now; he can't help both of us."

Stallard was quick with the answers. The Mets were traveling on a commercial flight that was not nonstop. When the plane was ready to continue after making the intermediate stop, the pretty flight attendant was counting the passengers and asking for their destinations. She more than met her match in Stallard.

"How far are you going?" she asked.

Without missing a beat he said, "As far as you let me."

I've always admired people who are good with the quick comeback. Dick Allen of the Phillies and Cardinals never wasted words. When a TV reporter wanted to get an interview, Allen didn't want to talk. The reporter kept at it, following him closely as Allen walked out of the ball-park. "Dick, I hate to do this," the reporter said. "Then don't," Allen answered and kept on walking.

Billy Martin is my nominee for giving the best comeback that left an interviewer speechless. At a charity golf tournament in Tucson, this interviewer must have been the winner of the Mr. Obnoxious contest. He was baiting Billy and trying all kinds of questions to get him riled. Billy never lost control, and finally the big question came.

Mr. Obnoxious: "Billy, what has been your biggest thrill outside of being on this program?"

Billy Martin: "Getting off this program!"

With that Billy smiled and walked off, and Mr. Obnoxious looked like somebody had sprayed him with concrete. I think he may have even stopped blinking.

Some of my favorite stories are what I call "good lies." Guys always tell them with a straight face and an "honest, it really happened" or "if I'm lying I'm dying." These Storytellers go into a special category. It's up to you whether or not you want to believe them. I'm only the messenger.

If you think Bill Buckner's eyesight was special, here's what Charlie White thought about Ted Williams and what he could do in the batter's box:

We're playing an exhibition game, and I had never seen Ted Williams hit, so I'm ready to see a show. I'm catching, and we got Jim Wilson, a knuckleball pitcher, on the mound. Up walks Williams and I call for the "thing" (the knuckleball). It dances all the way up there, and it's strike one. I call for it again, and here it comes. The Splinter swings and misses, so we got strike two. I'm saying we got him now. I call for the "thing" again and motion to Wilson to put some extra on it. We got two strikes and nothing to lose. I gotta try to catch it or get in front of it when Williams misses it. Here it comes. It's dancing, bucking, dipping, and doing it all. I put my glove up ready to catch it when Williams turns around, looks at me and says, 'Never mind Charley, I'll handle this one.' Then he knocked it over the fence.

Watching Luis Tiant pitch was always exciting, with his turn-your-back-to-the-hitter delivery. He made so many twists and turns that if he pitched a complete game, at some time during the game he'd look every fan in the ballpark right in the eye. Luis had a great move to first, and the runner wouldn't dare take a big lead even though Tiant was right-handed. When you asked him about his move with men on he took great delight in giving his father credit: "I learned the pick-off move from my father, who was a star pitcher in Cuba. My move is OK, but my father had a better one. He would strike out batters with his move to first base."

Satchel Paige was my favorite Storyteller. He had a slow speaking style and would look you right in the eye and tell you the biggest tale (that's a polite way of putting it). If he started a sentence with, "I betcha," look out, because you were going to hear a blockbuster. You didn't know whether or not to believe him, but you'd be entertained:

I betcha you never saw my best pick-off move. See you have to be smooth. Got to be real smooth. I remember a game I pitched and came in with runners all over the bases. First thing I did was I picked off the lead runner at third, then I picked the runner off first, and I did it with a move so smooth that the batter swung and missed, striking out. So I done retired three men without pitching a ball. I was so smooth that the ump and the other team never knew what I did.

Asking Satchel how many different pitches he threw was an adventure. He'd say, "I threw the blooper...the looper...the hesitation, and the b pitch. It be high. It be low. It be where I want it to be." Argue with that, if you will.

The first time Satchel Paige pitched against Stan Musial was on a barnstorming trip. When he saw Musial's stance he stopped and asked, "Who is that in a knot? He doesn't have a chance to hit me all balled up like that."

How old was Satchel Paige? Everyone had a guess, even Cool Papa Bell who said, "Satchel always told the sportswriters that even he wasn't sure what year he was born. He said his mama wrote all of the children's birthdates in the family Bible, but one day their pet goat ate the Bible."

On a TV show called *The Baseball World of Joe Garagiola*, I did an interview with Satchel and Cool Papa Bell, and what a treat it was. Satch

Satchel Paige was my favorite storyteller. When he said, "I betcha..." you knew a great story was coming. Courtesy National Baseball Hall of Fame Library, Cooperstown, N.Y.

wanted to talk about Cool Papa's speed but wanted to stay away from a much told story about how fast Cool could run:

Joe, I gonna tell you how fast this man could run. Everybody knows about me telling he was so fast that when he turned the light switch off he would be in bed before it got dark. Everybody heard about that. But, one time, I was pitching against Cool and he hits a slow ground ball back at me. It was so slow it fooled me, and I missed it, went right through my legs. We got him anyway, Joe. This man was so fast that he was sliding into second for a double, but the ball hit him and he was out. You be believing that ball went through my legs and hit him going into second.

You could feel that Satch was the self-appointed president of the Cool Papa Bell Fan Club. "I'll tell you one more thing. If Cool was on first and the man bunted the ball to make the third baseman field it, Cool would score and make it easy. That man had to drink diesel fuel for breakfast."

When Connie Johnson pitched in the Negro Leagues he said his arm was so strong that he had to put alcohol on it to weaken it: "My roommate, Jesse Williams, used to do it. In Indianapolis, I couldn't get no

Cool Papa Bell sliding into third. Satch said he "had to drink diesel fuel for breakfast." Courtesy National Baseball Hall of Fame Library, Cooperstown, N.Y.

alcohol so nobody would warm me up. Joe Green didn't want to warm me up. I had to come in and warm up by throwing to the first baseman pretending I was trying to pick off the runner."

Connie Johnson's great stories didn't stop when he came to the big leagues with the Chicago White Sox. Connie and Ray Moore had a running contest between them for the biggest "lie." Their hunting dogs were usually the subject.

"Ray, what's your dog doing these days since it ain't hunting season?"

"Not much, just sitting around the house watching soap operas on TV."

Ray then asked, "How about your dog, Ol Blue. How's he doing?"

"Don't really know. Last I heard he was in Hawaii surfing."

Dodgers left-hander Preacher Roe is another one of my favorites who loved to tell stories about his hunting dog:

He was the smartest dog and could do everything but talk. I really believe he could read. I'll tell you why. We were out hunting and we hadn't had a shot all day. The dog is having a great time just running all over the place. I'm watching him, and all of a sudden he goes into a point. I quiet down and start looking around, and there are no birds, but the dog's still pointing. We were about to give up when we finally figured it out. One of my buddies picked up a menu that had blown off the train and right there on the menu was: Quail On Toast. That dog could read.

Left-handed pitcher Marshall Bridges was one of the best tellers of "good lies." I was broadcasting Cardinals games at the time, and it was a great ride if you were close enough to hear Bridges. Pinch-hitter deluxe George Crowe was his best audience. The subject was basketball, and everybody knew that George was more than an average basketball player. Finally he'd heard enough from Bridges and said, "You can't play man. At least I got mentioned when they talked about All-State players." Marshall paused and came back with, "All-State, man that was nothing. I was All-World."

Marshall Bridges had a slow delivery like he was chewing every syllable: "I was hunting rabbits and had my best dogs with me. Pretty soon we saw a rabbit, and the dogs were chasing him. I knew I'd get him."

Bridges knew exactly when to pause so he'd have complete silence. "You ain't gonna believe this, but this is gospel. I raised my gun, and the rabbit dropped dead. I cleaned that rabbit and not a shot in it." Then another pause. "I guess it knew I was a good shot because it dropped dead of a heart attack."

Joe Durham, an outfielder, and George Crowe, an infielder, commanded attention when they discussed anything. This time it was pitching: "George Bamberger had the best control I ever saw," Durham said. "He didn't walk anybody in sixty-eight innings, in tough games. That's something."

Crowe just looked at him and said, "That's nothing. Satchel was in some tough games, too, and he didn't walk anybody in fifteen years."

Joe Durham always talked about hitting and hunting. Instead of saying he hit the baseball, Joe always hit BBs and pitchers always threw seeds. When Durham and Bridges talked, you wanted to get there and listen because you knew it was going to be different. This conversation was about hunting:

"What kind of gun do you use?" Durham asked Bridges.

"A 410 Magnum."

"What's that?

The trap was set for Durham. "If you're hunting and an elephant is coming right at you and sees that 410, I'll tell you, all that elephant can do is stop and squat. Then you shoot."

A lot of stories came from the bullpen, and there were all kinds. Dick Hall, who became a good relief pitcher for the Orioles, once used a mathematical formula to figure out how many rain drops were landing on the dugout roof. Another player tried to figure out how many number combinations were in the lottery and how many tickets you would have to buy to win. I learned it would take you eleven years to count a million dollars if you used only five, ten, and twenty dollar bills. I don't know how accurate that is, but the man had a paper filled with numbers to prove his answer. I was just trying to figure out how to give simpler signals to my pitchers. There were some interesting guys in the bullpen who made you think about things.

Like pitcher Larry Anderson, who'd ask profound questions such as:

How do flies land on the ceiling? Do they fly upside down or do they flip over just before they land? Why is it when you send something by ship it's called "cargo" and when you send it by car it's called "shipment?" How do you know when you are out of invisible ink?

I'm sure that more than once a pitcher has left the bullpen not thinking about the trouble waiting for him but trying to figure out how you know when you're out of invisible ink.

See if you can come up with an answer to this question: If a relief pitcher's arm is a radial tire, how many miles would be on it? You won't get that question on a game show, but you might hear it in a major league bullpen.

I know those "good lies" stories didn't start with my breaking into the big leagues. They were there long before I got there. In 1951 and 1952 I played for the Pittsburgh Pirates. Even though we lost one hundred twelve games in '52, I enjoyed my time there. We were once described as a team that scored runs in bunches of one, or if the other team made ten or twelve mistakes against us we could beat them. Our reward was knowing we were in the big leagues.

One of the joys—a real privilege—was to sit on the bench with the legendary Honus Wagner. He'd put on his Pirates uniform, slowly make his way to the bench, sit, and watch everything. He knew his regular audience would come out and sit near him. I was part of that audience. He always wore a kind of pixie smile. Some of his stories were about baseball but hardly ever about himself. I know I heard this story from him more than once:

This was before I got to the big leagues. I was young and I could really move in the infield. I could catch anything. Well, we were playing this country team, and it seemed like every ball was hit to me. If it moved, I grabbed it and threw it to first base for the out. Well, it's the ninth inning, two outs, and the tying run at third when here it comes. I scoop it up and throw it to first, but it wasn't the ball. It was a rabbit, and we got the runner by a hare.

Left to right—Front row—Donald Pisera (bat boy), Jack Smith, Clyde McCullough, William A. Meyer (Manager)
Milt Stock (coach), John Merson, Joe Garagiola, Murray Dickson.
Center row—Jim Walsh, Tom Saffell, Pete Castiglione, Don Carlsen, Frank Thomas, Gus Bell, George Metkovich,
Paul LaPalme, George Strickland, Honus Wagner (coach), Bill Howerton.
Back row—Eddie Fitz Gerald, Mel Queen, Dick Cole, Ralph Kiner, Bob Friend, Ted Wilks, Bill Werle, Vernon Law,
Bill Koski, Lenny Yochim, Howie Pollet, Jack Phillips.

We were all so proud to be in a picture with the great Honus Wagner.
Courtesy Pittsburgh Pirates.

That kind of material won't get you on the *Late Show with David Letterman*, but if you can play baseball like Honus Wagner, you can also tell stories like that and get big laughs.

A couple of other legends were the Waner brothers. Baseball fans don't have to be told how good they were. To use the ultimate baseball phrase, "They could play." I remember listening to Paul Waner talk about hitting, something he could do as his twenty-year lifetime average of .333 proves. His nickname was Big Poison.

The story he told about speed, though, puts him into this "believe it or not" category: "My brother Lloyd and me would go hunting for rabbits when we were young. We did it a little different though. Lloyd would run alongside the rabbits and feel them to see if they were tender enough to eat. Now that's the way to hunt."

Stories make players come alive, and that's why I'd rather hear a story than a bunch of numbers. If a guy's six-feet seven-inches tall and weighs two hundred twenty-five pounds, you get the idea that he's big. But I'd rather hear that he's so big you can't pass him on the right, or if he passes you he honks. The numbers say he gets to first base in 3.9, and that's fast. I'd rather have a scouting report saying he turns stand-up-doubles into slide-in-triples and on defense turns doubles in the gap to singles. His fastball is between ninety and ninety-four mph. But I know he's fast when I hear it sounds like they're stacking lumber when that ball hits the catcher's mitt. Or as umpire Red Jones said of Bob Feller, "He could throw his fastball through four pounds of wet wash, and the ball would come out dry." That I understand.

Baseball has always been a game played by real people, and the Storytellers make sure the history lives on. If I were a manager, my bench coach would be a player like Gorman Thomas. The former Milwaukee Brewers home run hitter was probably one of the most popular players the team ever had. You could not get down about a slump—or anything else—listening to him talk about one unforgettable game:

> I struck out eight straight times and then hit into a double play
> in a series in Boston. I got a standing ovation for striking out, a
> standing ovation for hitting into a double play, and when I got
> out to center field a dog ran out in front of me and relieved him-
> self, and I got another standing ovation.

Now that's a player who understands what makes baseball such a great game. That's a Storyteller.

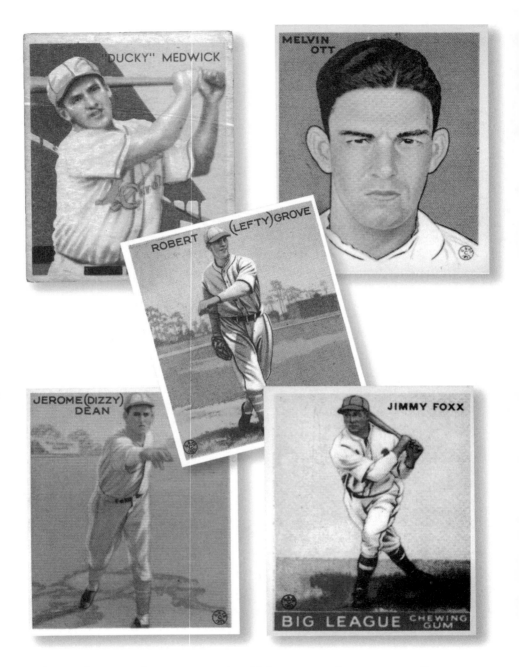

These cards were my biggest treasure. I couldn't wait to see these guys come alive.
Courtesy Joe Garagiola.

What Happened?

CHAPTER 7

I once traded Dizzy Dean, Mel Ott, Jimmy "Double X" Foxx, and Lefty Grove for Joe Medwick. There was no talk of a "no trade clause" in the deal. There was no rule of ten years in the big leagues and five years with the same team to keep me from making my deal, so I made it. My friend, River, was happy and I was happy. Pucci was mad because he wanted Mel Ott. True they were all from the 1933 Goudey Gum set, but I think of those cards when I read about trades.

Today, as soon as a youngster gets his cards he pulls out the calculator and his price book to see how much his cards are worth. The conversation about cards sounds like two rookie stock brokers trying to make a deal.

"I got a Jeter rookie card."

"Yeah, well I got an Albert Pujols rookie card, and the corners are sharp, and you can't find any creases."

"Well my Jeter card was graded eight. What was yours graded?"

"My Pujols is a nine, and that beats your Jeter."

"Wanna make a trade? I got a Willie Mays rookie card, and that's a nine."

It's more about no creases and sharp corners than home runs and hits. What happened?

Joe Medwick was our hero while we were growing up in St Louis.

When we heard France Laux, the Cardinals' radio broadcaster, describe him as "Ducky Medwick, the strong boy from Cartaret, New Jersey with the bulging biceps," we took out our cards to look for his biceps so we could try to bulge ours if only we knew what they were. Bubblegum cards were for collecting and trading to get "your guy." Nicknames always had us going through our cards so we could put a face to "Rabbit" Maranville or "Fiddler" Bill McGee or Harry "The Horse" Danning. There was no ESPN for an up-close and personal story of your favorite player. My remote control was either the 1933 Goudeys or Diamond Stars.

Fortunately, I can still call up those kinds of memory pictures whenever I want. Rather than listen to someone ask me, "Do you know how much _____ (fill in the name) is making?" then hear him break it down to how much per game, per bat, and even per swing, I have a better idea. I'd rather sit in the ballpark and think about what happened to the parts of going to the park that I used to really enjoy.

I think about how much fun it used to be to watch (and later as a player to be a part of) a "pepper game." This simple pre-game practice could involve just a couple of players or as many as seven or eight. The batter hit the ball softly to the "fielders," players who were about ten feet away. The pepper game was supposed to be a kind of bunting practice drill since the main requisite for the batter was bat control. But if the batter was having a problem with one of the fielders then "hit softly" changed. The object then was to get even by hitting one off his shins. It was called a "shinburger."

The rules were simple as were the stakes. Usually it was played for bets of a soft drink (translate to a beer). The fielder pitched the ball to the batter who continued to bat until he messed up. At that point the fielder in the Number One position became the new batter. If the fielder made an error he went to the end of the line. Compare it to a blackjack game with the batter as the dealer. The fielder makes an error and it's like he went over twenty-one and is busted. Batter mistakes and fielder errors were judged by the majority. This decision could get heated. The pepper game also helped the bench jockeys sharpen their wits because they threw zingers out according to who was playing.

I remember one pepper game where Stan Musial was the batter and two of the players were Gussie Busch, owner of the Cardinals and Anheuser Busch, and George Vierheller, director of the famous St. Louis Zoo. The third player was sure-handed infielder Red Schoendienst. Stan was hitting the ball so softly that if it had been an egg he wouldn't have cracked the shell. Schoendienst was playing like he was the bodyguard. That might have been one game that could have been approved by Good Housekeeping, but it didn't stop the zingers.

Tom Glaviano, a confident rookie, saw this and hollered, "Hey, Stan, what are you playing for, a keg of beer or a tiger?"

The Gas House Gang had a version of the pepper game that rivaled anything the Harlem Globetrotters did with a basketball. With ring leader Pepper Martin, players like Jack Rothrock and Rip Collins put on a show before the game. The ball was bunted back to a player who'd flip it into the air, bump it with his knee to the next guy who'd pass it between his legs three or four times, work it behind his back, and pretend to swallow it as he passed it to another player who would finally toss it to the batter.

A pepper game could be played anywhere but was usually played behind home plate. Even watching a straight game instead of the Gas House Gang sleight-of-hand version was fun. But then a sign went up in ballparks—No Pepper Games. A great pre-game entertainment went the route of dirt, and became obsolete.

Ty Cobb said pepper games helped him break out of slumps. Looking at his numbers I don't believe he ever had a slump. But Cobb said, "You hit the ball hard towards the pitcher, up the middle where there's the most room. Bat control is the key, and that's what you get from a pepper game. A controlled swing gets you back the groove."

Instead of a pepper game, today you can watch a coach with a bucket of balls sit on a stool and flip a ball so the player can hit it into a net. The other version is to let the batter hit it off a tee. I guess it helps some players, somehow, sometime, but I have yet to hear anybody give me a good reason except to say, "It loosens me up before batting practice."

I guess players need all the loosening they can get because these days

Ty Cobb. With that grip he had great bat control. He also said that Pepper Games helped sharpen his skill. Courtesy National Baseball Hall of Fame Library, Cooperstown, N.Y.

batting practice is more like home run derby. Although even in my day players took pride in keeping a book of how many batting practice home runs they hit. Gone are the days when a batter picked a field to hit to and worked his way around. Steve Finley, while with the Diamondbacks, was a delight to watch as he would start with hitting the ball to left field and work his way around with hits to the right field corner.

Hitting coaches used to stand behind the cage and holler things like, "shortstop covering" to see if the batter could hit the ball through the make-believe vacated spot. The next call could be, "need a sacrifice fly" or "second baseman covering." This always led to bench jockeying. If you took a pitch after hearing something like, "shortstop covering" a chorus of advice let you know that "take practice" wasn't allowed to end up with a base on balls.

If you miss seeing batting practice you might be in time for a pastoral scene that could be a page in a Thomas Kinkade book. Call it The Sprinkling of the Field—or is it? Soaking the area in front of home plate looks innocent enough, but it could be the tenth man on the team at work. If the home team has a sinker ball pitcher working that day, the dirt in front of home plate could challenge the Okefenochee Swamp. Any ball hit there will slow down considerably with no high hops that translate into infield hits. A groundskeeper with a hose can be the slow infielder's best friend. So, you could learn a few lessons from watching batting practice and infield practice that might help you during a game.

Certain parks were more suspect than others. Sportsman's Park in St. Louis was one. You knew the infield was hard because two teams—the Cardinals and the St. Louis Browns—played there, and the crew had little chance to work on the grounds. In Pittsburgh's old Forbes Field we kept the infield ground hard because we had plenty of singles hitters who could run. Airport runways weren't as solid as that Pirates infield.

Most people going into Wrigley Field admire the vines on the outfield wall, but players check the infield grass. Sometimes it was so high that a ground ball looked like a snake crawling through the grass as it made a path to a slow moving Cubs infielder. During infield practice one of the things I always watched was the outfielder's throw coming off the grass as he threw to the catcher. Did it pick up speed (short grass), or did it slow down because of high grass?

I still put the binoculars on the white lines between home and first and home and third to see if I can spot an extra coat of white to build up the line or a subtle mound of dirt equally distributed down the lines so the bunted ball stays fair.

If you believed what a Cubs teammate told us, the lines could get pretty high. Steve Bilko was a big man at six feet one inch and two hundred thirty pounds. He took a fall running to first that could have registered about a seven on the Richter scale. When he came back to the dugout we asked what happened. "Couldn't you see I tripped on the foul line?" he said. "It was too high."

Today, for the most part, infield practice is just a memory. You might see a team come out to the park early and work on a particular play, but rarely do they take infield practice. It used to be that the starting line-up took infield first. Then the "scrubinis" (utility players) took second infield practice. That was your time to shine, to let the opposing team know you could field or that there was nothing wrong with your arm. The regulars used infield practice to get ready for the game while the "scrubinis" used it as an audition. Today while the grounds crew is busy watering the infield or giving the grub worms their nightly drink, the players are in the clubhouse watching TV or talking on their cell phones. Guaranteed contracts give you that luxury.

Another part of the game that's become extinct is chatter. When was the last time you heard any player, home or visitor, holler anything? I remember walking out and hollering the number of outs; now they hold fingers in the air. If I thought the batter was a first ball hitter, I'd walk in front of the plate and holler to my pitcher, "Watch the first pitch." I know it would get to some hitters. To this day, the former Brave Johnny Logan doesn't say hello when he sees me but hollers, "Watch the first pitch." The only time you hear chatter in the infield is at a little league game, and most of the time it's the parents.

In the clubhouse meetings every manager I played for had his own version of the instruction to avoid collisions. It always ended up with the same words, "DON'T BE AFRAID TO HOLLER."

I spent only a month with the New York Giants when Leo Durocher was the manager, but that was enough to learn some of his pet peeves. If two of his players came close to a collision he would be on the top step of the dugout waiting for them to come in after the third out.

The only player who could break up Leo was Dusty Rhodes, the 1954 World Series hitting star. Dusty was different. I saw him come to the dugout in Wrigley Field after misjudging a couple of fly balls and get a batting helmet and go back to the outfield to play defense.

Dusty had a gotcha on Leo in the Polo Grounds after a near collision in the outfield. "Did you hear him holler for the ball?" Leo wanted to know when Dusty came in. "C'mon, Leo, I couldn't even hear him waving."

It seemed that if the ball stayed in the park, Willie Mays would catch it. So, one thing Leo didn't want was for anything to happen to Willie. Durocher's strategy was simple.

"Willie you cover from foul line to foul line and the rest of you get out of his way. If it stays in the park, Willie will catch it." It was interesting when you played against the Giants to watch the right fielder and the left fielder take a position and then move only toward the foul lines to get the ball. Durocher made it clear that no one should get in Willie's way. You got out of his way.

In the early days of the Mets, every bizarre play seemed to happen to them. Elio Chacon, the shortstop, didn't speak English. Richie Ashburn, the center fielder, didn't speak Spanish. The ball was hit and they both went after it hollering, "I got it" in their native tongues. The result was that they collided and the ball dropped for a hit. Ashburn, leaving nothing to chance, learned how to say, "I got it" in Spanish so there'd be no collision next time. It wasn't too long before the same situation came up. The ball was hit and there they went again; Chacon went out and Ashburn charged in. This time Ashburn screamed, "Yo tengo...yo tengo!" Chacon heard this and pulled up short, but Frank Thomas, the left fielder, who didn't speak Spanish, crashed into Ashburn. The ball fell for a hit.

Our shortstop at Pittsburgh was George Strickland, who had a great

*Willie Mays's theory was, "When they throw it, I'll hit it. When they hit it, I'll catch it."
And he did. Courtesy National Baseball Hall of Fame Library, Cooperstown, N.Y.*

sense of humor. On a routine pop-up in the infield, he never said something as simple as, "I got it." The byplay usually happened on a foul ball that both he and the third baseman were chasing. As soon as Strick got close you heard him holler, "It's up there…it's up there." The look on the third baseman's face after he made the catch was enough to make a highlight film. The next thing you heard was the third baseman saying, "Where the hell else is it going to be?"

The other little zinger was that as soon as George heard the other player holler, "I got it," he'd back away and say, "Now that you got it, let me see you catch it."

Tom Seaver, a Stanford graduate, not only made the play but always used correct grammar. He never hollered, "I got it," but said, "I have it."

Maybe now it would be comforting to hear a "C'mon Baby…keep humming." Even hearing a fan holler, "You swing like a rusty gate" would sound good. If you think the third base coach has the "itches" as he flashes signs, take a good look at the catcher when he flashes his defensive signals with runners at first and third. He looks like an old navy semaphore flag man with bad twitches. Yes, I miss the chatter.

Looking around any modern ballpark today makes me wonder what happened to the good old-fashioned scoreboard. The JumboTron is the main focus now as highlights of the week or great plays are shown with commercial messages in between. The most important phrase in baseball seems to be stream of revenue. Airlines sponsor home runs to let you guess "How far did it fly?" Automobile engine cleaning products show you a home run and tell you "It's clean outta here." You'd think relief pitchers come in from the bullpen only because of the direct connect sponsored by a telephone company.

A clip from a Three Stooges movie always entertains me, but not like the signs in the old ballparks that made me laugh because of their location.

Abe Stark, a clothier, had a great sign in Ebbets Field. At the bottom of the scoreboard in right field it said something like, "Hit me for a free suit." You certainly couldn't hit it on the fly. You might have had a chance to hit it on one hop, but for the most part you had to do it with a ground ball. With Carl Furillo playing right field for the Dodgers you had a better chance of seeing the Pope take batting practice than seeing somebody hit that sign.

Another sign like that was in the old Kansas City park where Charley Finley's Athletics played. The park had two fences from center to right field. Hit one over the inner fence and it was a home run; hit one over the back fence and it was a miracle. Finley had goats patrolling the hillside eating the grass. He didn't have the expense of mowing, and it kept the goats healthy and happy. I always expected to see Charley Finley make a trade for a shortstop and a goat to be named later.

The sign in that park that always put a smile on my face was from a jeweler. The batter was rewarded with a diamond ring if he hit it. I don't know how far it was from home plate, but most players thought it was about a fifteen dollar cab ride. I never saw any player come close to hitting it or even reading it without binoculars.

I only heard about this particular sign, but I still wish I had seen it. Lifebuoy soap, a sponsor of the Phillies, advertised with a sign in old Baker Bowl that read: The Phillies use Lifebuoy soap. That simple sentence got a lot of attention when someone wrote beneath it, "and they still stink." That ranks right up there with another of my favorite ones I used to see on my way to Yankee Stadium. The sign read, "Who is Jesus?" Underneath was added, "Matty Alou's brother."

Along with the modern scoreboard are the modern statistics you might see displayed there. For example, do you know what AVGPAP is? The stat sheet describes it as Average Pitcher Abuse Points per game started. How about asking a player what his BABIP is? That means Batting Average on Balls put In Play. Not long ago a fan asked me at a game what a GADIP was, after seeing it on the scoreboard. I thought he was confused until I saw it up in lights myself—GADIP, meaning Grounded into a Double Play. Later I was given eighteen pages of similar BABPIP and AVG-PAP information that made me realize there's no end to the statistics that can be put together.

How about this stat I read in the newspaper: "In a six to five Cardinals loss to the Cubs, Albert Pujols swung and missed on three pitches for a strikeout. The strikeout marked the first time that season and only the fourth time in Pujols' career that he had swung and missed on three pitches in one at-bat."

Here's are a couple of statistics you might be more likely to hear on Sesame Street. On May 26, 2002, Mark Quinn of the Kansas City Royals hit his forty-fourth career home run. How can a forty-fourth career home run be historic? That home run, believe it or not, broke a tie with former Royal Jamie Quirk for the most home runs by a player whose last name starts with the letter "Q."

In 2006, pinch-hitter Carlos Quentin hit a home run off Chad Qualls to give Arizona a seven to four lead. That was the first time in major league history that a hitter whose last name starts with a "Q" hit a homer off a pitcher whose last name starts with the letter "Q."

The scoreboard is a lot more than an electronic sign to display statistics. It might show a noise meter that urges fans to get louder. A hot dog race starring relish, ketchup, and mustard, entertains between innings. In Milwaukee, if Bernie Brewer isn't sliding into a beer keg, then a bratwurst race is going on. Mascots in the park are a must, from the Philly Phanatic to Baxter to Fred Bird. Kids can't wait until T-shirts are shot from a bazooka so they can scamper to catch one. So the fun is still at the ballpark, only now it's high tech. What happened?

I sit in the stands and think back to when I was a Knot Hole Gang member. The scoreboard was exactly what the word implied. It told you the score and nothing else unless you consider the scores of out of town teams important. There were no races, no smile-cam pictures of fans, no wedding proposals to witness. Scores and batter counts and seeing "3 balls 2 strikes" wasn't too exciting, so we made our own entertainment. Counting the warm-up pitches was easy. Seeing how many guys were sitting and how many were standing in the bullpen was even easier.

The Knot Hole Gang was like a real club, except we didn't pay dues. You got your membership card at school at the beginning of baseball season, and then you showed your card and got into the game free. I don't know if you could go to any game because we only went on Saturday. It wasn't every Saturday either, only when it was your turn to go.

In our neighborhood, you could never expect your mother or father to take you to Sportsman's Park to watch a baseball game. My father's answer when I asked if I could get a pair of baseball spikes tells you everything you need to know about whether or not he was a baseball fan. Papa wanted to know if I could wear the shoes I wanted to church. I tried to explain spikes to him, but when I finally admitted that I couldn't wear them to church he simply said no.

So all of us Knot Hole Gang guys had to look somewhere else if we wanted to go to the ball game. A nice lady named Domenica, who happened to be a big Cardinals' fan, took care of us. Domenica spoke English, a big plus because most grown-ups on The Hill were immigrants who spoke only Italian. I tell everybody that when I went to school I thought the other kids talked funny since all we ever spoke at home was Italian.

Domenica was our transportation ticket to the game, as she paid for our bus rides to Sportsman's Park. We were excited for days before, building up to the big event like a pitcher who needs four days rest between starts.

Walking to the bus stop to get the Lindenwood bus, knowing we still had a ride on the streetcar coming, was the start of a great day. The route took us down Market Street, and when we caught the smell of the packing house we knew the bus ride was near the end and it was on to the streetcar.

The Grand Avenue streetcar was a great ride past the big church, St. Alphonsus Rock Church, and the big beautiful Fox Theatre. Every time we passed the Fox you'd hear somebody say, "When I start my job, the first thing I'm gonna save up for is a ticket to the Fox." Utopia was Grand and Dodier, the address of Sportsman's Park.

Since the Knot Hole Gang kids sat in a special section, Domenica would take us to our gate and point out where we would meet her after the game. As if the bus and streetcar rides weren't enough, we knew there was a lot more to come.

We sat in the left field section, perfect because we were close to our guy with the "bulging biceps." Domenica would give each of us fifteen cents to buy a Brown Cow ice cream on a stick. Even that was special. You made it last a long time because you were able to buy only one. Even when it was gone you still had the thrill of checking the stick. You really took your time looking for the word FREE. You knew if you saw the magic word you had another Brown Cow coming. The adrenalin was pumping when you got close to the last bite, and if you saw FREE on the stick the biggest cheer of the day went up.

We were all on our best behavior because we knew that any problem would mean the end of this pilgrimage, and that's exactly what it was to us. We were at the shrine. Our Vatican. The excitement didn't stop when the game ended, either.

If the Cardinals won it was almost a perfect day. But there was more. Many times fans were allowed to walk across the field and leave by a gate in right field. That meant that if we were lucky to be there on that day we could walk on the "sacred ground" too. You walked most of the way on the outfield grass and partly on the infield. You were walking with your dream. But you had a job to do.

Even though you had on your best pair of pants, you had to scoop up a handful of infield dirt, put it in your pocket, and take it home. That night, sitting by the lamppost in front of Pucci's house, you showed the guys who didn't get to go the real dirt from the infield at Sportsman's Park. Then you told them everything you did at the park. It was like that every trip regardless of who went to the game.

Back then, we did different things to stay busy between innings. One of the most interesting games (it didn't take much) was to count the number of gloves left on the field. Deep down you thought how great it would be if you could be on the field and hold the glove until the player needed it again.

Most of the time, the first baseman and third baseman threw their gloves into foul territory near the coach's box. The second baseman and the shortstop threw their gloves a little behind second base. The outfielders dropped their gloves in mid-outfield or brought them into the dugout. Some pitchers carried their gloves into the dugout while others tossed them in front of the dugout. The catcher always brought his glove into the dugout. (I always felt he was ashamed of that big pillow and the fewer people who saw it, the better.) The number of gloves left on the field varied and whoever had the exact number won. Of course, he didn't win anything; he just won. Make no mistake that it was just a fun game. Some of the guys kept notes on who left his glove on the field and who took it into the dugout. Today's player looks at his fielding glove like it's part of a set, so he wants to keep it with his batting glove and his base running glove in the air conditioned dugout.

Leaving gloves on the field happened in the minor leagues, too. From 1942, my first year in the minor leagues, until I finished in 1954, I never saw a player trip over a glove; neither did I ever see a ball, batted or thrown, hit a glove on the field. Sure, I think about that sometimes between innings. I laugh when I think of a game being held up because our left fielder, Ralph Kiner, didn't bring his glove into the dugout. Instead, Ralph threw it toward the bullpen along the left field line. We were both with the Cubs and playing at Wrigley Field. For the most part it was like a valet service for Ralph. After the third out he'd run to the dugout and flip the glove toward the bullpen. When he had to go back out on defense one of the guys would hand it to him. But that wasn't the case this time.

It was one of those well known hot, humid days in Wrigley Field. As was the custom in those days we were two runs behind right after the National Anthem. After the third out was made, Kiner started for the dugout and flipped his glove toward the bullpen. It hit catcher Walker Cooper in the back of the neck. Bad mistake.

Big Coop grabbed the glove and spent the whole inning packing the fingers with anything he could find—grass, dirt, gum wrappers, mustard-stained napkins, used tobacco wad, and unused tobacco. The glove was a five finger toxic waste dump that should have had a warning: Using this glove could be dangerous to your health.

When Ralph ran by he grabbed his glove and didn't try to put it on until he reached his position. I'll let you use your imagination to picture the scene. You can understand why the game was held up as Kiner went to the dugout for another glove and, on the way, canceled his bullpen valet service.

Another thing I wonder about as I sit in a modern ballpark is what happened to the grounds crew racing out in the rain to cover the infield with a tarp? What a cheer went up, especially from the Knot Hole Gang, when the grounds crew guaranteed us a game because they got the infield covered in time. But now as I think about it, what happened to rain? With domed stadiums or a retractable roof like the one at Chase Field, home of the Arizona Diamondbacks, rain has gone the way of the complete game.

Modern technology has me sitting comfortably in a ballpark while the big screen TV in the outfield shows me the weather outside. I'm in an air conditioned park watching the streets around it getting soaked. Many a time my memory takes me back to the minor leagues.

No way would a minor league owner lose a Sunday double-header crowd because of rain. If double-header sounds like a foreign expression, let me help. Seems like it's in the dinosaur section of baseball because you rarely see them any more, but they were almost always holiday and

Sunday events. The teams played two games, and you paid only one price. Later on, in the major leagues, some owners changed that by playing what they called day-night double-headers, which were two games separated by a couple of hours and two separate admissions.

The minor league owner had a last resort remedy to save the field from a rainout—a good old country solution. He'd burn the infield. The grounds crew, usually two or three at the most and some volunteers who'd get free tickets to any upcoming game, would simply spread gasoline on the infield and then light it. When it burned itself out the infield was ready for the sand. It could be a fun afternoon if the rains came again. Even the fastest runner moved like he was running in quicksand. But the main goal had been reached; the gate receipts could be counted instead of refunded. This philosophy has reached the big leagues, but it's always been the mantra of the minors: it doesn't make any difference whether you win or lose, it's how many fans come to the game.

If a game is really important, look for an even bigger and better method to get the field ready. I remember walking into Candlestick Park in 1962 to do a World Series broadcast between the Giants and Yankees and seeing an unbelievable sight. It had rained all night, and the weather forecast was for the rain to stop by game time. To be sure to get the game in, two helicopters were brought in to hover over the outfield with their rotor blades at full speed to dry the field. I remember thinking that if the helicopters could fly upside down they could dry the field and cut the grass at the same time.

Sometimes a creative player could take advantage of a rain-soaked field. We had a pitcher who loved it when it rained. Whenever I see a ground crew member hurry out with a shovel and a bucket of dirt to fix the mound or the landing area, I remember this guy. His prayers were answered when the crew came out and spread sand over the mound to dry it out. Sand covered the pitching rubber too, and this was perfect for my man.

He'd deliver the first pitch from the pitching rubber and just stand where he finished his follow through to wait for the return throw. Instead of going back to the rubber, he'd go into his windup and deliver from his new spot about three feet closer to the batter. I saw him take at least two steps closer; it was funny to hear a batter say something like, "Damn, he looks faster today." The whole time I'm thinking that if he goes to a count of three and two he may knock out the batter with a punch in his follow through.

For ballparks that are still at the mercy of the weather, there's not much entertainment value in a rainout. After the field is covered, fans have nothing to look forward to except periodically seeing some player stick his head out of the dugout, raise his hand over his head, then turn to a teammate and say, "Still raining."

But that's another thing that's getting harder to find, a player in the dugout, even during a game. I sit in the stands with binoculars and sometimes wonder where all the players went. Are they in the clubhouse watching a basketball game or Oprah? What happened to sitting on the bench and watching the game?

Some managers had their own game show on the bench to keep players alert. Eddie Stanky, while managing the Cardinals, would walk down the dugout and suddenly turn to a player and almost scream, "Count." And he didn't mean to start counting 1-2-3; he wanted to know what the count was on the batter, and you better not look at the scoreboard for the answer. Not knowing or sneaking a look meant a fine that was put in the kitty for the end of the season party or a donation to a charity. Stanky wanted you in the game whether you were on the field or on the bench. That's changed and in many ways for the better.

Now in a lot of parks, adjacent to the dugout, you have (among other things) a bathroom, hitting cages, and a video room. A player anticipating pinch-hitting can get loose by actually getting in the cage and taking light batting practice. Players can leave the dugout to go into the training room to be treated for an injury, or to the video room to look at their last at-bat or a pitch sequence that resulted in a key strikeout. That viewing could turn into a horror movie. Watching yourself strike out or seeing the home run you just gave up doesn't usually get a two-thumbs-up review.

Some fun things have disappeared from the game, but I also see great improvements—for example, with coaches. What happened to the coach being the manager's best friend? That good ol' boy system is pretty much gone because today's coach is a specialist.

In 1946, the year the St. Louis Cardinals won the World Series, our "brain trust" consisted of the manager and three coaches. None were designated to a specific duty like a hitting coach or pitching coach. Now strength and conditioning coaches are on staff to help players. The bench coach is another new creation. This job has to be more than what Don Zimmer, who was the bench coach for Joe Torre and the Yankees, says it is. When asked what he did Zim had a great answer. "When Joe puts on the hit and run play and it works I say, 'Nice going Joe.' If it doesn't work I get up and go to the other end of the bench and get a drink of water." Zimmer also has been accused of using the stop watch to time the person singing the National Anthem before the game.

Some things don't qualify as improvement or progress—they're just different. What happened to using dirt or rosin to make the bat feel better in your hands before you hit? Now it's the pine tar rag with the pine tar halfway up the bat. Craig Biggio uses so much pine tar he even gets it on his uniform and helmet. By the third inning his uniform and helmet look like they came from a bad swap meet. Luis Gonzalez was the first player I heard about who was the victim of too much pine tar. After taking a few practice swings before getting in the batter's box, he laid the bat on his shoulder. But Gonzo had so much pine tar on it that the bat stuck to his shirt.

What happened to a base runner picking up a handful of dirt and holding it as he ran the bases to make sure he didn't open his hand and risk a broken finger while sliding? Now it's a sliding glove. I always felt that the base runner needed a different glove so he would be more fashionable when he got to the next base. If you think I sound like an old ball player, I can still hear Hall of Famer Frankie Frisch moaning, "Now the player comes out of an air conditioned dugout with a bucket (batting helmet) on his head to hit and gloves on his hands so he doesn't get blisters and puts different gloves on when he's on base so he doesn't get dirt under his nails. They don't wanna play; they wanna go to the prom."

During that tirade he referred to his favorite pitcher, Dizzy Dean, and said, "When Ol' Diz was pitching I'd like to see a guy put up his hand to hold up the game while he's digging a hole in the batter's box and doing it while wearing that bucket. Old Diz would holler to him to dig it deeper because he was going to bury him, and if he missed him he would play the *Wabash Cannon Ball* (Diz's favorite song) off that bucket."

I also wonder what happened to signatures that you could actually read. Who was the first player to give an autograph that you could easily mistake for an EKG? I have two baseballs I got signed when I was doing NBC's *Game of The Week,* and I defy you to tell me who the players are. You can see the scrawl but no way can you decipher a name. Whenever I see the autographs of the greats like Babe Ruth, Lou Gehrig, Jimmy Foxx, and my guy Joe Medwick, I wonder what happened to penmanship.

None of these changes keep me from enjoying a game. Still, just one more time I'd like to see a pepper game during batting practice, maybe have it rain so the ground crew can put down the tarp, and be able to talk to the fan next to me instead of listening to a scoreboard sell me something or tell me when to make noise. Most of all I'd really like to see a youngster with a bubble gum card in his hand asking his guy to sign it rather than having a book in his hand to see what it's worth. Baseball has changed, and that's why I sit in the stands and sometimes wonder, what happened?

Yogi Berra. Everybody knows him; everybody quotes him. Courtesy National Baseball Hall of Fame Library, Cooperstown, N.Y.

We're All Yogis

CHAPTER 8

One of the first speeches I heard when I joined the St. Louis Cardinals' organization was about the opportunities baseball had to offer. I still remember hearing something like, "In baseball, if you bear down, you can go as far as you want." I wish I had counted the number of times I heard the line "as far as you want." I wanted to go to the Hall of Fame, but as I've said a million times, I'll have to buy a ticket to get in. I'm thrilled and honored to be in the broadcaster's wing, but I'm talking about being with the BIG GUYS! Once I made it to the big leagues and saw some of the other players I knew that Cooperstown wasn't a stop on my itinerary. The line really should have been, "If you give the game all you've got, you will go as far as your ability will take you."

I soon knew I'd never be as good a hitter as Stan Musial or Enos Slaughter. I'd never throw like Del Crandall. I'd never run and steal bases like Jackie Robinson. When I got right down to it, the reality of living on Elizabeth Street in St. Louis came home. I was a good enough player to make it to the big leagues. That usually means you were an All-Star in high school or made the All-City or the All-State team. But I wasn't even the best player on my block because a kid named Lawdy Berra lived across the street. He grew up to be Hall of Famer Lawrence "Yogi" Berra.

Not many days go by that I don't hear that famous question. When people don't know what else to say they go to the old reliable, "How's Yogi?" It's almost like we're joined at the hip. When I get to the Pearly Gates, St. Peter will probably look at me and say, "Hey Joe, before you go in let me ask you something. How's Yogi?" I don't mind because, as I have often said, I can't remember not knowing Yogi. I heard Yogiisms before he was Yogi. I've talked about him. I've written about him. I can only say there isn't much about my friend Yogi that has remained a secret. I've seen him grow from being the kid who ate banana and mustard sandwiches to a cottage industry. And his famous way of talking seems to have caught on with a lot of people.

First, let me say that it's not in Yogi's personality to get before an audience and be funny. But I will guarantee you that in any group he will say something that will make you stop and give your head a quick "one turn" tightening because you're not sure of what you just heard.

I remember a winter night when he was driving home and skidded into a fire hydrant. He hit it hard enough to make it look like a mini Old Faithful. Water was shooting straight up and all over the place. Yogi's explanation for the accident? "I couldn't help it. There was ice on the road and it was slick, and the horn didn't work." Now that could have you walking away mumbling.

As a manager, Yogi didn't hold press conferences. He just talked to the "guys." He could not have been more honest when he said, "I wish I had an answer for that because I'm tired of answering that question."

Yogi will tell you, "I don't think of those things, they just come out." Like at the dedication of his Yogi Berra Museum and Learning Center in New Jersey. On that big day he described his feelings with a perfect Yogiism. "This is great. You either have to be dead or gone to get one of these." Who can argue with that?

Yogi says it's like a game around the Berra house as his kids wait for the next Yogiism. The victory cry is, "There's another one." This one is vintage Yogi. It came from a conversation that all of us have in our wonderful (?) golden years. When it's time to go to the big bullpen in the sky, where will we be buried? If you stay in the city where you were born and grew up, it's an easy decision. When you move to other cities it becomes more difficult.

With perfect logic, Carmen, Yogi's wife, asked a simple question: "Yogi, you were born in St. Louis, but you played in New York, and we have lived most of our life in New Jersey, and our kids and grandchildren live here. Where do you want to be buried, St. Louis, New York, or New Jersey?"

"Surprise me," Yogi said. I don't think Carmen, or anybody else for that matter, was ready for that answer.

I enjoy watching other people react to a Yogiism because they often don't recognize it right away. Yogi and I were having breakfast before getting ready to play in the Bryant Gumbel golf tournament. Mike Eruzione, the captain of the great United States Olympic hockey team that beat the Soviet Union, came over to say hello. During the conversation Mike said to Yogi, "Yog, you got the Devils and the Rangers right in your backyard. Do you go to many hockey games?"

"Yeah, but I only go when I'm there. When I'm not there then I don't go," Yogi replied.

Eruzione was frozen in time. He just looked at Yogi and started to laugh. "I think I know what you said." Eruzione had been hit with a Yogiism.

But Yogi's not the only guy who's mastered this way of talking. TV and radio broadcasters lead both leagues in sounding like Yogi. To use a Yogiism, close your eyes and read these profound statements aloud and tell me it's not Yogi.

I know I am not the only one who made this profound statement:

"This is a really good crowd for a Monday night. There are no 'no shows' here tonight."

On catcher Rick Dempsey, Hall of Fame manager Earl Weaver said, "Dempsey's agility will never continue to amaze me."

"I know you believe you understand what you think I said, but I'm not sure you realize that what you heard is not what I meant." No surprise that whoever said that one wanted to remain anonymous.

When and if you figure that out, try this one. "You know, before you came in we were talking about you, and you weren't there."

In 2006, Jim Leyland came out of retirement and did a great job with the Detroit Tigers. In late August, Leyland had the Tigers in first place in a tough series against the Yankees. His argument with the umpire makes Leyland eligible for the We're All Yogis Award.

Right before the bottom of the seventh inning, Leyland came out to argue an umpire's call. His timing was bad because that's when the Yankees play *God Bless America*. So Kate Smith started to sing, and Leyland had to stop arguing and with cap in hand against his chest, stand next to the umpire and listen to Kate Smith. When the song was over Leyland started up his argument again. As usual, the umpire won, and when Leyland said the magic words he was ejected. In the press conference after the game his explanation makes him eligible for the Yogi Award. Yogi couldn't have put it any better: "I venture to say that I say less to umpires than any manager in the league," Leyland said, "and at this time of the year, I say even more less."

Yogi is often described as a malaprop, but he's not. I looked it up in my dictionary and it proves my Yogi point. Malapropism: an act or habit of misusing words especially by confusion of words that are similar in sound. An instance of this is "Lead the way and we'll precede." Yogi doesn't do that.

Broadcasters are easy victims of malaprops since they're on the air for hours at a time, and there's no script in sports. You see it. You say it. Sometimes you wish you could get a second chance, but there are no second chances in live sporting events. Malaprops, spoonerisms, and just plain bloopers happen. As a broadcaster and as a fan, as soon as I hear one or read one I save it.

When a malaprop happens on a broadcast it gets your attention because you're not sure you heard it right. It's the same reaction to a Yogiism except there's no explaining it. It's just funny to hear.

RALPH KINER: "Todd Hundley walked intensely his last time up."

"Pitching has been good, but they've been welding a hot bat."

RON FAIRLY: "The Giants are trying to make a trade, but I don't think Atlanta wants to depart with the player the Giants want."

Jerry Coleman told his audience one night that the umpire behind the plate was wearing a check protester. And on one of my broadcasts I had a player making an impoverished plea rather than an impassioned one.

Pete Vuckovich, then the Pittsburgh Pirates pitching coach, was ejected from a game against the Cardinals for arguing from the dugout with first base umpire Randy Marsh. If what he said about it were true it definitely could have been worse, as Vuckovich explained, "I was a victim of circumcision."

Some of the explanations I've heard from pitching coaches have really gotten my attention. I was hoping this statement had been true because it would have made for great TV. "We were worried about him because he was so dehydrated he had to have an RV stuck in his arm."

With another pitcher it wasn't an RV but another device. According to his coach, "They put an IUD in him so he could get some fluids, and he went out and pitched a shutout." Bruce Del Canton, then the pitching coach for the Atlanta Braves, told pitcher Terry Blocker that his fastball had "good movement and philosophy."

I was never sure about a couple of my teammates when they would drop a malaprop into the conversation. Whether it was a prepared ad-lib or not, I enjoyed every one, and I grabbed the pencil and pad right away. Clyde McCullough and I were teammates on two teams, the Pittsburgh Pirates and the Chicago Cubs. In Pittsburgh there was more than one time when I grabbed a pencil rather than the shin guards.

Once Les Biederman, a writer for the Pittsburgh Press, came into the clubhouse to invite the players to a banquet. Clyde didn't hear the announcement, so he came out of the trainer's room to ask Les "if everybody was secluded."

Playing in Wrigley Field could get hot, but McCullough had the solution. Bill Serena, an infielder, was taking infield practice and started complaining about how hot it was and how tired it made him. When McCullough heard him he walked over to the cooler, got a big cup of ice cold water, and poured it over Serena's wrists saying, "Now tell the truth, doesn't that survive you?"

Gus Bell was having a great day hitting the ball all over the place, but it took Mac to put a smile on our faces. "What a day he's having! You know that's his fourth hit in concession."

I can't leave out a beauty I heard at a banquet in Pittsburgh. It was the famous Dapper Dan dinner, and one of the speakers was heavyweight champion Rocky Marciano's trainer, Jake Mintz, a hometown hero. While telling everyone how happy he was to be home Jake said, "I've been to so many Catholic churches that pretty soon I'm gonna be a convertible."

Players liked to play cards on the long train trips, and one of the favorite games was Hearts. If you've ever played it you know it doesn't take much to get tempers fired up. In the heat of battle Ron Northey got so worked up after Sam Narron slipped him the Queen of Spades that he called Narron a "Masonic S.O.B." We were all laughing and sure that Ron meant "moronic," but in the next hand Narron tested him again. As he slipped Northey the Queen of Spades, Sam said in his best Southern accent, "Ron, you got a college education, and I'm just a cotton farmer, let me see you get out of that." This time, Northey baptized Narron as a moronic S.O.B.

Milwaukee had a player who could make a conversation interesting or have you thinking you were a game show contestant as you tried to decipher the sentence.

Jim Gantner, who played seventeen years for the Milwaukee Brewers, told how he missed a radio show because he "must have had ambrosia." He once argued with umpire Ken Kaiser that a base runner had interfered and that it was construction. Describing what he did one winter he said that he went on a hunting trip to one of those Canadian proverbs.

I didn't know this about Roger Clemens, but he was quoted as saying that when he loses his location he gets erotic. That could be a new way to spell erratic.

What could infielder Bernie Allen do when pitcher Dave Boswell told Bernie that they ought to go down the street and endeavor into a movie.

Boswell was once asked if he was ambidextrous and he said, "Oh, yeah, I've always been a hard worker."

The press conference has become the big thing in sports. Win or lose, it's to the press room to give the reasons why. In my day the manager dealt with the writers who were with the club every day, and it was not unusual to hear the manager say, "Hell, you were here, you saw what happened, and you know my players, so write your story." That usually signaled the end of the press conference.

I can't help but have that picture in my mind when I see and hear some of today's press conferences, regardless of the sport. The questions haven't changed over the years nor have the answers, just the faces and the names. The reporter asks the question and you can almost hear the gears meshing to come up with the brilliant answers. You'll hear words that for the most part are foreign to the manager or player. (It's the same when you see a police official being interviewed. It's never the criminal or the burglar. It's the perpetrator. Nothing is for sure as most every answer is prefaced with the word "alleged.")

Listen carefully and you'll hear some great explanations from baseball managers, football coaches, and everybody in between. The press conferences have convinced me that most of us are like Yogi, he just gets better coverage. This is an equal opportunity section, not limited to one sport, one player, or one manager. The only yardstick I want you to use is the question, could Yogi have said it any better?

Sparky Anderson, talking about his pitching staff: "Our pitching could be better than I think it will be."

Sparky talking about a young player: "What I like about him is that he's scared, but he's not afraid."

Trying to explain the difference between an injury and playing with pain, Sparky simply said, "Pain don't hurt."

Rick Wrona: "You don't get your first major league home run too often."

Anaheim Angels 2002 World Series hero Darin Erstad, returning to the lineup after missing seven days with a concussion, told the press, "I feel like I haven't played in a week."

Wayne Fontes, while coaching the Detroit Lions: "Our defense has been playing very poorly on third down. Maybe it's because they have been playing very poorly on first and second down."

NFL quarterback Michael Vick, on the secret of his success: "I have two weapons—my legs, my arm, and my brains."

George Allen, while coaching the Redskins: "Every time you give ground you usually lose yardage."

Jean Peron, hockey coach: "It's a good change. A good step backwards."

Barry Beck, New York Rangers hockey player: "We have only one person to blame and that's each other."

This Yogiitis happens to people in all fields. During one of baseball's labor meetings, baseball negotiator Ray Grebey said, "Even if I said it, I don't think I'd make a statement like that."

Brooke Shields was a spokesperson for an anti-smoking campaign when she let us all know that "if you're killed you've lost a very important part of your life."

Fred Couples, professional golfer: "I'm playing as well as I've ever played except for the years I played better."

Don Zimmer, managing the Cubs, after the team went four and four on the road: "It could have easily gone the other way."

Gaylord Perry was once suspended for throwing a spitball. Bob Stanley, a Red Sox pitcher, was accused of "loading one up" and also was suspended. Perry asked Stanley what he learned from his suspension. He said, "I'm not going to throw it anymore, if I ever did, and I can't remember."

Those are all English words, but if you were part of that conversation you might have to take two aspirin and hope you're feeling better in the morning.

I'm sure there have been times while listening or watching a broadcast you've heard the announcer say something that made you wonder and left you hoping he'd explain it a little more in-depth. These lines fit that description, and I know Yogi couldn't have said it any better.

After the catcher held the ball while the base runner was stealing second, what did the announcer mean when he said, "He had mentally made up his mind to throw to second."

This one really had me stretching my imagination. Word for word it came out like this: "Here's a swing and a miss for strike three. There's a bluff throw down to third base...not in time." Here's the first cousin to the last one. The announcer told me, "He fakes a bluff."

Explain how this can happen: "Stargell keeps his feet closer apart."

Try to figure these out: a trainer announced that the bad hop hit the player "in the left front eye."

Sam Jethroe, an outfielder for the Braves, was asked why he started wearing glasses.

"I got a bum eye," Sam said.

"Which one?"

"The one I hit right-handed with."

Dukes Duford was the football coach at St. Louis University. Fred Broeg was his quarterback. During a game Broeg took a big hit, was bleeding, and he had to be helped off the field. Duford asked the trainer about Broeg's condition.

"How bad is he hurt?"

"I think his nose is broken."

"Which one?" That question makes you wonder who took the hit.

How about the pitching coach who told me, "He's doing better throwing the ball when he's throwing the ball." Could Yogi have said it any better?

Managers always try to find explanations for a losing streak but it took NFL coach Hank Bullough to put it in focus. "We keep beating ourselves, but we're getting better at it."

I can't wait for the dictionary to come out with the definition of a Yogiism. Malaprops we know. Spoonerisms are still another part of the language that makes us shake our heads and wonder.

My dictionary defines a spoonerism as the transposition of initial or other sounds of words, usually by accident, as in a blushing crow for a crushing blow. Named after W.A Spooner, an English clergyman noted for such slips.

Pirates announcer Bob Prince, wrapping up a broadcast, wanted to give pitcher Bob Friend credit for a two hit shutout, except that it didn't come out that way. That night the "s" came before the "h" and Bob Friend pitched a "two shit hutout."

Plenty of broadcasters will identify with me on this spoonerism. I was doing a football halftime show and kept referring to the "toin coss." It must have taken me half the program before I realized that I wasn't saying "coin toss." Makes me wonder how many times a referee has walked to the middle of the field and asked the players if they were ready for the "toin coss."

My roommate with the Cardinals, Tommy Glaviano, complained in spring training of having "splin shints."

Willie Wood, the great Green Bay Packer, made plenty of great plays, but did you know that on one broadcast, "Willie Wood made the packle for the tackers." He was on the field so he knew that Bart Starr was still in the game although the announcer told viewers that the quarterback was Start Barr.

While Yogi has a unique way of looking at things, plenty of us go beyond that to a whole new way of talking. If you listen, it won't be long before you hear a word you've never heard before.

I was getting on a plane at O'Hare and was greeted by the flight attendant who apologized for all the chaosity in the lobby. I didn't know what chaosity was, but she assured me that it was unusual.

On a Monday Night Football game, former player Dan Dierdorf praised the offensive line and kept talking about their tenacitisity. I tried to work it out with tenacity and elasticity, but I had the same feeling I get when my crossword puzzle gets wet. There's no answer. Let it go.

Pitcher Jose Rio will always be one of my favorite people. Win or lose he always had a hello, a smile, and an answer. While with the Cincinnati Reds, he had a particularly rough road trip. He had just lost a thirteen to nothing game and got into a fight with teammate Chris Sabo in the dugout; then the team bus got stuck on the freeway for fifty minutes because a produce truck overturned. He summed up all this with one sentence: "We have just reached the height of embarrassivity." The reporter covering the story joined in the fun by reporting that if you look on the map, embarassivity is just south of humiliarity.

Jose Rio put the importance of the League Championship Series and the World Series in focus: "There's less pressure in the World Series than in the LCS because when you get here...you're there."

I like trying to figure out new words, and my favorite is one that Dandy Don Meredith coined, and I felt right at home with. The word is camoning. If you say it slowly the meaning will come to you. Don explained the word by telling us that camoning is when your parents keep telling you, "We're late c'mon." Your answer is, "Well, I'm camoning."

I called this chapter "We're All Yogis," and to prove it, all you have to do is look and listen. The real test comes with everyday people in their own surroundings. In addition to the usual question, "How's Yogi?" I get letters and calls from people telling me about the Yogiisms they've heard. For the most part they're right on target, or as Yogi might say, "If nothing's gonna happen you can't make it."

Ed Liberatore was a good friend and a lifetime baseball man. He told me about this conversation he had with his wife, Dee.

Dee: "Why didn't you answer my question?"

Ed: "I didn't hear you."

Dee: "Why didn't you tell me that you didn't hear me?"

Just keep listening. These are all from personal friends—and not one from Yogi.

When I was driving a car once I was told, "This is a good way to go. Where are we?"

"I only heard what I read in the papers."

"I explained it to you. I can't understand it for you."

"I don't want a check. I want to hold card cash."

"When you get old your shrine spinks."

How do you answer this question? I went into Home Depot and asked the clerk, "Do you have any silver polish?" He asked me, "What do you want to use it for?" I was tempted to say I had a sore throat and wanted to gargle with it, but I just shook my head.

People who work behind store counters are great sources. During the winter I had a terrible cold, and everything was either running or leaking. I went into the drug store and bought Kaopectate, Tylenol, Comtrex, and Preparation H. I was hurting. The clerk put everything in a bag and with a smile said, "Have a good day."

Growing up on The Hill, an Italian neighborhood in St. Louis, one of my favorite dishes was and still is ravioli. So I couldn't believe this sign I saw in a grocery store: Ravioli $3.95 a pound, filling extra.

When I read these next two stories I knew they belonged in the "just like Yogi" group. Mark Evans, a police dispatcher in Las Cruces, New Mexico, got this 9-1-1 call.

"Where is Spots?" the woman asked.

"Ma'am, I don't know what you mean."

"I'm worried about Spots. I don't want to go through there, so I'd like to know where it is."

"Ma'am?"

"I can't even find Spots on the map."

Dispatcher Evans finally figured out that the woman was doing some traveling and thought the warning phrase "icy in spots" meant there was ice in the town of Spots, New Mexico. There is no such place, but she is a candidate for the Yogiism award.

Computer manufacturers ran into a similar problem and had to add a useless key labeled "Any." That's because some users were confused about the often-used command, "press any key to continue" and kept calling the company's customer service line to ask where the "Any" key was.

Yogiisms are part of everybody's life. They make us wonder if we heard right, but we smile as we try to decode them. When we are criticized we could be like Luis Polonia, who responded to the criticism of a team-mate by saying, "If I have something to say, I won't say anything." Or Winston Burdett who said, "I don't want to be quoted, and don't quote me that I don't want to be quoted." Or we could go through life like one of broadcaster Mike Shannon's favorite players who is "an aggressive youngster who never made the same mistake once." Me, I'll stay with my pal Yogi, who has said it more than once: "If I had to do it over again, I would do it over again." How can you argue with that?

The Ballpark

CHAPTER 9

When you've been in as many ballparks as I have as a player or a broadcaster, the parks really become your friends. Walking into a ballpark is always an up feeling for me. While the park itself might jog my memory, it really comes alive because of the people. So, the first thing I do when I walk in before the game is to see what's happening on the field.

What a treat it used to be to watch a maestro of the fungo like Jimmie Reese of the California Angels at work. Pitchers ran to stay in shape, and usually the pitching coach threw baseballs for them to catch. Jimmie Reese would take the fungo bat and hit it just out of their reach, so they had to speed up or stretch out to catch it. When I hear someone talk about bat control I think of Jimmy, with his absolutely perfect fungo bat control.

One thing that always gets my attention is when a bunch of players are standing around, as if someone has called a meeting, instead of running or shagging fly balls. You don't see it too often today, but if you ever see a group of players gathered in the outfield instead of scattered around shagging balls it either means a challenge or a race. Challenges can run from: "Can you throw a ball out of the park?" to "Can you throw a ball up to the last row in the third deck?" to "Can you hit that sign between the hot dog stand and the foul pole way up there in the left field bleachers?" Throwing a ball onto the roof in right field in

Pittsburgh's Forbes Field was always a good challenge. In Sportsman's Park the big scoreboard high in the left field bleachers was the target. It sounds ridiculous, but I have seen All-Star outfielders to star pitching aces take the challenge that gives general managers a Maalox moment when they hear about it later.

The race is more fun because it can be between the two slowest guys on the team or the two fastest. This race many times is pretty well planned, a polite way of saying that most times it's rigged. Clint Courtney was always setting something up and usually had the percentages stacked his way. This Courtney-promoted race was between teammates Pete Ramos and Don Hoak. The scouting report said that Ramos, a pitcher, had speed and stamina but was a late starter—slow out of the blocks. Hoak had great speed and came out of the blocks very fast. Courtney marked off the course and gathered the friendly bets. The race agreed upon was supposed to be a one hundred-yard dash. It looked like it was marked off at one hundred yards. The race started, and true to the scouting reports, Hoak came flying out of the blocks with the lead, but as the race went on Ramos caught him, passed him, and won. As usual, Courtney collected his winnings. Then somebody decided to measure the course. It was one hundred twenty yards long.

Once I take my seat in the stands, I enjoy listening to and talking with the fans around me. You can learn a lot about a fan by listening to him root. Mike Kennedy, my good friend and a real baseball fan, is also a lawyer. Upset at the umpire, he didn't holler for him to bear down or to wake up. Mike hollered, "Show some accountability." Only a lawyer would use that kind of language while giving an umpire a blast.

I put that right next to the most literate argument I ever heard from a big league player. Luckily it was caught on tape.

Bud Harrelson, the Mets' shortstop, thought he was safe on a close play, but umpire Augie Donatelli called him out. Harrelson, who was halfway to the dugout thinking he had scored, came charging back, got right in Donatelli's face and said, "I'm not going to be penalized for your inadequacies!"

One of the most literate and well-spoken fans of the game was Commissioner of Baseball, Bart Giamatti. He had been president of Yale

University. I'm sure he was the right man for Yale, but for me, Bart Giamatti was all about baseball. He loved being at the ballpark. After only a few months on the job, Bart Giamatti died suddenly on September 1, 1989. It was our loss. He loved the game before he got the job and loved it even more after he had the title Commissioner. In his book, *A Great and Glorious Game*, he wrote this about the game of baseball:

> It breaks your heart. It is designed to break your heart. The game begins in the spring, when everything else begins again, and it blossoms in the summer, filling the afternoons and evenings, and then as soon as the chill rains come, it stops and leaves you to face the fall alone. You count on it, rely on it to buffer the passage of time, to keep the memory of sunshine and high skies alive, and then just when the days are all twilight, when you need it most, it stops. Today, October 2, a Sunday of rain and broken branches and leaf-clogged drains and slick streets, it stopped, and summer was gone.

> That was Bart Giamatti's game.

Sitting in the ballpark watching a game with him was hard because no fan was denied a hello or an autograph. For nine innings he visited and he signed, but he didn't miss a play.

This was a typical hot day in Scottsdale, Arizona where the Cubs were playing the Giants in spring training. The Commissioner was making the rounds of the baseball camps, and he didn't just drop in like the Welcome Wagon. He came to visit with the players, to watch the game, and enjoy being in the ballpark. That was his favorite thing—being in the ballpark. In fact, I learned later how much he disliked watching the game on television. He wrote: "The real activity was done with the radio—not the all-seeing, all-falsifying television—and was the playing of the game in the only place it will last, the enclosed green field of the mind." All-falsifying television? It was during that game between the Cubs and Giants that I finally learned what he meant.

Shawon Dunston, the Cubs' shortstop, made a tremendous play in the hole. He covered a lot of ground, then back-handed the ball, braced himself, and fired a strike to first to barely get the runner. The crowd went wild, and I turned to the commissioner and said something like,

"What a play! What a play! I'd like to see it again on replay." That was a big mistake. I had really said the wrong thing.

Commissioner Giamatti looked me in the eye, moved in closer like a player getting ready to argue with an umpire and said, "Replay! Replay?! Let me ask you something. If you had a chance to see the Lincoln-Douglas debate live or on tape, which would you rather do?" He was really worked up, almost yelling.

I remember leaning back and saying, "I don't even know Lincoln or Douglas. I'd just like to see Dunston make that play again." We had a good laugh, and I told him, "You're the only guy I know who could bring Lincoln and Douglas to a ballgame and make sense out of it."

Many times I've seen a great play at the ballpark and said to myself, *I'll bet even Bart Giamatti would like to see the replay on that one.* Certain plays remind me of him, and certain plays remind me of Mr. Branch Rickey, one of baseball's great general managers. It's not that you needed a dictionary to have a conversation with them, but when they spoke, you not only listened but you wished you had paid more attention in English class. I would pay to hear a discussion about baseball between Comissioner Giamatti and Mr. Rickey.

Mr. Rickey's role in baseball is well known, especially when the name Jackie Robinson comes up. Mr. Rickey had the courage to break the color line by signing him to a major league contract with the Brooklyn Dodgers.

My first meeting with Mr. Rickey is the reason why, even now, I never refer to him as Branch or even Branch Rickey. The memories are too powerful. My association with him began when I joined the St. Louis Cardinals organization and he was the general manager. Is he a hero of mine? He just might be. But it wasn't always that way. The first time I met him face-to-face he scared me out of his office.

I had spent most of the summer in Springfield, Missouri. The Cardinals had given me a job to help the groundskeeper and to catch batting practice. I was only fifteen years old and had not signed a contract. I'd never been farther from my house than going to Sportsman's Park. Springfield seemed like the other side of the world.

*I could never call him Branch
Rickey. He was always Mr. Rickey
to me, and he still is.*
Courtesy Los Angeles Dodgers.

A wonderful widow by the name of Sue Wicker ran a boarding house where some of the Springfield Cardinals lived. That was my home, too. I remember names like Roy Broome, Wes Cunningham, Hal Olt, and Archie Templeton, who never made it to the big leagues but took care of a scared kid. I still have the newspaper picture of that team, and there I am in the front row. The description reads, "Above left, front row, are Joe Garagiola, 15-year-old St. Louis hopeful, whom the parent Cardinals sent here for safekeeping." Even after I got to the big leagues some managers kept me on the bench for safekeeping.

At the end of the Western Association season I went back home, and that was when I met Mr. Rickey face-to-face. My older brother, Mickey, and I went in to talk about a contract. The Cardinals' offices were in Sportsman's Park, and the two of us must have looked fresh off a Norman Rockwell painting as we both tried to act like we knew exactly what we were doing. But our actions gave us away. We were actually scared silly.

A lady I got to know really well, secretary Mary Murphy, made us feel like we belonged and were expected. I can still hear her, see her, and remember her friendly smile. Miss Murphy had us sit down and asked if we wanted a drink of water. Mickey and I thanked her and said no, but I know that if she had asked if we wanted to go to the bathroom we would have gone together.

The time for our appointment came, and Miss Murphy said, "Mr. Rickey wants to see you." I remember it so well because she said "wants to see you" and not "will see you."

Strangely enough, when we went into his office, the first thing I noticed was not Mr. Rickey but the big chalkboard behind him. It had all the names of the St. Louis Cardinals on it by position. I was trying to say hello and read the names at the same time. Then I saw him, and I think I lost my breath.

He was big. I noticed his eyebrows first because they were so thick, almost as if they needed a haircut as they drooped over his horn-rimmed glasses. His hair was just as thick and might have been combed that morning, but it looked like he had been running his hands through it all day. He had an unlit cigar in his mouth that didn't look like it had ever been lit, but it still wasn't a whole cigar. He sat behind a big desk with papers piled so high he could have hidden behind them if he'd wanted to.

I remember Mr. Rickey sticking out his hand and saying, "My boy, how are you, and who is this with you?" When Mr. Rickey said, "my boy," it was like God talking, his voice was so loud and so deep.

Our only reason for being there was to talk about a contract, and the only preparation I had was a conversation with one of the Springfield Cardinals' players. Hank Redmond was an outfielder sent from Rochester when Stan Musial was called up from the Springfield team. Redmond had been around and had casually asked me if I had signed a contract yet. I told him I hadn't because I was too young and my father had to sign for me, and that would be hard because he didn't know anything about baseball and didn't speak English. Hank Redmond's advice was simple: "Get a bonus. Get money up front. If you get money up front you're one of the last players they'll release because they got money invested in you." It was good advice, but it was the spark that set off Mr. Rickey.

Mickey and I didn't know how much bonus money to ask for, but we did come up with a plan. Without telling Papa we found out how much money he still owed on the house, and that was what we were going to ask for. Truthfully, I don't remember too much of what went on before Mr. Rickey scared me out of his office, but I do remember that part.

"Now, my boy, about signing this contract to play in the St. Louis Cardinals' organization. Is there a problem?"

"No sir. I want to play for the Cardinals, but I want a bonus."

"A bonus? You want a bonus?"

He paused for what seemed like a month-and-a-half and then, in his low, deep voice asked, "How much of a bonus do you want? How much?"

Calling on my Catholic background, I asked the help of all the saints I could think of, including St. Christopher, who was later released by the Church. I took probably the deepest breath of my life and said, "Five hundred dollars."

Mr. Rickey stood up; his eyebrows seemed to get thicker and his voice got louder. "Five hundred dollars! You want five hundred dollars!?" His voice got louder as he came closer. "What are you going to do with all that money? Five hundred dollars is a lot of money."

I was so scared I didn't say a word. I just looked at him and then looked at my brother and said, "C'mon, let's get out of here." We left.

The St. Louis Browns had their offices down the stairs and across a small hall, and that's where Mickey and I were headed until Miss Murphy stopped us. She asked us to sit down and said she wanted us to meet Sam Breadon, the owner of the Cardinals.

We met Mr. Breadon, who brought in Mr. Rickey, and the four of us spent all of ten minutes together until they agreed to the bonus. I agreed to the contract and had the five hundred dollars.

The money turned out to be one of the biggest thrills of my life. We went right down to Laclede-Christy, where Papa worked making clay pipes, and during his lunch hour I gave him the money. Now he wouldn't owe a cent to anybody. To see my father, a hulk of a man with hands

Yogi's hero, Papa Berra.
My hero, Papa Giovanni.
Courtesy Bettman/Corbis.

like snow shovels, start to cry, and to watch those big gumdrop tears roll down his face is a memory I'll have forever. I had never seen my father cry, but I knew those were happy tears coming from an overflowing heart. It had been a bumpy beginning, but in the end, Mr. Rickey was a big part of one of my life's happiest moments.

Many of my memories of Mr. Rickey involve his speeches. Here's how he described baseball when he appeared before Congress: "A game of great charm in the adaptation of mathematical measurements to the timing of human movements, the exactitudes and adjustment of physical ability to hazardous chance. The speed of the legs, the dexterity of the body, the grace of the swing, the elusiveness of the slide—these are the features that make Americans everywhere forget the last syllable of a man's last name or the pigmentation of his skin." That was Mr. Rickey's game.

Whenever I heard one of his speeches I took notes. I still have my notes from a speech he gave on the value of a pitching machine. When you can make a pitching machine sound valuable you're more than a good speaker.

His quotes, called Rickeyisms by a lot of people, can be found every-where. Probably the most famous saying attributed to Mr. Rickey is: "Luck is the residue of design." He had others about luck: "Good luck is the by-product of planned effort. Bad luck will feature any team which is sat-isfied with mediocrity." When we didn't quite understand him and asked a question, my notes gave me his answer, I think. "If you hit a ball and you think it's an easy double and you don't run hard all the way but the outfielder does run hard and makes a strong, accurate throw to get you (BIG PAUSE) then don't charge your out to bad luck."

One of his speeches was about a champion player: "A consuming desire to be great is the important quality that will make ability and capacity meet. The greatest single factor that makes a champion player is his desire to be one. They want to win a pennant so much that they never ask the price, but pay it. The greatest quality of a championship team is a collective, dominating urge to win."

He once made a speech on base-stealing with Nobel Prize-winner Anatole France as his star. The thrust of his speech was taking chances. Here's how my notes read: "The manager signaled him to run...to steal. But you could see the runner was timid. He looked afraid. He was afraid. He wouldn't try. Oh, how that upset me. I am for the man who will embrace the rights and hazards of adventure. Like Anatole France who told the French Assembly, 'I prefer the errors of enthusiasm to the indifference of wisdom.'" I think about half of us in the room were try-ing to figure out how much Anatole France hit and in what league. Commissioner Giamatti brought Lincoln and Douglas to the ballpark, and Mr. Rickey brought Anatole France, and they all seemed to belong with Ted Williams, Willie Mays, Joe DiMaggio, and the rest of the greats.

During a banquet honoring one of his favorite teams, the Cardinals' Gas House Gang, Mr. Rickey was a spellbinder. He said he enjoyed being their general manager because of all the emotional twists.

He said, "This was a group willing to embrace the hazards of rational chance. A group full of adventure. They had no price on victory." Couldn't he just say they played hard to win? I was the emcee that night, and I was like a schoolboy taking notes for the final exam. Describing Leo Durocher

Gas House Gang. My favorite team. Mr. Rickey: "This was a team that had no price on victory. They knew how to play; they knew how to have fun." Courtesy St. Louis Cardinals Hall of Fame Museum.

he said, "Leo Durocher is a mental hoodlum with the infinite capacity for taking a bad situation and making it immediately worse. But if I owned a team I would want him as my manager."

Mr. Rickey was the first I heard describe a guy as "an anesthetic player." That might make you think of the TV show *Grey's Anatomy*, but he meant the player was not playing up to his potential. Although he gave you some good games he didn't give you enough to help win a pennant. "He's killing you, but you don't feel it." That's an anesthetic player.

One of my favorite Rickeyisms ended a discussion with Stan Rojek, an infielder with the Brooklyn Dodgers. In a conversation with Mr. Rickey, the subject of marriage came up. Here's how I heard the story:

RICKEY: "Stan, are you married?"

ROJEK: "No, I'm still single."

RICKEY: "Are you thinking about it?"

ROJEK:: "That's about it. I'm thinking about it."

RICKEY: "My boy, you are a matrimonial coward."

That was one of his favorite expressions. Like Bart Giamatti, he could put the words together.

Watching a game with him was always special. In fact, one of my most memorable nights at the ballpark was spent with Mr. Rickey. I was broadcasting for the Cardinals by then, and an off-day in our schedule took us to Pittsburgh. That not only gave me the opportunity to see the Dodgers play the Pirates but a chance to say hello to Mr. Rickey, then the Pirates' GM.

Many of the Dodgers' players came up through the system when Mr. Rickey was the Dodgers' general manager. He was a hands-on operator who knew the Dodgers' players as well as, if not better than, his own Pirates. The one he was most proud of was Jackie Robinson. You wouldn't be sitting with him five minutes before he used words like "daring" and "creative" when talking about Robinson.

When Jackie Robinson got on base you could feel the adrenalin in Mr. Rickey working overtime. This night Robinson had already stolen second base twice, and this at-bat found him at third base with two outs. My notes from that night may not be word-for-word, but you'll get the idea that listening to Mr. Rickey was exciting:

Be alert. This is an ideal situation for Robinson to steal home. He is sending out the bait. Stealing home is on his mind. He is so daring he is not thinking of not making it. He's not afraid to fail. He has a one-way lead, and a look from the pitcher will have him going back to the bag. He better look. Robinson has him measured. He didn't even move toward third as the ball headed for the batter. He's going to take a two-step extra lead, and it will look like the same lead, that he had on the last pitch since the pitcher didn't even look at him. If he gets those two steps he is gone and he will make it.

My eyes were riveted on Robinson. I still couldn't see the difference in the two leads. Then I heard, "He's got it. He's got the two extra steps. He's going, and he will make it."

No sooner had he said it, Jackie Robinson took off and the play wasn't even close. Stealing home is one of the most exciting plays in baseball, and I not only saw it but was in on it from the beginning. Mr. Rickey had the blueprint for the steal and explained it all the way.

Jackie Robinson could beat you so many ways; this was just one of them. Courtesy AP.

Mr. Rickey knew the game so well there's no wonder he understood what it took to succeed. He often talked about three points to stardom. "A young man must...

1) Feel that the job is worthwhile.

2) Have a consuming desire to be great.

3) Pay attention to the small details.

I remember the way he summed up a batter who he felt was thinking too much in the batter's box. Mr. Rickey simply said, "Full mind, empty bat." That other great philosopher, Yogi Berra said, "You can't hit and think at the same time." Different words, different school, but the same result.

Mr. Rickey had a sign in his office that was a lesson. It read:

He that will not reason is a bigot.

He that cannot reason is a fool.

He that dares not reason is a slave.

I really got to know Mr. Rickey after I was traded from the Cardinals to the Pittsburgh Pirates and he was the Pirates' GM. One of the first things I learned was that he was a man ahead of his time. Baseball now has an Arizona Fall League where the best players from the different organizations play with and against each other. I think the idea came from the fertile mind of Mr. Branch Rickey.

One year, after the big league season was over, he had a camp in Deland, Florida. He brought in all the bright Pirates' prospects. These were the youngsters who, in his mind, were going to be big league players. I was at the camp having just finished the year with the Pirates. I'd never seen so many great arms, so much speed and ability in one place in my life. Ron Necciai, who struck out twenty-seven batters in a minor league game, had the best pitching arm I had ever seen. Jackie Brown and Ed Wolfe had curveballs that would make grown men cry. Felipe Montemayor, an outfielder, could do everything: run, throw, and hit. Dick (Dr. Strangeglove) Stuart, had just hit fifty-six home runs. Bobby Del Greco, Tony Bartirome, Jim Waugh, and Ron Kline were all gifted players who later made it to the big leagues. I was impressed with the camp, and thought I was in on the beginning of a dynasty, but unfortunately injuries devastated the plan.

To watch Mr. Rickey teach a young pitcher control his way was worth the price of admission. He'd walk in, talk to the pitcher about confidence, and then place his Indiana Jones-style hat on the ground some three feet in front of the pitcher and ask the youngster to hit it. The youngster would hit the hat, and Mr. Rickey would back him up to five feet…same routine…ten feet, and so on until he was back to about pitching-mound distance but still hitting the hat on the ground. Then it was not unusual to see Mr. Rickey pick up the hat that had just gone through the practice, dust it off, put it back on his head, and leave.

Mr. Rickey's sense of humor showed even stronger because of his voice and delivery. With all the young players in the Deland camp, practical jokes were bound to happen. Mr. Rickey's sense of humor was put to the test when a practical joke backfired.

We were all living in a barracks-like situation, and this night a couple of the pranksters wanted to soak some of the other rookies while they were asleep. Taking the fire hose down from the wall and putting it through the transom they managed to flood the room. The execution was perfect except for one detail. It was the wrong room. They flooded the room full of coaches. The next morning at the daily meeting everyone was expecting a real blow off. Instead, Mr. Rickey delivered an appeal: "If the player responsible will come forward I will guarantee him a job with Ringling Brothers because he must have the biggest bladder in the world." The meeting ended with smiles, and many believed it saved the post-season camp experiment.

Mr. Rickey's sense of humor wasn't well publicized, but he could use a sharp needle. He once described a player as having "feet of clay with a head to match." I especially like the story of the scout who hadn't signed too many players but came in asking for a raise.

"Why do you think you deserve a raise?"

"This is my third year, and I haven't had a raise."

"That's why you've been here for three years."

Whenever I hear talk about the live, juiced-up baseball I go right to my Branch Rickey file and quote, "The trouble is not the rabbit in the ball but the quail in the pitchers."

This one involved an American League general manager who came to him for some advice. "Mr. Rickey, I've got a good young outfielder who puzzles me. Sometimes he plays great. Other times he limps like his right leg is broken. My doctors can't figure out what to do. What do you suggest?"

Mr. Rickey nodded. "Best thing to do, my friend? The next time he doesn't limp, sell him."

Mr. Rickey wanted his base runners to be creative and daring and not necessarily in that order. So many times when I'm at the ballpark I can almost hear Mr. Rickey speaking. Again, from my notes:

"Speed is the only common denominator on offense and defense. Speed never goes into a slump. A speedy outfielder can outrun a bad jump or the wrong turn. Speed can be the eraser." Great notes, but with my speed they did me about as much good as keys to Fort Knox. When would I use them?

Mr. Rickey often started his speeches and seminars with a far-out thought. One was a question: *Does he wear suspenders or a belt?* That took him to the different leads for a base runner:

A two-way lead…where the base runner can go either way. Back to first or try to steal. A big one-way lead. This is to draw a throw. At the first move of the pitcher, break back to the bag. Then there's the lead the runner has to have so he knows he can go and make it. If a runner gets only a few feet off base, he probably plays it safe all his life and ends up wearing suspenders. The question is, *does he wear a belt or suspenders, or does he wear both?*

I've had that thought many times while watching a runner get just a couple of feet off the base. Does he wear a belt? Or suspenders? Or both?

Mr. Rickey made even going to the dentist a reason to be alert and ready to learn something new:

I go into the dentist's office and I look around. The waiting rooms are usually spotless, so I feel good. I find answers in the magazines on the table. Are they current? If they are I anticipate newer techniques and expect better treatment because of these newer techniques. Old magazines tell me he may not be willing to learn anything new. He's satisfied, maybe even complacent.

Everything was a scouting trip to Mr. Rickey. The look you had when you met him, the grip of your handshake, the speed of your answers, all were included in his scouting report on you.

Mr. Rickey once gave me a personal lecture about catching, and he wasn't talking about technique. The entire conversation revolved around the shin guards and the mask. When he was talking to the team as a group it was more of a lecture or a speech, but when it was one-on-one it was like a question-and-answer session.

"Let me ask you, what do you think when you see the opposing catcher in the on-deck circle and he is still wearing his shin guards?"

"I think he's just waiting to hit."

"The shin guards tell you nothing?"

"No." (I still think that if shin guards could talk they would be talking to Mr. Rickey.)

"Those shin guards are sending a message to your pitcher. They are telling him that his own catcher doesn't think his teammate will get a hit. Wearing shin guards in the on-deck circle is not a positive sign for your team. It helps the opposing pitcher by giving him added confidence." All I could do was agree.

Picking up the mask once for the opposing catcher meant another one-on-one session. I may not remember his words exactly, but to sound like Mr. Rickey, let me say that his lessons are indelibly impressed in my mind. This is the conversation we had after I picked up the opposing catcher's mask:

"After you hit a foul ball, why do you pick up the catcher's mask?"

"No real reason. It's on the ground, and he's coming back."

"Do you do it so he likes you more?"

"No, it's just there. It's not that big a deal. It seems the natural— maybe even the decent—thing to do."

"Why would you expend your energy to do that? Let him expend his. Let him stoop over. Don't let him rest by picking up his mask."

I played in Pittsburgh part of 1951, all of 1952, and part of 1953. Back then, the Pirates were in a rebuilding mode. They were still in that planning mode when I was traded to the Cubs. The previous winter, when I signed my contract, Mr. Rickey had told me I figured in his plans, but I didn't realize what he meant until he traded me. After that, I went into broadcasting. It was then that I learned a lesson from him that showed how he noticed even the smallest things. For example, when most of us see a catcher go after a pop foul we simply wait to see if he catches it or misses it. At least that's the way it was for me until I heard Mr. Rickey on the subject.

I knew the correct method of catching a foul ball, although it was never easy for me. As soon as the ball is popped up the catcher must try to find it, hold the mask in his hand until he finds it, and then fling the mask in the opposite direction so he doesn't trip over it. It was a difficult lesson for me to learn. As soon as the ball was hit, off the mask would come, and away I'd go. To this day I marvel at catchers who do it right and make it look easy.

On a trip to Pittsburgh when I was broadcasting for the Cardinals, I saw a young catcher the Pirates had brought up to the big team. I liked him and thought he would be in the major leagues a long time.

A foul ball went up, and the young catcher flipped off his mask. Mr. Rickey's scouting report said it all: "He still hasn't learned to hold that mask," he said, "and if he can't learn a simple technique like that he will never stay in the big leagues for any length of time." Again, he was right, as the young catcher who I thought would make it easily was in the big leagues less than five years.

Is it any wonder I admired him so much? A theory about whether someone wore suspenders or a belt told him how daring a base runner was. Not being able to hold on to the mask told Mr. Rickey a catcher was not long for the major leagues.

Every player who knew Mr. Rickey grew to respect him. In fact, he's the only general manager I know of who was scouted by the players. In those days, signing a contract was not complicated. But because nobody was represented by an agent it was up to you to make the deal. The contract came in the mail, and the battle was on. You sent back your answer, and then it really got interesting. What came back by return mail might upset you, confuse you, and sometimes even make you laugh.

Tony Kubek, my partner on the NBC *Game of the Week*, told the story of sending back a contract asking for more money by writing a short note to George Weiss, the Yankees' general manager.

"Your offer is unsatisfactory. I can make more money here in Wisconsin by shoveling snow." Mr. Weiss's answer was short but not sweet. "Received your answer. Suggest you get a big shovel."

Usually after a few more exchanges like that, a player was summoned to the home office for a face-to-face meeting with the general manager. Here's where the player's scouting report helped. Players compared notes; it was word of mouth either by running into each other in the office or by telephone. You might call a player who had just signed or was in the middle of a contract fight.

This classic story shows how two players, Gene Hermanski and Chuck Connors, (from *The Rifleman* TV show), teamed up with a plan before a contract session with Mr. Rickey. On the flip of the coin, Hermanski went in first. After about an hour he came out and Connors asked how it went.

"I didn't sign. I know he's a pretty religious man, so I thought I was ready for him."

"What did he ask you?" Connors wanted to know.

"He asked if I smoked, and I said 'not too much.' He was okay with that. He asked me if I went out with women; I said 'not too much.' He didn't say anything, just looked at me. Then he asked me if I drank, and I said 'a little bit,' and that's when he went through the roof." Connors listened, and then went in next.

"Do you smoke?" Mr. Rickey asked.

"No, Mr. Rickey."

"Do you go out with women?"

"No, Mr. Rickey."

"Do you drink?"

Connors, the aspiring actor, jumped out of the chair, slammed his fist on the table, put on an indignant face and yelled, "If I have to drink to stay in your organization, I'm leaving." That's the only time I ever heard of Mr. Rickey being a victim of "gotcha."

I don't know what kind of a contract Connors got that year, but I do know that in negotiations, your fatal mistake was to bring up your average or runs batted in. You'd lose in a hurry. Mr. Rickey loved to debate—he never argued.

After my 1952 season I thought I had decent numbers. My best weapons were: games played, one hundred eighteen; RBIs, fifty-four; and batting average, .272. Besides, I wasn't looking for that big of a raise. When I finished stating my case and Mr. Rickey took over, I felt like the guy who was hunting elephants and rhinos with a BB gun. I was ready to take a job with the grounds crew. I became an expert on knowing that on-base average and power were the best weapons.

Later, I found out in a 1954 *Life* magazine story that Mr. Rickey had worked out a formula to determine the value of a player. Today you hear about the value of on-base average and power, but Mr. Rickey made his statement fifty years ago: "If the baseball world is to accept this new system of analyzing the game—and eventually it will—it must first give up preconceived ideas. Two measurable factors—on-base average and power—gauge the overall offensive worth of an individual." He used his formula on me in 1952, and it proves both that I was overmatched and that Mr. Rickey was way ahead of his time.

Ballparks are my friends, but that's because they remind me of the people who've created the memories there. I think of Willie Mays's great over-the-shoulder catch off Vic Wertz in the 1954 World Series in the Polo Grounds; Kirk Gibson's game-winning home run in Dodger Stadium; a double hit by Tony Womack to tie the seventh game of the 2001 World Series; and the single hit by Luis Gonzalez to win the game for the Diamondbacks. I've seen no-hit games, perfect games, and games where records were set and broken, like the night Henry Aaron broke Babe Ruth's all-time home run record.

Events like those are historic. To be able to share some of those moments with friends is a bonus. I've watched an All-Star game with President Gerald Ford; when you're both eating hot dogs and rooting for the same team, you can't get any more American than that. I sat with my *Today* show co-host Barbara Walters who, bewildered, wanted to know what had just happened when Tommie Agee stole home to win a game for the Mets, and the crowd was going wild. And leaving Riverfront Stadium one night, Tony Kubek and I walked out with the man who had walked on the moon, Neil Armstrong.

Ballparks scratch out the year on my birth certificate. Whether the park is full or empty, it makes me feel like getting out my bubble gum cards to see if the guys on the field are the same guys on my cards. It's a reminder of the great day when I got the card of my favorite ballplayer, Joe Medwick. Do you remember the day you got your favorite player?

All Be Chasing Grandma

CHAPTER 10

The great sportswriter Red Smith once said that baseball is a dull game only to dull people. It's true. When people come up to me, and before they even say hello, tell me they never watch baseball, I only look at them and almost feel sorry. I know some people are not baseball fans just like I don't go to symphony concerts that often. I like Broadway musicals, but I can't remember seeing a Shakespeare play. That's the way it should be. My friend, Gary Mule Deer, a comedian who can always make me laugh, puts it best: "Grandpa says that if everybody liked the same thing then they'd all be chasing Grandma."

"It's too slow," is the lame reason I hear most often. I disagree because plenty is going on if you look for the action as hard as my non-fan looks for a hot dog stand. My eyes are all over the place.

For example, the pitcher is standing on the mound with the ball. Nothing is going to happen until he throws it. Does he have it in his glove? Does he have it in his bare hand? Is his wind-up the same on every pitch? Where is he standing on the rubber? Is the first base coach or the third base coach almost straining his eyes as he watches the pitcher? These are just a few of the things to study before the ball is thrown.

If the ball is in the pitcher's glove, watch his free hand. Does it go into the glove the same way every pitch? Does it change with the catcher's signal for a curveball as opposed to a fastball? If he sets his grip with the ball in the glove does he do the same thing every time? Look for changes in his routine. I remember batting (notice I didn't say hitting) against a pitcher who set his grip with his hand inside the glove, but he might as well have told us what was coming. His hand wasn't deep enough into the glove, so if you saw part of his palm it was a fastball, and if you saw the back of his hand it was a breaking ball.

Another pitcher I faced would stop his windup at the top of his head for a curveball and go behind his head for a fastball. Moving around the rubber can give you a clue as to where his target was.

If the catcher moves too soon after giving a signal, that can alert the coach who is watching or even a player on the bench. If the catcher gives a curveball sign and inches forward, this could tell you he wants to catch the breaking ball before it hits the ground. If he gives the signal and just spreads his legs, it's a sure fire fastball.

Where the catcher places his arm to give the signal is most important. Moving the arm in close could mean a fastball, moving it out could mean a curveball. Gene Mauch, a big league manager for many years, was always looking for the edge. He claimed he could see the veins move in the catcher's arm when he'd wiggle for a change of pace. Believe that or not, it probably forced catchers to wear a long sleeve shirt when they played against a Mauch-managed team.

As a batter you can't see any of this, but a coach or another player can, and they can tell you the pitch immediately. How? A pre-arranged signal like a shrill whistle or hollering a key word like your first name or a city. "Hit one downtown" is an easy signal for a player. All this and the pitcher hasn't even thrown the ball.

Many good base runners try to steal a look at the catcher right after he has given his signal to see where he sets up. This may give the runner the edge, knowing whether it's a fastball or a curveball. I know it's easier to steal on a breaking ball. I'm not saying that from my base running days but from my days of trying to throw out those base runners. Many times a base stealer guarantees the hitter more fastballs because the catcher wants the edge in throwing out the runner. Go ahead and play this game in the stands. Watch a good base stealer as he gets his lead, and then see how many fastballs the pitcher throws.

While runners are taking their look at catchers, the opposition is watching the runner carefully. Roger Craig was good at picking up tip-offs by runners. His thinking was simple. A thief is a thief whether he is robbing a bank or stealing a base. He will do something different. Find that difference and you have the edge. Dull, no way.

On winning teams, every player on the field moves on every pitch. The center fielder is usually my key guy. He will tell you by where he positions himself how they are trying to pitch a certain hitter. Infielders, especially the second baseman and shortstop, will also tell you certain things.

Since the middle infielders have to cover second base they make up their own signals for a particular pitch. The standard was to put your glove in front of your mouth, then look at your partner; the open mouth could mean fastball and the closed mouth a pitch other than the fastball. The by-the-book procedure was if the runner breaks for second the shortstop covers with a left-handed batter and the second baseman covers with the right-handed batter. Many times infielders make up their own defense. It's always fun to see if they played it the "book" way or their own way.

The danger here is tipping it off early. The scenario you're watching breaks down like this: The runner could be running on this count. The catcher gives the signal for the pitch, but the infielder who you think is holding his ground is a bit anxious. Did he just pat his glove and not move? Might be saying, "I'm not covering on this fastball." Did he move a couple steps toward home plate? If he is covering, did he move toward the bag? All those are tip-offs, and they happen more than you think. You can't be sure, but it adds to the game you are watching.

I'm not forgetting about the first and third baseman, but they're in a different world on defense. Both are reaction positions. Most of the time you either make the play on the hard hit ball or you don't. You may see the first baseman cross his arms with a runner on first and that tells the pitcher he's playing behind the runner. He is trying to keep his pitcher from committing a balk. The first or third baseman may talk to the

*Roger Craig looked for an
edge, and he usually found it.
Courtesy Los Angeles Dodgers.*

pitcher and set up a defense against the bunt. But then there's a time
when they come running in to talk to the pitcher after he has made his
pitch. What's that all about?

The first and third basemen really hate it when a pitcher changes
speeds on his own. Murry Dickson and I were teammates on the Cardinals.
We nicknamed him Tom Edison because he started experimenting from
the time he walked into the clubhouse and then took his experiments
out to the mound. For example, he had a theory that went against all
baseball strategy. He liked to pitch when he was behind the hitter. He
wanted the count two balls, no strikes or three balls, one strike because,
to listen to him, "They're looking for a particular pitch, so I can throw
them something else." Some days it worked. Some days it didn't.

Murry Dickson was always changing speeds on his own. You would
put down the fastball signal and the third baseman would play accordingly. But if a strong, right-handed power hitter was up there the last
thing a third baseman wanted to find out was that it was not a fastball
but a change of pace that the big guy could really pull toward third base.

I remember third baseman Whitey Kurowski running to the mound after surviving the decision change almost screaming, "If you're gonna do that let's get the married men off the infield." The same act was performed by the first baseman if the batter was left-handed.

Many times in the clubhouse meeting I heard, "I'm gonna play him straight away," but I always felt it was a misnomer. Very few center fielders lined up directly with the second base bag or the mound. The good ones shaded one way or the other even if just a step. As a batter you may have an idea, but don't go to the bank with it. I think all players live by the code that you can't trust what you see. If you're a left-handed batter and you see the left fielder toward the line and the center fielder in left-center, logic tells you they're pitching you outside and will make you hit that way. But that could be a set up.

It's easy to believe the action begins when the pitcher releases the ball, but that isn't the case. Watch the hitter. In the batter's box a hitter may look like he's just running his hand up the barrel of the bat or maybe fixing the bill of his cap. As a catcher, any such movement alerted me that it could actually be a signal to a base runner that a play was on.

One of the first things I learned as a rookie catcher was to watch certain batters, and number one on the list was Hall of Famer Billy Herman. Nothing ever got past him, and he was always looking for the edge as a player and then later as a coach and manager. He didn't do anything illegal, nor did he ever cheat. But if, as his opponent, you were careless he was going to take advantage.

Once, at an Old Timers game, I asked Billy who he concentrated on while he was batting, other than the pitcher:

You know I was probably going to put on a hit-and-run play if I had a base runner, so I would watch the middle infielders. One second baseman in the league couldn't have told me any better what the pitch was going to be. They had me figured to hit to right field on a fastball and hit to left on a curveball. So when I saw him pound his glove waiting for the ball, I knew a fastball was coming. When he didn't do a thing it was the tip-off that a curveball was coming.

Billy Herman's nickname was "Bulb Eyes," a tribute to his ability to see everything and everywhere. In the batter's box he always fidgeted with the bat, his belt, and especially the bill of his cap. He was probably the best hit-and-run man I ever played against. This story gives you an idea of how good he was.

We were both in the American Association, and he was finishing up a great playing career. The strategy against a hit-and-run batter is to crowd him, not to pitch him outside. The right field fence in old Nicollet Park, in Minneapolis, was very short and full of advertising. Billy was always very friendly, and I'll never forget this conversation. He never called me by my baptismal name:

"Dago, I don't care where you pitch me, and you know I like the inside pitch better when I'm gonna hit-and-run, and you know that's what I'm gonna do, but you don't know which pitch."

I didn't say a word. (What an upset.) Billy fouled off the pitch with the runner breaking for second. Stepping out of the box and picking up a handful of dirt Billy said, "Tell you what. I don't want to tell you which pitch, but see that heating sign on the fence in right? I'm gonna dot that 'i'."

"He didn't dot the 'i,' but he could have crossed the 't' with the line drive he hit.

When Billy Herman came up to hit, I'd look directly at his eyes to see if he was trying to steal my signal. One game Billy was fooling with his cap, and I made eye contact. He was looking for my fingers, but instead of putting down one for a fastball or two fingers for the curve I delivered a message by putting down my middle finger. He backed out of the box laughing and called me everything except Joe. So next time you see a batter get out of the box, he may be visiting with the catcher while he takes those practice swings.

When I was playing and a relief pitcher came into the game, nine times out of ten I guessed his first pitch would be a fastball so he could get ahead of me. If I was right, I'd have a good swing, and if I was wrong and it was a strike, I was behind in the count. Another "look for" pitch was the one after throwing something soft. I always felt the pitcher would come back with something hard—never two soft pitches in a row.

Now, in the stands, I still play my guessing game. You could call it "Check List" or "You Guessed Wrong, No Wonder You Didn't Hit for a Better Average." There is no bat in my hands, but I'm still looking for my pitch. That kind of thinking may have put me in the stands before my time.

You can also find clues by watching the pitcher warm up between innings, further proof that something's going on every minute. I don't know how many players in my day or today subscribe to this theory, but I used it. Maybe this theory made me a broadcaster, but it's fun to watch.

Even if you're in the upper deck you can see the pitcher tell the catcher what he's throwing by using his glove. If he flicks the glove straight ahead it will be a fastball; if he flicks it with a downward motion it will be a breaking ball. In the minor leagues I first heard this theory about pitchers and the start of an inning. The pitcher will start the first batter of the inning with the last pitch he threw during the warm-ups. That seemed a stretch, but I did believe this one. Usually the pitcher will throw his best pitch on the last warm-up toss, and that means a fastball. I smile every time I see a pitcher throw a breaking ball on his last warm-up toss and then start the hitter off with a curveball.

As a catcher, I was always looking for danger signs from my pitcher. Even now sitting in the stands I'm leery when I see a pitcher shake off the catcher in the eighth and ninth innings when he has hardly shaken off a sign all game. It's another red flag if he keeps asking for a new ball from the umpire when most of the game he didn't care if the umpire gave him a cantaloupe to throw. Early in the game, and even in the middle innings, he didn't care, but now he handles the ball like a surgeon with a scalpel—or your pitcher suddenly becomes a gardener, fiddling with the mound, smoothing it out or digging around with his spikes. Throwing over to first base is another S.O.S., especially if the runner is not known as a base stealer and is practically standing on the bag. As a catcher you're always checking the defense, but now all of a sudden your pitcher, who hardly knew anybody else was out there, is checking the defense and moving them even though they're playing the hitter the way it was discussed in the meeting. So nothing is actually happening, but the wheels are spinning in the dugout. When do you make the change, or when does the ghost of the famous "did-I-leave-him-in-one-batter-too-long" appear in the dugout?

That's the biggest gripe you hear about a manager—he left his pitcher in too long. Unless you're in the dugout and privy to the conversation you don't know what the pitcher said to his manager. I've heard pitchers working on a shutout say to the manager, "I'm about on empty. You better get me some help as soon as I get in trouble." To me, that's the sign of a good athlete and a team player. The mound is no place for heroes. Sitting in the stands you can play manager and think about taking a pitcher out before he gets rocked. Even though you don't know the condition of the bullpen or the pitcher, you can still play manager. The manager has seen his danger signals. Did you see yours? It makes the game a little more interesting.

For years I've listened to baseball people give tips on all the positions, and now when I watch a game I get to check it out. One example is the between inning warm-up. I had managers who would read the riot act to his catchers if they just lobbed the ball to second base.

Bill Meyer at Pittsburgh was the best manager I played for. True we lost 112 out of 154 (remember, not in a row), but we didn't lose them because of him. He didn't miss a trick. Being a former catcher he had his method, and he preached it. To this day I watch for it at every game:

—Always throw the ball back to the pitcher on his glove side and the target is the letters. Don't have the pitcher jumping all over the place.

—Throw it back hard so your arm stays loose in case you have to throw to second on a steal attempt.

—If you want to let the pitcher know you are not happy with the last pitch, throw the ball back even harder.

—Between innings throw the ball to second like a man is stealing, and make sure you are throwing from behind the plate and not two steps in front. When I see a catcher just lob the ball to second I halfway expect to see a delayed steal attempt by the other team.

—Make sure you're wearing all your equipment, especially the mask, when you're warming up the pitcher between innings. It can save you from an injury.

Since I was a catcher I watch that position more than the others. Whenever the catcher goes out to the mound or even a couple steps in front of the plate to set up a defense, I really watch him when he walks back to his position. Most catchers will never step on home plate when they go back. I wonder why? Check it out the next time you go to a game.

Terry Moore, a great center fielder with the Cardinals, was another guy I always listened to even though he talked mostly about outfield play. Terry always said, "If there is a need for a throw, back up, come into the ball, and catch the ball on the throwing side." It appears to be such a small detail but is so important. When I see there's going to be a play from an outfielder that picture always jumps to my mind.

I never saw Terry catch a ball one-handed unless he had to. He was sure-handed and almost always used both hands. He placed a lot of importance on the webbing of a glove and felt it should be lacing, not solid, so as not to screen yourself on the play. Outfield play has changed considerably because most outfielders now make one-handed catches of everything. Some have even perfected the one-handed dropped fly ball. This play is called an error.

When I see an outfielder just stand there and wait for the ball to come to him I always think of Terry. "It ain't room service, man. You gotta go get it. Any outfield that will not charge the ball is a second division outfield," he would scream. Is it any wonder he was the captain of the team?

Curt Flood was another of the better center fielders. I don't think he got enough credit for his ability. He had a theory that sounded good but was hard for me to understand. Curt played a shallow center field and so took many singles away from hitters. "I play by the bill of my cap," he said. "When the ball is hit, if it's over my bill I head back for it. If it is below my bill I come in." It worked for him, believe me.

This one came from a groundskeeper. During batting practice, watch how many players are around the cage. If too many players are standing

Curt Flood was a much-
underrated outfielder who
had a unique way of tracking
the baseball.
Courtesy St. Louis Cardinals
Hall of Fame Museum.

around talking, you don't have to check the newspaper to know you're looking at a second division team.

I still find myself looking at the third base coach on the two ball, no strike count or the three ball, one strike count. As a player, I didn't look at the third base coach on the three ball, no strike count because I knew they wouldn't give me the hit sign, so why should I look? The third base coach is the man in the spotlight when it comes to giving signals, but for the most part I like to look at base runners, especially those on second base. They see what the catcher is flashing, and if worse comes to worst they can at least flash whether the catcher is setting up outside or inside. This is most valuable to some hitters. It really is an easy system. The key is to pre-arrange it with the player who wants the information.

If the runner leads off second with his right foot, set up is inside. Lead off with a cross-over step, the set up is outside. If you think you have the actual signals (and they must be verified) getting that information to the hitter is a breeze. The more obvious ways involve the hands and arms.

Arms straight on the knees means fastball. Arms bent means crooked or curveball. Using just the hands it could be hands on knees fastball, off the knees, off-speed, or breaking ball. Any time I touched above my belt (fixed my cap, tugged at my sleeves) meant fastball. Any time I touched below my belt (rubbed my pant leg, etc.) meant off-speed or breaking ball.

Changing battery signs is a simple matter. Just touching your mask before giving a signal could change the whole sequence. Instead of the last finger flash, the touch of the mask switches it to the first finger flash the pitcher sees. If your pitcher is really paranoid about somebody stealing signs he can call the pitches. Again, watch the catcher before he gives the signal. Does he do the same thing every time? Is he standing the same way every time? Maybe his feet are together this time. Next time they are not. Is this a signal? I played with two teams in the big leagues where the catcher did exactly that to give the signals.

If we saw a player or coach sitting on the bullpen bench with a towel around his neck, he was a suspect. We'd watch to see what he did with the towel when he took it off. One team had a coach in the bullpen in right field, and the towel around the neck meant fastball, off the neck was a breaking ball or an off-speed pitch. He was about four hundred feet from home plate, but another player using a pair of binoculars brought home plate right to the bullpen.

One instance when managers don't get too fancy with the signals is in the All-Star game. That is a time when players finally get a chance to needle the manager.

MANAGER: "Let's get some signs for today's game."

PLAYERS: "Let's use the ones you use for your team. The whole league's got 'em anyhow."

I've said for many years that the beauty of baseball is its unpredictability. Football has its set plays. Basketball has its set plays. Both are run by a clock. What starts out as a set play in baseball doesn't guarantee that it will end up that way.

Even the so-called injury can give you something to watch. A batter will foul a ball off his foot and go to the ground like hunting season just opened and he was the target. He'll get up and limp and give the impression he could be on the disabled list for months. Former Diamondbacks coach Brian Butterfield even has a name for him—Crybaby Deke. Then this guy shakes it off and decides to tough it out. Back in the batter's box he tops the ball, and with a base hit in sight he's running so fast you think he made a side trip to Lourdes for the miracle. Go through the same scenario except that he gets a clean single. It wouldn't surprise me one bit to see him try to steal second on the first pitch. I learned the hard way during my career, never trust a limping player.

Something else that triggers a few thoughts for me during a game are airplanes flying over the ballpark. Shea Stadium, a close neighbor to LaGuardia Airport, is the champ when it comes to the statistic, "Park with most planes flown over." Whenever the roar of a jet disrupts the broadcast for a few seconds I think of broadcaster Jack Buck's great line, "Well, there goes another load of lost luggage."

The Dodgers' private plane made an unscheduled stop because of an engine problem, but Don Drysdale assured the team, "We won't be here too long. We're just gonna change a couple of spark plugs and forty-two pairs of shorts."

How can you argue with Casey Stengel's logic or not think of it when you see a plane over a ballpark? "Old Timers games and airplane landings are all alike. If you can walk away from them they're successful."

Jesse Gonder, a catcher for the Yankees, hated to fly. During a flight the weather got bad, and the plane was bouncing all over the place—the kind the great Minnie Minoso described as a "knuckleball flight." Minnie always wanted a "fastball flight," fast and straight. During this turbulent flight Gonder was close to panic when he started yelling to let him out. He wanted to get off. "You can't get off. We're too high and besides, we're over water," he was told. "I don't care. I can swim, but I can't fly."

One of the things I like most about baseball is that the pace allows for a relaxing time at the ballpark. And one of my most enjoyable experiences in all my baseball life was to sit in the stands with my good friend, the late Frank Slocum. Frank was a great storyteller with a fantastic memory. We'd play games pertaining to people or situations. One was called "Initials." The idea was to name a team, then give the initials and position of a player. The only rule was he could not be a star. He could be so obscure that his family might not have known how he was spending his summers. Usually it was the twenty-fifth player on a roster or someone who was brought up to the big leagues for the famous "cup of coffee" that seemed to last fifteen minutes—the kind of player whose name went on his uniform shirt with Velcro. I'm not going to embarrass any players by listing them, but to bring home the point, Joe Garagiola (JG) would not be eligible for this game. You had to play less than JG.

The other game was "Quotable Lines," but they had to be related to something happening in the game you were watching. You delivered the line the best you could remember. The other person then had to try to name who said it.

I'll play one game to give you the idea. The batter breaks a bat. So I'd turn to Frank and say, "I got one. 'I never broke a bat until my last year. I ran over it backing out of the garage.'" If Frank answered, "Lefty Gomez," he'd get the next chance to stump me.

Passed Ball— "You know you're in trouble when you say nice catch and it's the catcher you're talking about."
HANK GREENWALD, announcer, after four passed balls.
Manager— "The workout is optional. Whoever doesn't come is optioned." BOBBY VALENTINE.
"He's not happy unless he's unhappy."
COACH ELROD HENDRICKS on Earl Weaver.
Player Talking About Manager—"Playing for Yogi is like playing for your father. Playing for Billy Martin is like playing for your father-in-law." DON BAYLOR.
Stolen Base— "When we played softball I would steal second base, feel guilty, and go back." WOODY ALLEN.

I think you get the idea. Can you see why I find it hard to understand why some people say baseball is too slow? I kind of like it, though, when people call the game of baseball old-fashioned. I'd rather have it be like the sound of a waltz than rap or even classic rock. Sure, the walk-off home run in the bottom of the ninth is exciting, but during the game you can visit, strategize, and reminisce. You don't have to wonder if the clock is going to run out before your team can get the winning run. You can start a group conversation in your section by simply asking, "Is it just me or does the throw from home to second seem longer than a throw from first to third?"

That's not to say the sport hasn't changed. The biggest changes I've seen are expansion, the designated hitter, inter-league play, and sky-rocketing salaries. People keep making suggestions for more changes, like giving a team two or even three runs if a runner steals home, or counting a base on balls as a hit, or eliminating the intentional base on balls. I hope these suggestions keep getting turned down. One idea I would vote for comes from former player and manager Clint Hurdle. He wants to give the hit by a pitched ball (HBP) a new ruling. The batter who is hit would be awarded a base (or bases) according to the velocity of the pitcher. If you get hit by a Randy Johnson fastball some hitters swear the ball doesn't come out, it just stays imbedded in your body. For this you should get more credit than if you get hit by a soft tosser. Hurdle said he was hit by Dwight Gooden so hard one night that he could have had an inside the park home run HBP.

Can I be objective about baseball? No. I had a dream and I lived it because I walked through those clubhouse doors. The bubble gum cards are a little fancier now in their three and four colors. The players look a little younger, and too often these days I see the son of a former teammate on a card. What really drives it home is when I remember what a good player Gus Bell was when he was a teammate at Pittsburgh. Later I saw his son Buddy have a great career and go on to managing. Now David Bell, Gus's grandson, is a full-fledged major leaguer, and even played in a World Series.

When grandsons make it to the big leagues the scorecard tells you that you've seen a few games. I don't know how many, but I never saw a dull one. The parks and the domed stadiums look a lot different, but the air is the same. It's just easier to breathe because your bat isn't in the bat rack. The carpet in the clubhouse feels softer because you can't get picked off first base anymore. The lockers seem to know you but don't talk to you because now there's no worry about trades or being released. The pressure is gone. Now you can sit back and watch what happens on the field, and nobody has a clue as to which way the ball will bounce. Baseball is unpredictable.

Bill Rigney was one of the best guys in baseball for a lot of reasons, but I always looked forward to a Hall of Fame "Hot Stove League" session with him. We were in Scottsdale Stadium at a spring training game, and I asked him what was the most unpredictable play he ever saw. His eyes widened, and he got so animated you thought he had just left a Disney movie:

Ever saw? Hell, I was in it.

I'm managing the Angels. We need a double play, and here it comes, a routine ground ball to my shortstop, Fritz Brickell. I know he's gonna make the play. He comes up with it and throws it into center field. I'm on my feet now, and I see my center fielder, little Albie Pearson, grab the wild throw and let it fly right to the middle of the infield. I'm thinking, 'Who are we gonna get with that throw?' and now I see my pitcher, Ron Kline, pick up the ball, and he's gonna get the guy going to third. He throws it wild to third—might have thrown a spitball as far as I know, but the runner who hit the ball scores. They got three runs in. We got three errors on the same play. Now the ball is bouncing toward the dugout and stops in front of me. I stare at it. Three errors on one play. Hell, I pick it up and put it in my pocket and tell the ump to put a new ball in because I'm keeping this hand grenade in a safe place.

Like Red Smith said, baseball is a dull game only to those who have dull minds.

Clydesdales and King Kongs

CHAPTER 11

As a kid, I was the happiest when I was telling somebody, "I'm going to the ballgame." Until I actually walked into Sportsman's Park, all the pictures of it in my mind came from the descriptions of France Laux, the Cardinals' broadcaster. Some of the names were easy to remember, like "Big Poison" Paul Waner. The poison part made him sound scary. What was a Van Lingle Mungo of the Brooklyn Dodgers? We didn't have any names close to that one. We identified with Tony "Poosh 'Em Up" Lazzeri, Ernie "Schnozz" Lombardi, or Joe "Yankee Clipper" DiMaggio. I wanted to see the Arkansas Hummingbird, Lon Warneke. As soon as I knew the day I was going to the ballgame, I'd get out my bubble gum cards and make out team lineups. I didn't know or care where they batted in the lineup. It was enough for me to read about them on the backs of the cards and know I was going to see them in person.

When the day came, my eyes were all over the ballpark. I wanted to see everything, especially the players I had heard about on the radio. All I had to do to enjoy the game was follow the ball and keep looking around. Being a Cardinals' fan was easy then because I didn't know what a loss meant in the standings or what a slump was or that a particular slide was called a hook slide. It looked to me like they just fell down but knew what they were doing because they got up right away.

The explanation of a double play got lost because when I saw the ball moving so fast the next thing I knew it was time for the other team to bat. When the ball was hit into the bleachers I knew it was a home run, and even though I was in the ballpark, in my mind I could hear France Laux telling everybody about it.

Baseball started to change for me when I signed a professional contract to play for the Springfield Cardinals in the Western Association, a Class C league. I knew early on that there was more to it than just following the ball. I was going to school to learn how to play the game. As I moved forward I learned that every ballpark, regardless of the location, is different. Even the weather and groundskeepers could make a difference.

Now I'm a fan sitting in the stands, but my years growing up and my time as a player and a broadcaster let me use my memory and imagination to really enjoy watching a game. With a ticket in my hand, on the way to my seat, I still do many of the things I did as a player.

Unless the ballpark is a domed stadium, one of the first things a ballplayer does when he gets inside is check the flags. If the flag is blowing toward home plate, the hitter starts to moan even before he gets to his locker. His mind set is that it will be tough to hit one out or even get an extra base hit. I remember a teammate who could see the flags in Wrigley Field from his apartment. I think he checked the wind before he said good morning to his wife. If the flags were blowing the wrong way the Wheaties probably tasted like they had been sprinkled with rosin. If the flags were blowing out the Wheaties tasted like Eggs Benedict. The only people smiling about the wind blowing toward home plate are the pitchers. Only one pitcher likes it when the wind is blowing out—the knuckleball pitcher. He knows the wind provides resistance to his evil pitch.

The wind can tell you plenty, but many players look for more of an edge. When Keith Hernandez was playing first base for the Mets he found another way to learn which direction the wind was blowing—LaGuardia Airport. "When the planes are landing over your head that means the wind is going to left field. That's the day I like to hit line drives that way." Why not pick up grass to see how the wind is blowing? "You never know. The wind swirls." He had the edge, and as Casey

Stengel used to say, "You could look it up." Hernandez had a fielding percentage of .997 in 1985, and .996 in 1986, just two of the years in which he led the league.

The second checkpoint for the player is the sky. Are there any little, puffy white clouds that really help when a ball is hit in the air? If there are no clouds, the day could get exciting. Some outfielders will look like they just left a wine tasting party as they stagger under a fly ball. Without little clouds up there to help it can be tough.

At Wrigley Field you became part meteorologist and part gardener. It was simple to check the flags on the scoreboard and to check the sky, but what about the grounds? I played there when the grass was so high a ground ball left a trail as it fought its way through the infield. The area in front of home plate is another key area. The first bounce will tell you the condition of the field.

I always look at the starting area around first base to see if the runners get a good jump or get stalled by the texture of the dirt. If the visiting team has base stealers you can look for the ground to be so soft you may need four wheel drive shoes to get started. I remember the year Maury Wills was stealing so many bases for the Dodgers. Once, when they played the Giants at Candlestick Park, the umpires held up the game and called out the groundskeepers to remove much of the sand that had been dumped at first base. As a player you're not checking this area for beauty. It can be made so hard that you think you're on a freeway or so soft the first base coach could be a retired guide from the Everglades.

My entire baseball career was spent behind home plate or near home plate. If I was successful and got to bat and even more successful and got a hit, I always remembered what Charley Dressen told one of his players.

Having just been traded to the Dodgers the player asked Dressen, "Is there a Dodger way of playing this game?" Dressen, who was never at a loss for words, answered, "Yes; when you leave home plate try to get back to it as soon as you can."

Comic George Carlin talks about the peaceful and comforting words used in baseball. "Instead of saying a player scored, they say, 'He came home. It sounds like he's coming back for a reunion.'" But it's not always peaceful when a runner comes home.

In his book, *Take Time for Paradise*, the late Commissioner Bart Giamatti wrote about home plate. When I read it I wished I could have visited *his* home plate:

Catcher and batter, siblings who may see the world separately but share the same sight lines, are backed up and yet ruled by the parent figure, the umpire, whose place is the only one not completely defined. This tense family clusters at home, facing the world together, each with different obligations and instruments.

Commissioner Giamatti's home plate must have had a yellow brick road leading to it with Judy Garland as the guide. But I never felt it was that peaceful around home plate. I was either watching a parade of runners score or trying to land safely after a collision. I spent only one part of my career with a winning team, the St. Louis Cardinals. Outside of a month with the New York Giants, the rest of my career was spent with the Pittsburgh Pirates and the Chicago Cubs. In both places the highlight for the fans was unique—at almost every home game they got to see the bottom of the ninth inning. For me, home plate was not Shangri-la. It was more like urban renewal visited by unfriendly people.

In Pittsburgh, Sam Narron was our bullpen coach. He put the seed in my mind while we were sitting out in the left field bullpen watching the game. His favorite line was, "I got the best job in the world, and they can't fire me 'cuz I won't quit." He went on:

Look at being a third base coach. You wanna get somebody fired put him there. A slow-ass runner gets thrown out at the plate, and everybody blames the third base coach. I don't wanna be the first base coach either 'cuz he's got all kinds of things to do like write down how fast the runner is, how fast the pitcher throws to first to try to pick you off. Don't want that job. Pitching coach, forget about it. He don't get to watch the game 'cuz he's got to write down every pitch and then he's got to go out and talk to a pitcher who's mad when he gets there. Who wants to be a manager with all the headaches and talking to the writers when you lose and all that other stuff that don't have anything to do with the game? I'm telling you I got the best job.

Sam Narron, a good ol' boy who felt he had the best job in the world.
Courtesy Pittsburgh Pirates.

Then it was like we were playing a game called "Why My Job Is The Best." Everybody was chipping in. The pitchers in the bullpen said they had great jobs because if you're a starter you work every four or five days. If you're a reliever the most you work is two innings and sometimes you pitch to only one batter. They had convinced themselves that only a dummy would want to be a catcher. All those foul tips and no credit. And the outfielders had a tough job because they had to worry about running into walls. Who wants to be an outfielder when you're so far from the bench and have to run in every inning? Infielders have a bad job because they have to back up every play, so they're running as much as the outfielders. Never did figure out who had it best, although I think Sam knew the answer.

One of the things I used to do as a player was imagine what the other guy was thinking. You can't do it too often during a game, but when you're not playing it can be fun.

It started when I was with the Cubs, and we had an outfield of Ralph Kiner in left, Frankie Baumholtz in center, and Hank Sauer in right.

Frankie Baumholtz. The battle cry when Frankie played center field was, "Lotta room, Frankie." Courtesy National Baseball Hall of Fame Library, Cooperstown, N.Y.

Kiner and Sauer were out there because they had to be somewhere, but they were in the lineup because of their big bats. Both were tremendous home run hitters. To describe our outfield defense, all I can say is that we didn't have one collision all year. Baumholtz could have used help from the Illinois Highway Patrol.

The real clincher came when I read Stan Musial's answer to the question, "What do you do out there?" He said, "Well, I back up the infielders now and then. Oh sure, you have to be ready out there, but it isn't a nervous readiness. You just feel comfortable while waiting to hit again."

More than once I'd check the defense and see both Kiner and Sauer out there swinging imaginary bats. They'd go into their stance and then swing. I'd ask myself what was going on. We're on defense and those two are practicing hitting. And they were not alone. I'd check other teams' outfielders and some of them were doing it, too.

That's how I got started trying to figure out what the other guy is thinking out there. Now from the stands I do it more than ever. Body language tells you a lot, and that's what I look for. Especially on the mound, pitching coaches, managers, and catchers look for those tell-tale signs.

I remember one of the more dramatic speeches by manager Leo Durocher, to a pitcher who gave off all the signs of wanting to come out of a game. If you had to name the speech you could call it "The Hope Pitcher":

> Throw the ball. Let it loose. You're a hope pitcher out here. You hope you throw it for a strike. You hope he hits it. You hope one of the guys catches it. You hope...hope...hope...you're gonna hope your way right to the minor leagues.

All players give off vibes. So, have some fun. Pick a player and try to imagine what's running through his mind.

Start of the Game or Early Innings

THE STARTING PITCHER

You know what? Nothing happens until I throw this ball. All these people in the stands and they have to wait for me to start things. I've got a captive audience if I just tie my shoestrings. It's showtime! Oh man, is it going to be one of those days when the strike zone better be high and outside, or I'm in trouble? I can get this ping hitter out. I'll throw it right by him. First inning, first batter, first pitch, and dumbo behind the plate is squeezing the strike zone on me. Great. First batter and I walk him. Listen to the pitching coach hollering for me to bear down. I gotta keep my eyes and ears out of the dugout...my own dugout.

Start of the Game or Early innings

THE CATCHER

Look at him; he doesn't want to pitch, he wants to audition to be Grand Marshal of the Rose Parade. He picks up the rosin bag and uses it like he's in makeup for Jay Leno's show. He turns around to check the defense. He doesn't have a clue. I'm not sure he can count to seven to make sure there are seven guys behind him. I know that in his mind the catcher doesn't even count. Looking at him you'd think he came down from the mountain with the Ten

Commandments. In the meeting to go over the hitters I'm positive you can mark him absent even though his body is present. You can't give him any suggestions unless you get a hammer and split that oak-hard head of his and drop a note in it. I don't know what's gonna happen, but if he wins it's a press conference—"Hey, you wanna meet the real Abner Doubleday? I'm the guy who invented the game." Get ready to hear it all: great command, good stuff early, really prepared for them. Don't wait for: they made some great plays behind me, we had a good scouting report, didn't have to shake off a signal, it's great to have bear-down guys on your side.

If we lose I might as well put on the dunce cap because he's gonna be in the trainer's room where nobody can get at him and wait out the press guys. The error doesn't have to be critical, but if there is one he'll make it the turning point. He won twenty-two games four years ago, and he's still got the press clippings to show you. It's a wonder he doesn't have 22 and 6" tattooed on that, according to him, sculpted body. Oh well, maybe if he wins he'll give Santa Claus credit because nobody else will get any.

Start of the Game or Early Innings

FIRST OR THIRD BASEMAN

What a great day! Good crowd and I feel pretty good. I'm never choked up about being this close to the batter, but then nobody put a gun to my head and said I had to be an infielder. The only bad thing about today is that those guys have five left-handed hitters in the lineup (or right-handed hitters if you're thinking like a third baseman). Sounded great in the meeting because the genius on the mound was going to pitch them all away, but we'll see. I'm ready for "the pitch got away." They usually say that after the trainer leaves and my shin looks like Popeye's arm. I'm ready to play the retired bullfighter when this guy pitches and 'olé' a few of those bullet ground balls, but hell, when they come my way I try to make the play. I'm just glad I'm not a catcher because they know going in they're gonna get nailed with foul tips. Five left-handed hitters. You know what it's like to have to play in for a bunt when you got a big strong guy looking down your throat and you're not sure what he's gonna do? It's like being the rookie on the bomb squad and the boss wants you to be the first one in. Oh well, I just hope he pitches fast because I don't wanna be on my heels when those King Kongs start swinging the bats.

Start of the Game or Early Innings

ANY OUTFIELDER

Another game…another day…another day in the pension plan. Out here it's nice and peaceful without all the stuff you have to put up with in the infield or behind the plate. The only thing I might get is a wave from a coach on the bench to move because I wasn't paying attention and I'm a little out of position. You don't know how many times I've wanted to wave back when I see them on the top step of the dugout with a towel. I know it's a towel, but when they're waving it at me it looks like a bed sheet. Besides, as soon as he turns around I'm moving back to where I was. It's already hot out here and I'm looking at the shadow of the light tower, and that's where I'm playing everybody. Unless it's almost an over-shift, what's the use of moving? Most of the time the pitcher will miss and you hear, "I didn't get the ball out far enough." Hey, I'm on grass, and the sun is shining; all I need are a couple of sheep, and I could be a shepherd.

Start of the Game or Early Innings

THE UMPIRE

I'm ready. I really like this feeling of walking out there behind the plate. It's my game. Like the old umpire said, "Until I call it, it ain't nothing!" Believe me I'm gonna call it. Why can't everybody be like they are when they exchange the lineup cards? Sometimes they even tell jokes.

For me, behind the plate is where it's at. Third base is a rest home. Most of the time the toughest call you get is whether it's a fair or foul ball. Second base can get busy if guys can run, but most of the time it's the double play, and all you have to do is see that the pivot guy is in the neighborhood and you make the call. First base keeps you going, especially if you have a sinker ball pitcher and you get a lot of ground balls, but that's not the problem. You're just too close to the dugout, and you have to put up with the chirping. What really gets me is it's usually the guys who never play and feel like they're on the team only when they take the team picture. It's these turkeys who chirp the loudest, and you'd like to run 'em in the first inning. Yeah, you're close to the stands, too, but you just let the fans holler and hope they don't spill their beer.

Behind the plate is a whole different thing. Every pitch ends up with you. The guy behind the plate today is a pretty good catcher but a lousy umpire. He's starting to believe that he's good at framing pitches. I got his framing pitches. He'll know my strike zone early, and you know what? It's the only strike zone that counts. This guy thinks it's a strike as soon as he releases the ball. The guy on the mound doesn't have a clue, and he follows the guy behind the plate who doesn't have a clue either. He won't say much, but he'll try to stare me down and let me know about it after the inning. I've given him a lot of rope when he throws that rosin bag down, but he better be careful. They're both gonna know early who's in charge of balls and strikes. The worst thing about these two guys is that they have more meetings than the electrician's union. I hate to keep walking out to the mound because they let me get all the way out there before they break it up. Last game with these two rock piles I must have heard, "Here he comes" about five times. Just so my mask is solid and the foul tips stay away. I'm ready.

Bases Loaded

THE PITCHER

He's the best hitter on this club, but I got the ball, and I'm gonna make him wait. He hit my fastball the last two times up, so he might be looking for something else. I'm gonna hold this ball a little while longer and see if I can freeze him. I'll shake my catcher around and hope I don't give him a headache because that's what happens when he starts thinking. I'm gonna stay outside with my fastball, and if that big muscle-head with a bat goes with me we're gonna hear an explosion and the bases will be empty. But, if he tries to pull me it will be a little pop-up. So here we go—either it's the Fourth of July or Christmas Eve. Look at my catcher; he's kneeling, but I don't see a target. Maybe the dummy is praying.

Bases Loaded

THE CATCHER

This is gonna be good because it's gonna be the big number four hitter's strength against my genius out on the mound. He's always got it figured out. I know what he said in the meeting, but he'll try to change it. He does it every time. If he gets the out he'll tell everybody, including Armed Forces Radio, that you have to remember how to pitch to a hitter, but it's more important to remember what he did the last time against you. I always wait for the part where he talks about having a picture in his mind about how he's gonna get the out. If you could ever see that picture he's talking about it would probably be close-ups of Curly, Larry, and Moe. Remember what he did the last time up? He can hardly remember what the last pitch was without getting a migraine. I wonder what the hell he thinks I'm doing back here. Does he think I'm the foul pole for bunts? I know what this guy did the last ten times he faced the donkey. If he does what I want— goes with his strength— and a base-hit follows, he's got all the reasons. I didn't set him up. I didn't have the right location. I didn't remember what he did the last time. He might as well say that I'm wearing jockey shorts. What's the difference? He's got his alibi. I'd like to just cross my fingers in the good luck sign and see what he does. Here we go, fastball pitcher to fastball hitter. It's either going to make me a nothing because he'll take all the credit or I better get earplugs to get ready for the explosion. Then he'll give me the credit for calling the wrong pitch.

Bases Loaded

FIRST OR THIRD BASEMAN

I'd go to the mound and say something to him, but he looks at you like your fly is open. He makes you feel like you have to make an appointment. There's not much I can say, but he wouldn't let me say it anyhow. What am I supposed to say? The last time I went in I said, "The bases are loaded, and we'll make a play for you and get you out of it." The big jackass looked at me like I was asking what he wanted for his last meal and he had twenty minutes before the electric chair. Geez, I wish he wouldn't look at me like he's got one of my sweaty socks stuck in his nose. I just keep my head looking right at the batter, so I don't have to look at Asshead if he happens to get a brainstorm and look my way. I think the last time he looked my way was in the last series when he wanted to know if I was going to use all my passes because he needed a couple extras. C'mon, throw the ball and let's get it going.

Bases Loaded

ANY OUTFIELDER

This is when it's great to be an outfielder. The pitcher is prancing around like one of the Clydesdale horses, and I get a chance to check out the scenery. Too bad I don't have an attendance clause bonus because he gives me enough time to count the fans. Look at our catcher trying to get on the same page as the genius on the mound. I know he has a tough time remembering what fingers to use for the fastball. All I have to do is keep breathing. I'm like Elsie the cow out here just grazing. It could get busy, but right now I can think about anything I want: my family, what movie I wanna see. But mostly I have to figure out how that guy got me out last time. I was looking for the fastball and he just shows it to me. Why? The time before I really ripped his curveball and he's got a good one. He has to know I was guessing. He shows me the fastball. I think he's waiting until a game situation spot and then he'll throw it. Whoa! I just took a practice swing, and I'm on defense.

Look at my pitcher. When is he gonna make a pitch? Maybe he wants to go into the dugout and see the video of what happened last time. Man, I hate it when guys take so long. You lose the spring in your legs, and it makes it longer before I get to bat again. I wish I didn't have to run in after every inning. It's hot, and the ground is as hard as the parking lot. Why can't I just run into the bullpen and sit down? And how about that banana hollering for me to come over and give him an autograph?

Bases Loaded

THE UMPIRE

Guys like him run me right up a tree. He hasn't said a word, but he has delivered more messages than Fed Ex with his staring and throwing the rosin bag to the ground. He ain't looking at me like he wants to have dinner with me. He's got that look that says, "I'd like to cross up the catcher and nail you with my best fastball." I can't make him move any faster because he's on the mound looking for a sign, but he's staring like either he can't see or doesn't believe the signal the dummy in front of me is putting down. These two guys don't need an umpire. They need a babysitter and a playpen. He's been three and two on almost every hitter, so what's gonna be different this time? If he walks in a run I'm gonna make sure that the runner on third tags home, and then I'm dusting off the plate so he can get the message from the back of my fat ass. Guys like him make you want to check the classifieds. There has to be a better job. Throw the ball. No, he's shaking off the third sign when he's got only two pitches. I've heard the manager right on this mound tell him where he can stick his change of pace. If he's gonna get beat it's got to be with his fastball. I'm looking for it. The batter is looking for it, and the way he's pitching they're gonna be looking for it in the bleachers. Throw the ball. If I could, I'd follow him into his dugout, grab him by the shoulders, and shake him to see if the rattle in his head is as loud as I think it is. Throw the damn ball.

Getting Hit Hard But They're Not Scoring

THE PITCHER

I don't have it today, and I should take roll call after every inning. The infielders are doing a great job, but they should get hazard pay. I've thrown more garbage than two trucks can hold. I feel like I'm pitching under water. My arm is heavy, but I don't think the genius manager sees anything yet. Another inning like the last one and the fans will need earplugs. What the hell are they swinging that makes it sound so loud when they hit the ball? I wouldn't even make an American Legion team with that last curveball. The damn ball feels like a bowling ball, but I ain't throwing any strikes with it.

I wish it would rain. He's putting down the fastball sign. That's funny. I better check Will Call in this park because I think that's where my fastball is. And I wish the umpire would stop throwing the new ball to me. He looks like he's got better stuff than I do. Hell, he must be fifty years old. Another line drive, and another great catch. So far I've got everybody except the catcher and the batboy in the running for the Gold Glove Award. Well, it's the sixth inning and they've got only one run. With the crap I'm throwing up there today I could get a Purple Heart for being just sixty feet, six inches away from a bat. I'm not asking out, but what the hell game are they watching on the bench? Maybe they're trying to get even with me. I hope they don't show me the pitching chart for this game. It's gotta look like they used a post office pen to chart this crap.

Getting Hit Hard But They're Not Scoring

THE CATCHER

Is this some kind of bad joke? I could catch this guy with a pair of tweezers or two Kleenexes. With the junk he's throwing up here I don't need a glove—

I need a garbage disposal. His damn curveball is breaking down because of lack of speed. And I wonder if the radar gun can clock a twenty-nine miles-per-hour fastball because that's what it looks like. Maybe this would be a good time to work on a new pitch because he must have left all his old pitches in the bathroom when he shaved this morning. The stuff he's throwing is coming right out of the toilet. This is one of the best days I've ever had, although my eardrums might be punctured from the booms. I know I haven't had a foul tip off me all day. The ball is stopping about two feet from me, and I get to watch an infielder or an outfielder go on a kamikaze mission. I've never seen so many healthy foul balls. The little pissant shortstop hit one foul in the upper deck, and that means he finally pulled a ball. He couldn't pull a ball if it had a chain on it. I hope they don't ask me what kind of stuff this turkey's got today. All they have to do is look because it's all over the park and in the stands. This is the first time the fans down both lines in the upper deck need life insurance. Hell, I don't know what to call for. That last fastball came up in spurts like it had the runs. Everything he throws is a rocket leaving here. I wish I had a signal for a batting tee. Then he could just place it on the tee and let 'em hit it. You talk about room service fastballs. Hell, if I was on the other team, the next time he pitches I'd send a cab for him to make sure he gets here. They might have to have a lottery the next time to see who gets to play. Our guys will head for the training room rather than the infield.

Getting Hit Hard But They're Not Scoring

THE FIRST OR THIRD BASEMAN

My mother told me there would be days like this. Old Jock Strap Arm had to pitch today with five left-handed hitters in the lineup (change to right-handed hitters if you're thinking like a third baseman). Those guys almost got their own first base coach twice with foul balls. I mean it's a blur when they hit it. I remember one of those old infielders saying once that most of his pitchers had the FDR pitch, and he wasn't talking about Roosevelt. He meant fire, duck, and run. I'm pretty close to him, and he doesn't look fast getting rid of the rosin bag. If it even looks like they might bunt— and I can't think why they would—I'm not looking at our bench. They may have to come out here with the sheriff's posse to make me play in. If I'm in, I have a plan. As soon as he turns it loose toward the plate I'm hitting the ground. I may look silly if the batter takes the pitch, but I ain't making my wife a widow yet. I knew we were in trouble in the second inning when I couldn't tell the difference between his fastball and his change-up. When I asked him about it he said it was his slider, but it wasn't breaking. I went right into the clubhouse and put on the metal cup because that plastic one ain't gonna get it done. If I get hit there it will be bad for me but a concert for the fans because it's going ring like a church bell gone wild. What a play. You know that's about the tenth time I've said that, and we're only in the sixth inning. Safest guy on the field is the catcher. Hell, he's safer than the guy operating the scoreboard.

Getting Hit Hard But They're Not Scoring
THE OUTFIELDER
Usually it's pretty safe and quiet out here, but with this guy pitching it's combat pay time. I've never seen so many ricochets off the wall, and then here comes a line drive screamer and it's a double play. He must have gone to Lourdes before the game today. It's a miracle we're still leading. It's a miracle nobody's been killed, and it's a miracle he's still out there. If you didn't know our numbers before you sure as hell know them today because I've had my back to the stands all day. When they hit knuckleballs out to you it's scary, but today the ball coming back off the wall can tear your head off. It's like playing handball the way they're bouncing 'em off the wall. When he gets ready to pitch I wanna holler, "He's got it again, and I'm getting outta here." How can they hit 'em so high and so far? They must be using aluminum bats. When he gets to two and two I feel lucky, but I'm ready to get going because I know they're going to hit the next one. Closest he's been to a strikeout is two strikes and two foul balls. I need track shoes and insurance playing behind him. We're still leading, but it's roll-call-and-report-your-injury time after every inning. Usually I can tell his fastball from his curveball, but today the only difference is they're hitting one pitch harder than the other. I'm afraid to ask which one. It looks like he's throwing batting practice; everything gets up there in slow motion. If this were a fight they'd throw in the towel to stop it even though he's leading. My mother was right—I should have gone to law school.

Getting Hit Hard But They're Not Scoring

THE UMPIRE

Without a doubt, this has been my best game yet. I haven't missed a pitch all day, but then neither have the batters. It's hard to concentrate back here because you wanna watch the action out there. With the stuff he's got or hasn't got I don't have any pitches to call because the hitters are doing all the work. No griping from these guys. They're either so happy at getting all these hits or they're too tired to complain. I'd love to run a couple of those hitters today so they don't get a chance to fatten up with the marshmallows this guy's throwing up there. He better not say a word to me the rest of the season after this performance. Hell, if he was a Broadway show it would have closed yesterday. Fastball is so slow it's a rumor. Curveball's got about as much spin as a fat lady on a dance floor. His change of pace ought to be called a change of scenery because that's what happens to the ball every time he throws it. He couldn't fool Ernie from Sesame Street *today.*

The bad thing is, the innings are so damn long. I mean I've seen more runners than in the Boston Marathon. When the troops come in from chasing all those bombs he's throwing they don't wanna go back out there. It's almost like you need MP's on the bench to get them out there. My feet are killing me, but I can't say anything because the guys playing behind him must be worn out. If the sun stays out like it is now they're gonna need sun block on their tongues. What I don't understand is how the hell he's still leading and why he's still out there. Those guys on that bench must be watching another game. I've seen every hit I can think of today and a few I didn't think of. Hell, last inning the big guy on first must have been tired because he stretched an easy stand-up triple into a slide-into-second double. I think he just wanted a rest stop. Must have thought we were playing on Highway 66—stop, get some rest, change the oil, get gas, and then be on his way. You know I might need a foul tip off the mask just to keep me awake.

I'm going to use a disclaimer here, kind of like the ones I see on television. The preceding is not about real people living or dead. The characters are fictional and presented solely for your entertainment.

Now for a personal disclaimer—these are my thoughts, and I was thinking about real players, managers, and umpires when I wrote them all down.

When I walk into the ballpark, my memory and imagination take me on a trip of my choosing. I visit plenty of places right from my seat. When I hear a manager say, "We had the match-up we wanted," I think the same thing. The perfect match-up, the seat and me. The next day in the paper the pitcher will say he made a couple of bad pitches, and I try to figure out which ones he's talking about—and they don't have to be the key hit or the walk-off home run. I also know that good hitters hit good pitches, too. It's not always a bad pitch. Maybe it's that base on balls before the hit. Like pitching coach Art Fowler always said, "You can't catch a walk."

One of the things that make baseball unique is that it doesn't have a play book like football or basketball. You can't design a set play between innings to fit the situation like you see during timeouts in the other two sports. The biggest strategy move is making out the lineup card. When you get right down to it, the intentional base on balls or pitching around a batter like Barry Bonds could turn out to be a major strategic move. A manager can't really get his strategy wheels spinning until he gets a base runner. I think that's why the designated hitter has caused so much controversy among fans. Do you want to watch a power hitter who's in scoring position as soon as he steps in the batter's box, or do you want to watch a manager think his team into a run?

Baseball is unpredictable. After all, Babe Ruth stole home ten times. But just how unpredictable is it? That's up to you to see. It's there. Let your eyes wander. When I walk out of the park and people say to me, "Hey, Joe, how'd you like the game?" I always paraphrase Will Rogers and say I never saw a game I didn't like. Depending on the team you're rooting for, the scoreboard will make you want to laugh or cry. But as Tom Hanks said in the movie *A League Of Their Own*, there's no crying in baseball, and I agree. There are a lot of laughs, though.